Programs to
Employ the
Disadvantaged

Programs to Employ the Disadvantaged

EDITED BY

Peter B. Doeringer

ASSISTANT PROFESSOR
DEPARTMENT OF ECONOMICS
HARVARD UNIVERSITY

WITH A FOREWORD BY

John T. Dunlop

Prentice-Hall, Inc. • Englewood Cliffs, N.J.

C–13-730556-7
P–13-730549-4

Library of Congress Catalog Card Number: 79-100102

Printed in the United States of America
Current printing (last digit):
10 9 8 7 6 5 4 3 2 1

Case material of the Harvard Graduate School of Business
Administration is made possible by the cooperation of
business firms who may wish to remain anonymous by
having names, quantities, and other identifying details dis-
guised while maintaining basic relationships. Cases are pre-
pared as the basis for class discussion rather than to
illustrate either effective or ineffective handling of administra-
tive situations.

PRENTICE-HALL, INTERNATIONAL, INC., *London*
PRENTICE-HALL OF AUSTRALIA, PTY. LTD., *Sydney*
PRENTICE-HALL OF CANADA, LTD., *Toronto*
PRENTICE-HALL OF INDIA PRIVATE LTD., *New Delhi*
PRENTICE-HALL OF JAPAN, INC., *Tokyo*

Foreword

The insistent demands of black citizens, the growing public concern with the problems of our cities, and the fact of continuing high employment have combined in the last half of the 1960's to focus attention on the employment of the disadvantaged. While programs to improve education, housing, medical care, transportation, welfare, and social services all have a major role, jobs for the disadvantaged—and better jobs —provide the most direct and immediate amelioration for many of our citizens in poverty.

For managements, an increase in the employment of the disadvantaged involves, at a minimum, changes in policies and new problems of supervision. Under collective bargaining agreements, labor organizations directly affect many of these employment-related decisions. Government agencies have been playing a greater role in the recruitment and in some cases in the financing of additional costs of training of the disadvantaged. Civil rights organizations and community groups are much involved in programs to employ and to upgrade those at the back end of the employment queue.

As the volume and variety of programs to employ the disadvantaged have grown in recent years, it is clear that substantial adaptations in conventional procedures to recruit and train workers are often required. Some new institutional forms and new policies are arising in the private sector, and new relationships between the world of school and work have emerged in some localities. The employment of the disadvantaged will require considerable institutional rebuilding in the labor market and new devices for cooperation between governments and private parties.

It is appropriate in 1969, particularly with a new administration in Washington, to review carefully and critically a few of the more interesting and significant of the recent experiences of managements, labor, government, and civil rights groups with programs to provide job opportunities. The Conference on January 30, 1969 at Harvard University, under the sponsorship of the Meyer Kestnbaum Fund, provided the occasion to examine and compare some of the more important *Programs to Employ the Disadvantaged.*

In 1961 Harvard University received a unique gift from the Amalgamated Clothing Workers through the Sidney Hillman Foundation, the Hart Schaffner and Marx Company, and the family and friends of Meyer Kestnbaum "to support various activities in the field of industrial relations, industrial affairs, and the problems and opportunities of industry and labor in a changing world." The Committee which administers the bequest brings together the Faculty of Arts and Sciences, the School of Business Administration, the Law School, and the John F. Kennedy School of Government.

The terms of the gift to the University provide that once every ten years it shall sponsor a program such as was held on January 30, 1969: "to hold a series of conferences, some for policy-making labor leaders, some for top business executives and some for both together, and some with government representatives, in a university atmosphere for systematic discussion of vital issues confronting labor and management and their relations to the community."

Mr. Kestnbaum was a graduate of Harvard College, Class of 1918, and of the Harvard Graduate School of Business Administration in 1921. He began his business career with Hart Schaffner and Marx in the labor relations department and served as president of the company from 1941 until his death in 1960. Meyer Kestnbaum was an energetic and scholarly public servant as well as a far-sighted statesman of industrial affairs.

The Amalgamated Clothing Workers and the Hart Schaffner and Marx Company have an enviable record of industrial peace and constructive labor-management relations. Secretary of Labor Willard Wirtz recognized this distinguished relationship by providing that a plaque be placed in the Labor Department in recognition of this achievement. Both of these parties have had a deep and continuing interest in community affairs.

It is appropriate to acknowledge that *Programs to Employ the Disadvantaged* was suggested by Mr. Robert Kestnbaum, son of Mr. Meyer Kestnbaum, and Mrs. Meyer Kestnbaum, both of whom attended the January 30, 1969 sessions and participated in the workshops. My colleague, Professor Peter Doeringer, arranged for the individual case studies and has edited this volume. These studies will be of wide interest to all those interested in translating national aspirations into solid accomplishment.

John T. Dunlop

Contents

Introduction

BY *PETER B. DOERINGER*

The 1960's witnessed the first stages in the development of a comprehensive federal manpower policy in the United States. The earliest programs under the Area Redevelopment Act (1961) and the Manpower Development and Training Act of 1962 provided vocational skills to experienced, but unemployed, adult males. Since then the concern of federal manpower policy has turned gradually toward less qualified workers, and the remedying of a broad range of deficiencies in education, training, and health.

During the late 1960's a parallel trend emerged in the manpower policies in the private sector. The combination of a buoyant economy, the civil rights revolution, and the urban riots of 1967 encouraged many employers to lower their hiring standards, to begin to recruit from among the disadvantaged, and, consequently, to expand formal and informal training programs at the work place. These influences have also encouraged unions to initiate programs along similar lines.

Labor market disadvantage, while often summarized in terms of education and other socio-economic variables, is fundamentally a concept shaped by the costs of adapting workers with various traits to the performance requirements of particular work places. Too little is known about the nature and magnitude of these costs. Low learning ability may be one factor; problems of tardiness, absenteeism, turnover, and motivation are certainly others. These are, of course, problems which must be resolved with any labor force, but they appear to have a higher incidence among the disadvantaged.

Disadvantaged workers themselves perceive their employment problems somewhat differently. While work is not always scarce, jobs that are stable, pay good wages, and pro-

1

vide pleasant working conditions are difficult to obtain. Accustomed to low wage, dead-end employment, undesirable working conditions, and inequitable supervision, the disadvantaged worker often develops both work habits and expectations about jobs that are incompatible with the performance norms of higher wage enterprises.

The disadvantaged customarily find employment in the low-wage labor market, where turnover and absenteeism are often tolerated. Work in low-wage enterprises may be unstable, and therefore ideally suited to a casual labor force. Alternatively, such work may be low skilled or organized so that the costs of worker instability are minimized. Even where such instability is costly, it may be less so than discovering and implementing corrective measures.

High wage, or otherwise preferred, enterprises can partially avoid the costs of worker instability through selection procedures which, in effect, exclude the disadvantaged. To the extent that problems of motivation, attendance, and stability are derived from the character of previous employment, programs for providing better jobs will by themselves remedy the symptoms of disadvantage. The first task of manpower programs, therefore, must be to open such employment opportunities to the disadvantaged labor force. But expectations change slowly and previous work habits may have to be unlearned, so that many of the disadvantaged will require additional types of assistance.

Employer and union manpower programs are instruments for improving access to better jobs and for developing job-related remedial training and counseling. Such programs have the advantage of decentralization, which permits the design flexibility needed to accommodate both the diversity of work and the heterogeneity of employment problems encountered in the disadvantaged population. Moreover, such programs can draw upon managerial and training resources that are not often available to institutional programs.

RECENT EXPERIENCE WITH MANPOWER PROGRAMS

Given the current emphasis upon private initiative in manpower programs, it is important to study the recent experience of employers with hiring and training the disadvantaged. Nine studies of manpower programs are presented in this volume. These programs have been selected to represent a variety of problems and approaches, as can be seen from Table 1. Some deal with hiring and entry training, others with upgrading; both blue-collar and white-collar occupations are considered. The emphasis is upon programs designed and operated by private enterprises; this experience is contrasted with four other types of programs: (1) pre-apprenticeship training for

TABLE 1: DESCRIPTION OF PROGRAMS

1. *Western Electric*
   Newark, New Jersey

   Light electronics manufacturing facilities located in the low-income Newark Central Ward. Facilities are designed to train workers on the job for eventual transfer to the company's Kearny, New Jersey, plant. As of December 1968, 191 persons were employed at the Newark plant and 90 persons had successfully transferred. The program is privately financed.

2. *IBM*
   Brooklyn, New York

   Light electronics manufacturing facility providing on-the-job training in light electronics assembly. No special transfer arrangements are included in the program. As of December 1968, approximately 195 persons were employed, and an employment level of 450 is forecast. (This 195 includes 87 indirect and 108 direct employees.)

3. *Westinghouse*
   East Pittsburgh, Pennsylvania

   Four week vestibule training program, followed by on-the-job training in specific skills. This program is supported by federal funds under the Department of Labor's MA-3 program and has a training capacity of about 25 at any one time.

4. *The Equitable Life Assurance Society of the United States*
   New York, New York

   A series of programs begun in 1962 for high school dropouts. Training emphasizes development of clerical skills and remedial education.

5. *Cooperative Steel Industry Education Program*

   A joint labor-management training program involving ten major companies in the steel industry. It provides incumbent employees with remedial education to facilitate their upgrading. The program is supported by federal funds through the U.S. Department of Labor.

6. *Woodland Job Training Center* Cleveland, Ohio	Cooperative training arrangement between the Cleveland Board of Education and participating employers. This program provides basic education and vocational training concurrently with on-the-job training. Trainees are eventually transferred from the training facility in the Hough ghetto to regular production facilities. The program is financed by public and private funds, including an MA-3 contract.
7. *Workers' Defense League Preapprenticeship Training Program*	A preapprenticeship program to prepare minority group youths for apprenticeship examinations in the construction trades. The program currently operates in ten cities with support from the Ford Foundation and the U.S. Department of Labor.
8. *Department of Defense Project 100,000*	A program for accepting persons into the military services who fail to meet current mental or physical standards. Some remedial training is provided.
9. *The Concentrated Employment Program* Boston, Massachusetts	Placement, institutional training, orientation, and work experience provided through the Concentrated Employment Program and other manpower programs operated by ABCD, Boston's community action agency.

the building trades with union involvement; (2) programs in the military services; (3) institutional manpower programs operated by a community action agency; and (4) a cooperative program between industry and a public school system.

Program Initiative. There has been considerable speculation concerning employers' and unions' motives for becoming involved in special programs for the disadvantaged. Some attribute recent efforts to pressure from civil rights groups or from government agencies responsible for fair employment practices. Others trace it to the urban riots and the deep concern with the future of our cities. Economists have suggested that much employer interest is related to full employment and the rising cost of recruiting, training, or otherwise adapting the labor force to the requirements of the work place.

In the programs studied, external coercion never emerged explicitly as an element in the program decision, although some companies and unions did express concern over their record of minority group employment. This is not to say that the companies and unions were unaware of the benefits such programs might produce for fair employment compliance reviews or for public relations. These factors, however, seemed to be subordinate to a larger concern with the problems of the cities and the ability of public programs to remedy them.

Labor market factors also influenced many of these programs. The training program at Equitable Life Assurance, for example, had to be continually adapted to trends in New York City's labor force, as the shortage of qualified clerical workers increased. Equitable, however, experimented with some programs which were more ambitious than labor market conditions required.

The steel industry had been experiencing problems with bottlenecks in promotion lines during the 1960's, the result of an inability to upgrade poorly educated workers hired under an earlier technology. Even the military services, with their power to recruit by fiat, were under pressure to accept a higher proportion of the available manpower pool as the armed services expanded after 1965.

Recruitment and Hiring. Eligibility for two programs, Westinghouse and the Woodland Job Center, was defined by the Department of Labor's criteria of disadvantage: (1) having a poverty level of income and (2) being either: (a) a high school dropout, (b) under 22 or over 45 years of age, (c) handicapped, or (d) subject to special obstacles to employment. Other programs were not bound by this definition, although their applicant populations possessed many of these characteristics. Equitable hired high school dropouts and persons under 22; IBM sought to attract persons living in the low income Bedford-Stuyvesant area; the Workers' Defense League recruited youths from areas such as Harlem and Bedford-Stuyvesant; and Western Electric relied upon the local Community Action Agency for referrals. Both the Department of Defense and the steel industry programs drew upon an undereducated or otherwise handicapped population.

The number of program applicants often outnumbered the available training or employment slots. IBM had to select less than 200 employees from among 2,565 applicants (11.7 percent); Westinghouse selected 112 employees from 632 applicants (17.7 percent); the Workers' Defense League prepared 816 persons for apprenticeship examinations out of 2,056 recruits in its Bedford-Stuyvesant program (39.7 percent); and Western Electric screened 590 applicants for 250 positions (42.4 percent). Other companies had less choice among applicants. Equitable, for example, agreed to reject no more than half of the applicants referred from the state employment service and the steel industry drew from a population of poorly educated employees who bid for program vacancies according to their seniority.

Criteria for selecting from among these applicants had to be consistent with a series of objectives—helping the disadvantaged, creating an effective program where there were few guidelines, and ultimately developing a qualified labor force. Selection strategies varied considerably, and these variations provide insights into differing perceptions of labor market disadvantage. IBM, for example, assigned priority to hiring males. To accomplish this, however, the company had to de-emphasize previous unemployment as a positive factor in the hiring decision. The Workers' Defense League has consistently concentrated upon male high school graduates because of apprenticeship entry requirements which are beyond its control.

In all the programs leading directly to entry level jobs, various barriers to employment—high school educational requirements, criminal records, and so forth—were lowered. Thus, there is no doubt that the trainees were disadvantaged, at least in the limited sense that they would not have been hired under previous selection standards.

The extent to which these persons represented the most seriously disadvantaged, however, is debatable. Some programs frankly admitted to selecting the most qualified of the disadvantaged. Sometimes this was for reasons external to its program, as with the Workers' Defense League program; other times it was part of a broader policy of recruiting persons who were motivated, who were likely to benefit from training, and who would make good candidates for promotion.

IBM, for example, sought explicitly to establish a core of motivated, successful employees early in its program before embarking on a more ambitious phase of hiring persons with less tractable employment problems. Similar screening principles were operating at Westinghouse. As it gained experience in the program, the company did waive criminal records and even drug addiction as a bar to admission, but the program continued to screen carefully for qualities associated with motivation. As Purcell reports [in "196 Men Find a Chance," page 64]:

Mr. Ross's (the program director) prime allegiance must be to the general success of the program, so he cannot afford to take needless risks. A risk, in Ross's judgment, is a man who does not really want to work or who is enmeshed in such serious problems that he is unlikely to work steadily. Ross might be able to reform someone who is not yet truly motivated, but he feels the chances are slim and his time can be better used for others.

Applicants were rejected for reasons other than lack of motivation, perhaps the most important being medical problems. Excluding applicants rejected for their age or because work was unavailable, Western Electric reports that 39 percent of its rejections were for health reasons and 28 percent for drug addiction. Drug addiction and alcoholism, as well as noncorrectable health problems, were cause for rejection at IBM.

Content of Training Programs. A number of the programs established *formal* training and counseling arrangements, often supplemented by informal, on-the-job training. The exceptions were IBM and Western Electric, which relied almost exclusively on on-the-job training and informal counseling procedures.

Because of the importance placed upon attitude and worker motivation, several programs emphasized counseling. The Westinghouse program puts forth the greatest efforts in this area by devoting a sizable portion of its four-week vestibule training program to group discussion, sensitivity training, and role playing. Some basic education is provided, but it appears to be incidental to the primary objective of developing stable work habits and motivation.

At Equitable, counseling and training are provided by ordinary training supervisors and special coaches, as well as by the regular supervisory staff. At Western Electric, where an entire vestibule training plant has been established, training and motivational activities are provided on the job by specially selected supervisors. To accomplish this, the ratio of supervisors to employees has been markedly increased. IBM uses daily orientation sessions during which IBM's personnel philosophy, emphasizing individual respect and reward for merit, is carefully explained. After that, the development and motivation of the work force becomes the responsibility of each supervisor.

In the Workers' Defense League program, counseling consists of exposing trainees to construction sites, informing them of the drawbacks as well as the advantages of construction work, and sustaining their interest in construction until apprenticeship vacancies are announced. Since no stipend is paid to trainees, the self-selection process helps to ensure a motivated group.

The Department of Defense program is the only one which does not emphasize motivation. Instead, every effort is made to conceal the fact that trainees are disadvantaged, and, apart from remedial training, no special assistance is provided.

The experience of Equitable, IBM, and Western Electric with the greater health care needs of the disadvantaged is suggestive of another important area for program development. At Equitable, for example, the whole nature of the company's medical clinic began to change from a diagnostic service to a center for remedial medical care. If, as it appears from these programs, health is related to reliability at the work place, expanded industrial health programs may also be important in developing acceptable work habits.

Work Habits. Most of the program administrators are reasonably satisfied with the performance of their trainees, although Equitable stressed the need to distinguish between poor work habits and those which were merely unconventional. IBM experienced the fewest problems of absenteeism and turnover. Of the 195 persons hired as of December 31, 1968, only two had quit and three had been fired; absenteeism has not been serious. The retention rate for trainees at Westinghouse was 94 percent over an eleven-month period. Three trainees were dropped during the training program, three were terminated for absenteeism on the job, and two quit. Of the 362 employees hired at Western Electric, 33 were terminated and 76 resigned. Ninety-one percent of the involuntary terminations were for absenteeism or tardiness.

In general, the incidence of poor work habits was directly related to selection practices. Programs able to select motivated trainees, regardless of other qualifications, had the least serious problems with turnover and absenteeism. When such problems arose, however, the inevitable result was a discharge or a voluntary termination when the remedial counseling program failed to correct the poor work habits.

Supervisory Attitudes. Just as employee attitudes towards work are important, so are supervisory attitudes towards workers. By virtue of the experimental nature of their production facilities, the Woodland Job Center, IBM, and Western Electric programs have been able to select foremen and supervisors for their sensitivity to human relations. In other programs, the disadvantaged were exposed to the same supervisors as other workers.

The Westinghouse program tried to minimize the potential problems of supervisory prejudice or insensitivity in several ways. Supervisors were given special help in understanding the problems of the disadvantaged. Prejudice was openly discussed and analyzed in the vestibule training program. Finally, the corporation's commitment to the program and its determination to pursue an active equal employment policy were emphasized. This determination on the part of corporate and plant officials to make the program succeed seemed to be most influential among the foremen.

Supervisors in other programs were assisted in other ways. Vestibule training and increased supervisory personnel both eased the foremen's training responsibilities. Sometimes counselors helped in training and served as intermediaries between the supervisors and the trainees. At Equitable a special budgetary arrangement was developed which treated the trainees as "over hires," and placed them on the corporate payroll to remove them as a cost burden on the supervisor's budget.

Industrial Relations Issues. Even under the most selective hiring standards, new hires are never job ready. They must be oriented to the plant, trained in their job duties, and gradually accustomed to the expected work pace and standards of performance. This process of acclimatization normally occurs informally and unsystematically through supervisory control, pressure from fellow employees, and the discipline mechanism. Where these procedures are not effective, the employee is terminated, typically during the probationary period.

Since adjustment to the work place seems to be more difficult for the disadvantaged, programs to employ and retain such workers may involve both overlooking, or treating more leniently, infractions of work rules and the acceptance of production norms which are at variance with customary standards. This produces a conflict that is difficult to resolve between the need for dual standards of performance, one for the disadvantaged and one for the incumbent employees, and the principle of egalitarian treatment of all workers.

Resolving this conflict while bringing the disadvantaged up to the performance requirements of the work place will sometimes necessitate the extension of the period of probationary employment. During the probation period, sub-standard performance can be tolerated without a corresponding deterioration in regular plant discipline. In enterprises organized by unions, however, the extension of the probationary period may revive longer standing disputes over union security and the rights of employees to utilize the grievance machinery. A number of companies and unions have recognized this principle by *informally* extending the negotiated probationary period for individual workers.

The Western Electric "feeder" factory arrangement accomplishes a similar purpose. Duration of employment in the feeder factory depends upon the learning progress of the individaul, and the normal probationary period does not begin until an employee is transferred to the Kearny plant. Moreover, a supplementary collective agreement covering the Newark facility eliminates the arbitration step from the grievance procedure, thereby relieving some pressure for consistency in the application of work rules.

It is, however, clear that isolating trainees from incumbent employees and granting special considerations with respect to absenteeism, tardiness, and so forth can be only temporary. Eventually, each program recognizes that the same minimum levels of performance must be required of all employees.

EMPLOYERS, UNIONS, AND THE SYSTEM OF MANPOWER SERVICES

The process of adapting disadvantaged workers to employment in the private sector will involve some or all of the following steps:

1. Outreach or recruitment.
2. Screening and selection.
3. Remedial education and training.
4. Placement.
5. Orientation to work and to specific job requirements.
6. Counseling and supportive services.

The particular combination will depend upon the type of disadvantage encountered and the kind of employment involved.

Models of Private Sector Participation. Responsibility for these steps can rest with various institutions—employers, unions, school systems, community action agencies, and so forth. There is no single program or set of relationships which will be appropriate in all cities or for all "employment relationships." From the programs presented in this volume, however, several significant models of private sector involvement in manpower programs can be distinguished.

1. Relaxation of hiring standards combined with formal or informal in-plant programs to employ and upgrade the disadvantaged. These programs may involve various cooperative

arrangements with out-plant agencies for recruitment, counseling, or other supportive services.

2. Establishing permanent production facilities in ghetto neighborhoods. This emphasizes making employment accessible to the disadvantaged community and may encourage further economic development of the area. Arrangements may or may not be made for using such employment as a transition step for permanent employment outside the ghetto.

3. Consortium or union-administered training programs for multiemployer groups.

4. Cooperative training arrangements between employers and educational institutions in which education and on-the-job training are combined.

Many companies will find it expedient to utilize various public and private outreach agencies for recruiting the disadvantaged. Only large and prosperous companies, however, are likely to establish special, large scale production facilities designed primarily to employ and train disadvantaged workers. More prevalent will be special hiring programs and in-plant training programs, undertaken mostly in medium-sized and large enterprises.

Cooperative and consortium training arrangements seem to offer greatest promise where remedial education is important or where the number of trainees for any particular company is small. Workshops simulating actual production conditions and attached to centralized training facilities are especially suitable for small enterprises lacking in-plant training resources. Similarly, where enterprises are small and in those industries, such as construction, where employment is casual, consortium arrangements or programs administered by unions are most appropriate.

FULL EMPLOYMENT

The state of the economy is the most critical factor in the planning and evaluation of manpower programs to aid the disadvantaged. The recent manpower programs have been developed in a period when the economy was prosperous. Continuing economic expansion is essential if employment gains are to be sustained and compounded. A slowdown in production will imperil further recruitment, and would presumably jeopardize the employment of low seniority disadvantaged workers.

11

What alternatives are available? Job security has not been a problem for a company like IBM, with its large cushion of subcontracts, good growth prospects, and considerable scheduling flexibility. In contrast, employment and upgrading in the steel industry is highly sensitive to the business cycle. Employment security for the disadvantaged under these circumstances is part of the much larger concern of job security for the enterprise's entire work force.

Some establishments may undertake programs to stabilize employment or to guarantee incomes for their employees. Others may extend recall rights so that newly hired workers have improved opportunities for re-employment. It is unlikely, however, that special provisions can be made to improve only the job security of the disadvantaged segment of an enterprise's labor force.

The recent proposals of the auto workers and the steel workers that inverse seniority be used to determine layoffs, and thus assist in retaining newly hired disadvantaged workers, runs contrary to this view. But the practicality of this arrangement has yet to be tested. Such a proposal is likely to be acceptable to a work force only where senior employees on layoff receive supplemental unemployment benefits. Even with such provisions, the equity of distributing layoffs to senior workers may be questioned by other employees. For the enterprise, acceptance is conditional upon the ability to absorb additional training and supplemental unemployment benefit costs.

Upgrading opportunities also depend largely upon economic expansion. Once the problems of employing and retaining the disadvantaged are resolved, programs to qualify them for promotion will become the concern of many employers. Basic education is apt to assume greater significance in upgrading than it has for entry programs, as the steel industry experience illustrates. This is especially likely if upgrading to supervisory positions is eventually anticipated.

CONCLUSIONS

The findings of these studies are, on the whole, optimistic. Although the severity of trainees' disadvantage is sometimes questionable, and although some trainees have not achieved stable employment, initial optimism is not misplaced. Useful experiments have been undertaken, and valuable experience is being obtained.

But such experiments must be judged over years, not months. These programs are small; their entry wage rates are above average; and working conditions are generally good. The capacity of other enterprises to duplicate these circumstances, the extent to which such programs can be operated on a large scale, and their ability to reach those with the most severe employment handicaps have not yet been determined.

If continuing progress is to be made in the next decade, the experimental quality of manpower programs, and the lessons of success and failure they teach, must not be lost. Hopefully, the experience of the burgeoning public and private manpower programs will be collected and disseminated more systematically than it has been in the past. While the disadvantaged will be the immediate beneficiaries of these activities, the most important product of these experiments may well be our increased understanding of the larger process of improving labor markets and upgrading the nation's labor force.

1

Employing the Disadvantaged

BY *JACK CHERNICK* AND *GEORGINA SMITH* *

INTRODUCTION

In the fall of 1967 three Bell System companies in New Jersey decided upon a program for hiring the disadvantaged unemployed, and in January 1968 announced a combined effort to employ 550 such persons in the central cities of New Jersey. This job target was later assumed as commitment to the goal in the area of the National Alliance of Businessmen. Of the total number, Western Electric undertook to employ 250 persons; while New Jersey Bell set a goal of 200, and Bell Laboratories pledged to hire and train 100 workers.

The Vestibule or Feeder Plants. Having reached a decision to employ hard-core unemployed—a decision which implies waiving or lowering some of its customary qualifications for

* Respectively chairman and associate professor in the Research Section, Institute of Management and Labor Relations, Rutgers University. Acknowledgement is gratefully made of the assistance of John Payne, manager, Community Relations and Public Affairs, Western Electric, in assuring the accuracy of descriptive detail.

The Research Section is engaged in a study of Western Electric's efforts in the Newark area to employ the disadvantaged. Utilizing data collected in the course of operations and supplemented by information derived from interviews with key participants, the research is intended to throw light on the techniques employed, the problems encountered, and the underlying causes of the results achieved. However, the stage reached in the study as of the date of this paper is not sufficiently advanced to permit any extensive report on findings. The paper is limited to a description of the Western Electric Program, aggregate statistics on the number served by it, and preliminary discussion of some key issues to which it gives rise.

employment—a company may choose between two broad approaches.

1. In the first approach, new hires are placed in regular entry jobs in existing work groups. Special arrangements may be made for on-the-job training and for counseling. The usual probation period may be extended.
2. In the second, new hires are grouped together for formal or informal training and counseling. Individuals are transferred to regular jobs in regular work groups when they are judged to have attained qualifications equivalent to usual entry standards.[1] This approach also involves the decision whether to locate training facilities within or in close proximity to an existing operating unit or whether to separate them physically from such units.

The New Jersey Bell Telephone Company adopted the first of the two approaches designated above. Eligible applicants were hired and assimilated into the regular work force. Although they were required to take the tests administered under usual hiring procedures, the test results were not taken into account in the hiring decision. At Bell Laboratories, trainees work a half day on the job and attend courses on the premises the other half day.

Western Electric chose to follow the second approach. It was decided to establish a separate facility in which new hires from among the disadvantaged population would be oriented to work in an industrial setting. While the company was unable to predict the exact number, it was expected that some would be prepared for transfer to regular jobs in one or another of the company's plants in the Newark area. Of particular significance is the fact that the company decided to establish this vestibule facility in the Newark Central Ward.[2] A building formerly used as an automobile showroom was acquired on a three-year lease and refurbished; known as "the 200 Central Avenue plant," it opened in March 1968. At the end of

---

[1] A variant of this approach is the hiring of persons who have completed a government-sponsored training course which in design and recruitment is intended to serve the needs of the hard-core unemployed. One such training program in the Newark labor market area, SEED II, started out with guarantees by employers in the area that jobs would be offered to its graduates.

[2] According to a sample survey conducted by the Research Section in the spring of 1967, the core area of Newark, roughly coincident with the Central Ward, had a population of 102,970, distributed as follows: White 9.6 percent, Negro 84.0 percent, and Spanish-speaking 6.4 percent.

July a second plant was opened nearby (609 Central Avenue), when the first was found to offer insufficient space to meet the company's purposes.

It was intended from the outset that two divisions of the company in the Newark area would supply the regular job outlets for persons ready to transfer from the vestibule plants. The 200 Central Avenue plant set out to train men for production jobs and a small group of women as key punch operators, in both cases with a view to transfer to the Manufacturing Division plant some five miles from Newark, in Kearny, New Jersey. However, space in the plant was allocated to preparing men for transfer to the drafting department of the Service Division and to training a small number of women as typists. The second plant (609 Central Avenue) has two units, both concerned with training men for jobs in the Service Division. One group is being given job experience in the repair of telephone hand sets, the other receives training in the installation of telephone switching equipment in central offices.[3]

UNDERLYING CONCEPTIONS AND METHODS OF THE WESTERN ELECTRIC APPROACH

The Decision to Establish Separate Vestibule Plants. The company starts with the premise that there exists a population of disadvantaged persons who are unemployed or underemployed and who are unable to meet the usual entry standards. So far as the Manufacturing Division is concerned, there are obstacles to introducing such persons under lowered entry standards into regular work groups. For one thing, work is organized in groups; an incentive compensation scheme makes the pay of individuals depend on the output of the group. A new hire who takes longer than the normal learning period to reach established output norms would affect the earnings of the entire group. A second obstacle was concern for the probability that double standards with respect to absence and lateness would develop if the hirees were directly assimilated into the regular work force.

The vestibule plant permits considerable flexibility in the duration of the orientation period. It was contemplated at the outset that learners at 200 Central Avenue might be kept on the rolls for as

---

[3] The program has emphasized job opportunities for males. As of the end of 1968, out of 189 workers on roll in the two Newark plants, 42 or 22 percent were female.

long as nine months. The separated vestibule facility also permits more intensive instruction and supervision. The supervisor:worker ratio at 200 Central is approximately 1:19 as against approximately 1:27, the average in similar work at the Kearny plant. A further innovation at the shop is the inclusion of two experienced production workers in each group who, as work leaders, assist the supervisor in training.

Conception of the Nature of the Deficiency of the Disadvantaged Worker. The vestibule plants are organized and operated in accordance with the concept that a person can perform entry grade jobs even if deficient in educational attainment, but providing he possesses average intelligence and dexterity, is reasonably motivated, and is prepared to meet minimum standards of industrial discipline. In this view, the orientation experience is regarded as affording those who wish to take advantage of the opportunity to pull themselves up by their own bootstraps, to overcome habits that interfere with progress on a regular job.

In recruiting workers for the Newark plants, company entry standards were adjusted as follows: pre-employment psychological and physical dexterity tests were eliminated; health standards were relaxed. Applicants were required only to demonstrate basic literacy. Lastly, applicants with criminal records were to be given greater consideration with respect to the nature of the crime and the age at which it was committed than is the case with those who enter through regular employment channels.

In order to approximate a normal work environment, the company selected jobs from among those being performed in regular plant locations. Training is for the most part restricted to instruction on task performance. No provision is made for programs designed to increase basic educational levels.[4] The training of draftsmen and installers for the Service Division does involve some formal classroom work, and, in addition, the latter group now receives two hours of instruction in basic mathematics during the workday.

Location of the Vestibule Plants in the Inner City. The decision to locate the vestibule plants in the inner city is related to the conception of the plants as a transition or orientation phase for the disadvantaged worker. Given the fact that most of the potential recruits

---

[4] Workers transferred to mainstream jobs at Kearny can participate in a high school equivalency program conducted outside of working hours in cooperation with the New Jersey State Department of Education.

for the program were likely to come from the area, the presence of the plants nearby would obviate the transportation problem. Another consideration undoubtedly was the visibility of the plants in the community, a factor which could serve to demonstrate forcefully the concern of the company for doing something about the problem of hardcore unemployment. Recruitment of applicants for learner jobs from among residents of the community was assured by relying almost exclusively for referrals on TEAM (Total Employment and Manpower, the Concentrated Employment Program agency in the ghetto area of Newark).

Supportive Character of the Vestibule Environment. While the company attempted to organize its program around a set of conditions which simulated those prevailing in the regular installations, it was recognized that its goal of helping the disadvantaged to adjust to the normal industrial environment required some flexibility in the application of usual standards. It was assumed that this would be true in respect to performance levels, but it was necessarily extended to standards with respect to attendance. These have been considerably looser in the vestibule plants. Moreover, supervisors have made considerable effort to deal on an individual basis with problems confronted by individuals with poor attendance records. However, such standards were by no means completely overlooked, and in the 200 Central Avenue plant most involuntary terminations have occurred for reasons of poor attendance.

Management-Union Relations in Respect to the Vestibule Plants. The decision of the Manufacturing Division to establish the 200 Central Avenue plant was discussed with the union representing workers in the Kearny plant. This resulted in a supplementary agreement covering the learners during the period of their work in the vestibule plant. The agreement provides that membership is to be open to these workers (approximately 80 percent have joined), but that any learner transferred to a regular job at Kearny would not be credited with time worked at the Newark plant for seniority purposes until he had spent two years at Kearny. A worker transferred to a regular job in one or another of the company's installations starts out as would any new hire, working his way through a probationary period. This means that, even though at the time of transfer his performance is well above the beginner's level, the expected rate of progress is the same as for any new employee. Expected performance follows the standards anticipated in the engineered learning curve for the job he is on.

A union steward and two assistants serve the needs of workers in the 200 Central Avenue plant. It is contemplated that grievances will be handled in the usual manner, but no provision is made for arbitration of grievances as a final step. In fact, no written grievance has yet been submitted in the Newark plants.

SUMMARY OF PERSONNEL ACTIONS IN THE NEWARK PLANTS AS OF DECEMBER 31, 1968

TABLE A: ANALYSIS OF REFERRALS

		200 Central Avenue	609 Central Avenue
Referrals *		570	93
Did not show		71	2
Net referrals		499	91
On Roll		157	32
Ready for transfer but not placed **	34		
Pending clearance		15	11
Not hired		122	20
Terminated		33	5
Resigned		76	4
Transferred		90	19
Leave of absence and deceased		6	—
		499	91

* Most applicants are referred by TEAM. In the 200 Central Avenue facility approximately 25 percent are referrals of other community agencies or are "walk-ins."
** Many in this group were transferred in the early months of 1969.

TABLE B: REASONS FOR REJECTION OF APPLICATION

	200 Central	609 Central
Medical	33	12
Narcotics	24	
Criminal records	8	
Overqualified	20	3
No work available	32	5
Under age	5	
	122	20

TABLE C: REASONS FOR TERMINATION

	200 Central	609 Central
Lateness and absenteeism	30	3
Insubordination	0	1
Not suited to industrial employment	1	1
Relieved for medical reasons	2	
	33	5

TABLE D: EMPLOYEES ON ROLL BY SEX, RACE, AND AGE

	200 Central Avenue			609 Central Avenue		
		AGE			AGE	
	On Roll	Average	Range	On Roll	Average	Range
Males	115	23.7	18–49	32	22.3	18–35
Females	42	24.6	18–38	0	—	—
	157			32		
Negroes	120	24.0	18–49	31	22.3	18–35
Spanish-Amer.	37	23.7	18–36	1	31.0	31
White	0					
	157			32		

SOME TENTATIVE OBSERVATIONS

1. Experience in the private sector with respect to policies governing employment without discrimination suggests that the elaboration of a policy of equal opportunity by top management is a necessary but insufficient condition for altering hiring practices. Such policy can be thwarted at lower levels of management, by supervisors and by staff members in personnel departments. Implementation will depend on how seriously the policy is regarded—how vigorously it is pushed by high officials of the company.

The establishment of a separate vestibule plant in an area in which the resident labor force is predominantly black and Puerto Rican implies a set of conditions in which employment policy is unmistakably clear. The plant is organized in such a way that managerial personnel cannot fail to understand that their assignment is met precisely to the degree that the target employee population is prepared for regular jobs with the company.

2. The decision to locate the vestibule plants in the ghetto area obviates the problem of transportation for the learners and undoubtedly increases the attractiveness of the opportunity offered by the company. Nevertheless, in such cases, it may be that the problem of inadequate transportation out of the inner city to surrounding communities in which regular jobs are located is simply deferred to the point at which a learner is transferred to a regular job.

In the Western Electric program transportation is not likely to constitute a problem. Roughly half of the transfers out of the program have been placed in jobs at the Kearny plant which is served by direct nonstop Public Service buses from Newark. Among persons transferred to regular jobs in the Service Division, the majority move to locations in the city of Newark. Only a small number of workers, those placed in a service center at Union and satellite plants in Clark and Hillside (all in New Jersey), have had to rely on private transportation.

3. Past experience with the composition of unemployment during recession phases of the business cycle supports the assumption that the current effort to employ minority groups, and among them the hard-core unemployed, will suffer a severe setback in the event that unemployment rates rise substantially above recent levels. Does the vestibule arrangement offer the disadvantaged worker an additional cushion, or is the effect the same as if he were hired and placed directly in a regular job where low seniority would make him vulnerable to layoff? Workers taken on as learners at the Newark plants are regarded not as temporary trainees, but as company employees. But the viability of the vestibule plant operation depends on the availability of regular job outlets for persons ready to transfer. It is possible that a prolonged employment cutback would place a severe strain on the operation of such a facility. To date this has not occurred.

4. Even though the learners are working on tasks drawn from the regular plants, the Newark establishments inevitably create an environment different from that in the regular plants. The employees are all hired under special circumstances (most are referred by TEAM). The environment is supportive through the personal interest and counseling of the manager and section chiefs. This could conceivably create a social milieu which satisfies social and psychological needs and breeds a reluctance to transfer. In the experience at the shops thus far, there is no evidence that this has developed.

Also a strongly supportive atmosphere is generally considered more characteristic of public training programs than of large industrial companies. Encountering such an atmosphere may generate cynicism among the workers—many of whom are "graduates" of previous training which did not lead to jobs.

In the Western Electric program there are some counteracting forces. For one thing, the transfer to a regular job permits a substantial increase in earnings; those who move to the Kearny plant have an opportunity to earn incentive rates. Moreover, seniority is accumulated only with placement in a regular job. Supporting these incentives to transfer is a supervisory mode which, while tolerant of slow progress in attendance habits and performance patterns, emphasizes that continued employment depends on overcoming deficiencies. Preliminary findings based on interviews suggest that learners are anxious to move on to regular jobs once they are placed on the ready-to-transfer list.

5. The supervisor-employee relationship at 200 and 609 Central Avenue differs from the normal situation in regular plant locations. The ratio of employees to supervisors is lower; the supervisor has the assistance of a work leader. As a consequence, supervisors can devote more time to exploring the causes of learner behavior and to counseling. Implicit in this organization is a relaxation of pressures to maintain output. But, equally important, unlike his counterpart in the main plant, the supervisor need not face the potential repercussions of differential treatment of disadvantaged and regular employees. Nor does he confront differences and tensions between white and black workers, between long-service workers and recent hires.

6. The vestibule plants are conceived as production units with assigned output quotas. Yet, the average cost of production cannot be used as a criterion of successful operation. In fact, the greater the company's success in transferring employees who are ready to leave the vestibule plants, the higher average costs of production will be in these plants. 200 Central Avenue runs at about the 45 percent efficiency [5] level and ranges up to 70 percent for some individuals. Those who are transferred have reached the 70 percent level as part of the criteria for movement to the mainstream.

7. Wage-setting for learners under a vestibule arrangement must be geared to the wage structure in the regular plants and yet provide an incentive for acquiring the skills and habits which make possible

---

[5] Efficiency is a measure of actual output compared to expected output on a given task. It is defined as follows: actual output/expected output $\times$ 100.

transfers to a regular job. In the present case, wage rates of workers in the Newark plants are related to entry rates in jobs for which they are being prepared; they range from $2.15 to $2.37 per hour. Transfer to Kearny opens the possibility of sharing in incentive bonuses which bring the average hourly rate there in entry grades to $2.70 and above. Those who tranfer to the Service Division distribution center will earn $2.64 per hour.

8. It is evident that the Western Electric program for assimilating disadvantaged workers into regular jobs involves training costs in excess of those incurred in the normal process of absorbing new hires. An unknown quantity as yet is the savings that many accrue by not having to train the disadvantaged workers at the regular work locations. No application has, up to the present, been made for government subsidy in meeting the costs of the Newark program.

9. The ultimate test of the effectiveness of the Newark program lies in the experience of learners who have been placed on regular jobs. It is still too early to analyze that experience in detail. For one thing, most of the transfers have been on regular jobs for relatively short periods. Also, in the Rutgers study now underway, analysis of existing data has not been completed. However, it is clear that the retention rate has thus far been high; no more than 5 percent of those placed in regular jobs have been terminated or have resigned.

Discussion *

BY   MICHAEL J. PIORE †

The hallmark of the Western Electric program for employing the disadvantaged is two vestibule plants located in the heart of (black) Newark, which feed "disadvantaged" workers who have demonstrated their ability to meet minimal entry demands to the company's Kearny facility on the fringe of the city. The use of the ghetto facilities as feeder plants distinguishes Western Electric's efforts from other approaches. Its rationale is well presented by Professor Cher-

* Materials in these discussions are derived, in part, from workshops conducted at the conference discussions of each case and are not based strictly on the cases as they are presented in this book. [The editor.]

† Michael J. Piore is Assistant Professor of Economics at the Massachusetts Institute of Technology.

nick. On the whole, I find my own views of the project, which I have expressed elsewhere,[1] in accord with his. Rather than recapitulate the ground covered in the paper, therefore—but at some risk of detracting from a paper and a project to which I am very favorably disposed—I will emphasize two points upon which I found the conference discussions of this case inadequate.

First, I would take issue with Professor Chernick's initial assertion that companies which adopt deliberate programs for hiring, training, and integrating the disadvantaged into regular jobs may be assumed to have a policy of hiring through normal procedures without discrimination on grounds of race or national origin. The point did not emerge in the conference—perhaps because the conference was too public—but I have been told by several companies participating in MA-3 programs that their major motivation was the number of minority employees this would permit them to show on the EEO-1 forms required by the Equal Employment Opportunity Commission. If their presumption that such a showing will stall off a federal review of their personnel policies is correct, special programs may be a *substitute* for nondiscrimination in normal procedures. It may thus become much easier for a black to be hired if he is disadvantaged than if he is not; or, more likely, the hiring of blacks may be channeled through special programs. The prospect is rendered particularly disturbing by the fact that so many of the special programs involve employment structures reminiscent of segregated employment patterns of the South: separate black and white plants, segregated seniority districts, and the like. One of the major attractions of the vestibule plant approach which Western Electric is utilizing is that it appears to prevent the institution of segregated employment patterns: the black worker's stay in the ghetto plant is limited; he *must* transfer to the company's regular facility.

Second, I felt the Western Electric case left unexplored the problem of *managing* efforts to employ the disadvantaged. There is clearly a trade-off in these projects between efficiency (e.g., cost and quality), on the one hand, and the degree of disadvantage of the work force on the other. How does a company decide upon the proper balance between these two objectives? Having decided, how does it communicate these decisions to managers responsible for executing its policy? How does it judge the success of these mana-

---

[1] "On-the-job Training in a Dual Labor Market," in Arnold Weber *et al.*, eds., *Public and Private Manpower Policies*, Industrial Relations Research Association Research Volume (forthcoming).

gers? That there is a problem of managerial control was, it seemed to me, indicated by the way the company personnel (and here Western Electric was not at all atypical) handled questions about policy choice. Question them about the efficiency of their operation and they would talk about the degree of disadvantaged; imply that they might be "creaming" [selecting the most qualified of the disadvantaged] and they would talk about the need for some minimal level of efficiency. On how a balance between these objectives is achieved, however, the managers were singularly uncommunicative. The conference left the impression that, at Western Electric, the plant manager had considerable discretion on this score, but neither the paper nor the verbal discussion was very clear about the context in which that discretion was exercised. One would, for example, like to know whether management operates with a fixed budget, and if so, how it is derived. What happens if costs are less than those budgeted? Does the plant then increase the relative disadvantage of the labor force or does it return the savings to the company? How, in fact, does the company monitor the degree of disadvantage of the labor force? Does not pressure for cost reduction produce a tendency toward upward drift in the quality of the labor force?

2

An Act of Corporate Citizenship

BY   *EDWARD C. BANFIELD* *

This paper describes how and why the International Business Machines Corporation established a manufacturing plant in the Bedford-Stuyvesant area of Brooklyn. The plant began operation on July 8, 1968, and it will not reach its full complement of 450 employees until the end of 1969; this account is therefore of beginnings only.

THE MIXTURE OF MOTIVES

In terms of paper market values, IBM is the most valuable business in the world. The most important factor in its success, according to the booklet that it distributes to all new employees, is its three basic beliefs:

1. Respect for the individual.
2. A desire to have the best customer service of any company in the world.
3. The conviction that an organization should pursue all tasks with the idea that they can be accomplished in a superior manner.

In addition to these basic beliefs, IBM is guided by a set of fundamental principles, the seventh and last of which is:

---

* Edward C. Banfield is Henry Lee Shattuck Professor of Urban Government and a member of the Faculty of the John Fitzgerald Kennedy School of Government, Harvard University.

Acknowledgment is due Donald E. Graham, on whose interviews this account is largely based.

To accept our responsibilities as a corporate citizen of the nation, and the world.[1]

So long as the company remained small, this last principle was not very demanding. By 1962, however, IBM had 80,000 employees, and the principle was very demanding indeed. As Thomas J. Watson, Jr., chairman of the board, remarked to an interviewer not long ago, "No one expects much in the way of business statesmanship from a company making a few millions, but from one making hundreds of millions a great deal is expected." A company as big as IBM could not, even if it wished, regard the making of profit as the be-all and end-all of its existence. The public expects it to take a broad view of its responsibilities, and if it fails to do so—or even to *appear* to do so—it might be subject to criticism.

When the Kennedy Administration took office, it was natural that Watson (who like his father, the company's founder, was a liberal Democrat) should be drawn into the various New Frontier undertakings—the Peace Corps and the Labor-Management Committee, among others. He and his wife—she particularly—had known the Kennedys for many years; and as he came into closer association with them, especially with Robert Kennedy, who was then attorney general, he became more concerned about poverty and racial injustice. A few years earlier such matters would have been too controversial for IBM to get involved in. But now public opinion, that part of it anyway that mattered most to IBM, had so changed that *not* getting involved might be considered a failure of business leadership.

Up to then IBM, like most big companies, had employed very few Negroes. When Watson visited one of his plants, he used to see a Negro here and there; he knew, too, that there were a few Negro executives, although none near the top. But after bringing IBM into Plans for Progress, a government-sponsored effort to encourage employment of minority group workers, he set out to make it live up to its obligations. He wrote to all of his division presidents, instructing them to hire more Negroes; it would not do, he said, simply to wait for qualified Negroes to apply; managers (in IBM a *manager* is

---

[1] The other principles: (1) To provide intelligent, aggressive, capable management; (2) To serve our customers as efficiently and effectively as possible; (3) To improve our products and our technology continually; (4) To provide a maximum degree of satisfaction on the part of our employees in their assigned tasks; (5) To recognize the obligation to our stockholders to provide an adequate return on their investment; and (6) To play our part in furthering the progress of the communities in which our facilities are located.

anyone who supervises employees, however few) should make energetic efforts to recruit them. Because the company was growing at a furious pace (from 80,000 in 1962 to 225,000 in 1968), Watson did not succeed in increasing the proportion of Negro employees by as much as he would have liked; however, he did increase their absolute number twelvefold. More than a few got managerial positions.

When the Office of Economic Opportunity solicited bids for operation of Job Corps centers, IBM agreed to run one. The experience was illuminating to Watson. The men and women who came to the center were poor, low status, unemployed, on dope in many cases, and, for one reason or another, badly demoralized. Hearing about them and the problems that they presented for the management of the center, Watson concluded that little could be done to help people who were completely unmotivated. The thing to do was to reach them at an earlier stage. And the way to do this was by providing a better economic base, one that would give them reason to think that work and effort would pay off. As he put it later, "I thought you had to go in there and try to change these conditions so that there'd be some relationship between effort, personal integrity, and end results."

At about this time Watson was moved by a book by the Negro poet and photographer Gordon Parks. "I had never realized what it is like to be a Negro," he remarked later. "I'm sure that I don't now. But Gordon Parks' book helped me to understand that."

After the riots of 1964 Watson felt that something ought to be done right away to give visible expression to business concern about conditions in the ghettos. His fellow members of the Management Review Committee, the body of high-ranking executives that passed on important executive decisions, agreed. For a time the committee considered setting up a plant for printing computer cards in the Watts district of Los Angeles. Such a plant could be established very quickly; all that was necessary was to install the machines; the demand for the cards was practically unlimited. The trouble with the idea was that the people in Watts could learn very little by printing cards. The technology of it was such that the jobs would have to be almost all low-skilled.

What was needed in Watts and places like it, the IBM executives thought, were plants in which people could acquire skills and also develop a sense of pride in their achievement as a group or community. If IBM could develop a model of this sort, other companies might follow its lead, and the total achievement might eventually be large enough to make a real difference. Developing a model would not be easy, and the attempt might fail altogether. If it failed, the loss of money would not be serious; as compared to the loss that would result from failure of a major product, it would be trivial.

What IBM had at stake in the ghetto was mainly reputation. Many people—employees, stockholders, customers, suppliers, and others—were accustomed to seeing IBM succeed at whatever it tried. Their confidence in it was, of course, a very valuable business asset. If the company suffered an embarrassing failure in the ghetto, some of that asset would be lost. On the other hand, by taking a successful initiative in such an important and difficult matter, it might further enhance its standing. Highly educated young people were especially likely to be impressed by an attempt to do something for the ghetto, and they were a clientele of particular importance for a company that had to compete strenuously for scientists, engineers, and other creative people.

PLANNING

When, in September 1967, Vice President Humphrey and Secretary of Labor Wirtz invited executives of large corporations to hear an official of the Aerojet-General Corporation tell what it had done to employ hard-core workers in Watts, the IBM representative went, knowing that his company was about to take the plunge. The government, the Vice President said, was ready to give financial support to efforts like Aerojet-General's. This did not interest the IBM man. He knew that government support was bound to entail some limitation on the freedom of the employer to hire whom he pleased and in general to manage things in his own way. If IBM was to try something at all ambitious, it would need the greatest possible freedom of action.

After the meeting in Washington, IBM assigned George Carter, a Negro executive who had come to it the year before from the Peace Corps and who was about to become head of IBM's equal opportunity programs, to head a study group to look into the feasibility of establishing one or more ghetto plans and to come up with immediate recommendations. At the end of October Carter's committee reported: IBM should establish a manufacturing plant in Harlem to employ hard-core and underemployed workers. In reaching this decision, the committee had considered several alternatives. One was to create a feeder plant, where workers would be recruited and trained for assignment to permanent jobs elsewhere. This was what Westinghouse was doing. Another was to provide financial backing for a black entrepreneur who would run a plant as an IBM supplier. Although the company had never financed a supplier and although its policy was to take no more than 30 percent of any supplier's output, this third-party arrangement had much to recommend it. For one thing, it would tend to insulate IBM against "industrial relations problems"—in plain language, unions. The Watsons had never opposed unions for those who liked them, but no IBM facility had ever been unionized, and union practices were obviously at odds with the IBM philosophy of reward for individual effort. For another thing, the onus of failure—always a possibility—would not fall upon IBM. The committee recommended against the third-party approach, however, because of three offsetting considerations: First, IBM could do a better job of training the workers than could any subcontractor; second, one of the main purposes of the undertaking was to make clear that big business was "standing up to its responsibilities"; and, third, it was essential to get a plant into operation before the next long, hot summer began, something that could not be done if any time were spent looking for a suitable third party and then negotiating a contract with it.

The choice of a location was relatively easy. One member of the committee proposed putting the plant in the rural South in order to discourage migration to the big city slums. Carter opposed this idea. Negroes, he said, would leave the South whether an IBM plant was built there or not; besides, except at Cape Kennedy and one or two other places, the company was doing very little manufacturing in the South and consequently did not have a management structure there into which an undertaking of this sort could be fitted. If the plant was to be in the North, New York was the obvious place for it because "we are primarily a New York State company." The two great Negro enclaves or ghettos in New York were Harlem and the Bedford-Stuyvesant area of Brooklyn. The word *Harlem*, Carter pointed out, was practically synonymous with *black*; because Harlem was a symbol, a plant would attract more attention there than anywhere else; besides, Harlem was more accessible than Bedford-Stuyvesant to the mid-Hudson Valley, the source from which the plant's supplies would mostly come. It was also, he thought, more stable politically: about 30 percent of Bedford-Stuyvesant's half million residents had come there since the days of the Brooklyn Dodgers— that was an indication of their lack of experience as a community. Although the advantage clearly lay with Harlem and the planning enterprise was therefore called "Project H," the committee's formal recommendation was for the establishment of a plant in either Harlem or Bedford-Stuyvesant.

The Management Review Committee quickly approved this recommendation and asked three of the company's divisions—Systems Manufacturing (computers), Federal Systems (space equipment and programming), and Office Products (typewriters and dictating equipment)—to put forward proposals for a plant. The proposal submitted by the Systems Manufacturing Division (SMD) was quickly chosen. It was put together in two months at SMD's headquarters in White Plains by a committee headed by Warren Lind, the engineer who had organized the production of the 650 computer and who was now director of planning. The committee decided that the plant should manufacture a simple product in its first year, shifting to more complex ones in succeeding years. It should begin very small and grow in size until finally, in 1971, it would employ 350 "directs" (production workers) and 425 "indirects" (supporting workers). It was assumed that, like all of the other SMD plants, this one would have a medical staff. That the others, which had 3,000 to 5,000 workers, were in a much better position to support large overhead charges did not cause anyone much concern. To find a site the committee enlisted the help of the Real Estate and Construction Division (Real Con). There was none in Harlem, Real Con reported, but in Bedford-Stuyvesant the company could rent, with an option to buy, an eight-story warehouse that stood at the corner of Nostrand and Gates avenues in the very center of the ghetto. To fit the building up properly would cost $3,781,000. Working from this figure, the Lind committee estimated that the plant would incur a deficit until 1971. In so doing, it would add $6,850,000 to the cost of the division's production. This, it estimated, was $1,450,000 more than would be added if the same number of people were to be employed in a new plant built on cheaper land outside the city and $4,850,000 more than if they were simply added to the work forces of existing plants.

In mid-December the head of SMD put the Lind committee's plan before the Management Review Committee. It was still called "Project H," although by now Bedford-Stuyvesant had been definitely decided upon. The lack of a suitable site in Harlem was not the only reason for this decision. Watson was a member of the Bedford-Stuyvesant Development and Services Corporation, a group of big businessmen that Senator Kennedy, aided by Mayor Lindsay and by Senator Javits, had organized the year before to improve the community's "access to funds and managerial expertise." When he was asked to serve on the corporation, Watson was assured that there was no intention to trap him into building a plant or giving money. Nevertheless, he felt that, because of his connection with the corporation, Bedford-Stuyvesant had some claim on him. There were, besides, several reasons for preferring Bedford-Stuyvesant. It was, he thought, a simpler and therefore more easily understood world than Harlem. Also, it was not getting as much help; in Harlem the Urban League and many industrial companies (including IBM itself, which was sponsoring a storefront school, or "street academy") had projects of one sort or another, whereas in Bedford-Stuyvesant very little was being done. Finally, Watson knew the principal figures in the Bedford-Stuyvesant Renewal and Rehabilitation Corporation (later the Bedford-Stuyvesant Restoration Corporation, or "Restoration"). This consisted of 20 civic and religious leaders of the community brought together by Senator Kennedy to make plans for the community in collaboration with the corporation of white business leaders. If trouble should arise, IBM could count on the wholehearted cooperation of these local leaders, and this was an important consideration.

Watson was troubled when (on December 29) the SMD proposal was put before him. Somehow he got the impression that the division was proposing to build another 3,000 to 5,000-man plant just like the eight it already had. That was too big a step to take without first feeling out the ground, Watson said. The plant should be a small one to begin with. And there were several questions that should be explored before even a small plant was started. Would it be possible to recruit the right kind of workers, and to do so without discriminating against whites? Would the area's high crime rate pose recruitment or other problems? How about drug addiction and vandalism? Some blacks, he knew, believed that a white business would locate in a black district only for the purpose of exploiting black people. Was that view widespread? Was it really clear that the black community wanted IBM there? So long as questions like these remained unanswered, he was reluctant, to say the least, to spend $3.7 million to renovate a building that might become a monument to a failure.

"How do we know," he asked finally, "that we can find any real IBM'ers who are willing to run a plant there?" This was a question for which there was a ready answer. SMD had already selected a man to manage the new plant, and he in turn had selected six key assistants. The manager-to-be was Ernest K. Friedli, a 42-year-old engineer who had graduated from Duke University after having attended a Navy officer's training school there. He had joined IBM in 1947, served in several staff capacities at the divisional headquarters, and was now assistant manager of the Kingston, N.Y., plant. Friedli had no experience with hard core workers and knew nothing about the ghetto. The reason he was chosen for the job was that he had proved himself to be a capable manager and had earned promotion. If he had stayed in Kingston, he might well have become manager there within a year or two.

As it turned out, Friedli had qualifications that those who selected him were not aware of. He had grown up in Brooklyn—his father was a Swiss immigrant—and had attended parochial school there. Although he had gone away as a young man and had become a Presbyterian, he still felt an attachment to Brooklyn, and he had a special feeling for the people who lived there now. The idea of doing something useful for the place and the people appealed to him very strongly, and when he heard that the company might start a plant there he said at once that he would like to be associated with it. He was not looking for a faster way up the job ladder. Managing a factory was what he liked ("I enjoy getting something out the back door"), and he was perfectly willing to go on managing one for the next 20 years. The attraction of the Brooklyn job was that it would be useful and challenging. Not until after he had made the move was any mention made of a change in salary.

Friedli had already found the men he wanted as his principal assistants. Knowing that it would be harder to find experienced blacks than experienced whites, he decided to look first for them. Working from a list of all black employees, he soon found six who suited him. On a Friday just before Christmas, he told them about the plan for the new plant and asked them if they would be willing to help run it if called upon. They could expect relocation assistance, he said, but they should not count on more than that: This was something that was going to take dedication. And he would have to have an answer by Monday. To his satisfaction, all six said they would like to go. As matters turned out, only four of the six were needed. Two white assistants were also employed.

Friedli did his best to make his assistants feel that they and he constituted a team.

"Holy mackerel," one of them had said when Friedli first approached him. "Do you think I'm ready for a job like that?"

"No," Friedli had answered. "But as a team we ought to pull it off."

A week or two after seeing SMD's plan, Watson asked Friedli to lunch with him and three or four other high executives of the company. When he heard Friedli call Brooklyn "my old neighborhood," he was pleased. They talked about the changes that had occurred there. Did Friedli think that it would be hazardous for employees, particularly white ones, to go to and from the plant? Did he feel that he understood the special problems of black people?

"I think it's questionable whether you can run an efficient plant there," Watson told Friedli. "If we go into this, we must do it with our eyes open. We must recognize that it's a business risk."

He went on to say that all too often he heard that things were done in a certain way "because that's the IBM way." Take the idea of air conditioning the Bedford-Stuyvesant plant, for example.

Were they planning to air-condition it simply because other IBM plants were air conditioned? At every point, they should consider the probable effect of what they did on other companies in the area. If they drove other employers out of Bedford-Stuyvesant, they might make matters worse. "I want you to throw away the book," he said. "Write your own book."

He asked Friedli to form a study committee to look into three questions:

1. Should IBM become involved in the ghetto?
2. If it should, what form should its involvement take? Direct operation? Operation through a subsidiary? Through a third party?
3. What should be the plan of operations?

The study committee was chosen in part from among those who had served on the Carter committee and in part from the group of six assistants-to-be.

Taking with him two of his assistants, Eugene Douglas, who would be production manager, and Alfred J. Iannone, who would be in charge of facility planning and plant engineering, Friedli traveled around the country looking at plants that employed hard-core workers. After that they spent several weeks learning about conditions in Brooklyn. Sometimes they would drop in unannounced and talk to the personnel manager of a factory. In view of the riots, they would tell him, big business must do something to improve the working conditions of Negroes, Puerto Ricans, and other minority groups. What did he think were the problems here and what should a company like IBM do about them? Franklin Thomas, the executive director of Restoration, the community planning body that Senator Kennedy had started, took the IBM men on a tour of Bedford-Stuyvesant once, pointing out evidences of growing community pride—houses that had been repainted, trees that had been planted, and vacant lots that had been cleared of rubbish.

After a month of this, Friedli and his assistants were ready to answer Watson's first question with an enthusiastic yes. The second question presented some difficulties. In the choice between direct operation and the use of a third party, there were many conflicting considerations. For example, the objective of speed implied direct operation whereas insulation from industrial relations problems probably (the case was by no means clear) implied the use of a third party. Friedli thought that if only business considerations were taken into account the third-party course was clearly preferable. On the other hand, if "emotional" considerations—those that were *not* "business"—were also admitted into the calculation, the advantage was probably the other way. If one placed enough emphasis on speed (an emotional consideration in that the reason for speed was to change the mood of the ghetto before the long, hot summer), one could certainly justify direct operation.

Following a procedure described in a book called *The Rational Manager*,[2] the committee identified 17 factors that seemed relevant and then assigned numerical values to each. In "prioritizing" (as Friedli put it) their criteria, the committee members had not much to go on but their own tastes, hunches, and surmises: No one had told them what relative values IBM placed on speed, reduced industrial relations exposure, or any of the other 15 items on their list. ("The manager's judgment as to the weight of each WANT objective is drawn from his own experience and from the experience of others.") They did their best, however, and found—to their great satisfaction—that the rational thing was to operate the plant directly.

Before going on to draw up a plan, they thought that it would be well to get approval of the conclusions they had so far reached. Before going to Watson, however, Friedli explained where matters stood to the senior vice president, Frank Cary.

"Who asked you to worry about emotional considerations?" Cary asked.

Friedli had to admit that no one had.

"Go back and make the calculation strictly business," Cary said.

Friedli was sure that, on a strictly business basis, direct operation could not be justified. Further calculations confirmed his opinion.

Watson had been of two minds about the third-party approach all along. At times he thought that operating a plant in the ghetto under the IBM name was exactly the wrong thing to do: The risk of embarrassing failure was too great. At other times, however, he felt that the greater likelihood of success by direct operation justified that approach. The other members of the Management Review Committee were torn too. When the Friedli committee recommended this approach, the corporate officers hesitated. The report was excellent, Watson told Friedli, but the company was not ready to proceed on that basis. For a week nothing happened. Then Cary called to ask for an evaluation of the idea of a consortium of three big companies to finance, staff, and provide a market for a plant in Bedford-Stuyvesant. This possibility was quickly disposed of; it would take too long to find two companies that would agree with

---

[2] Charles H. Kepner and Benjamin B. Tregoe, *The Rational Manager* (New York: McGraw-Hill Book Company, 1965).

IBM on the choice of a location, a manager, and a product or products. Whatever the advantages of consortium arrangement, they could not offset its inherent clumsiness.

That having been disposed of, Cary advised Friedli to put a strictly business proposition before the Management Review Committee. Do so, he said, even though you yourself favor a different approach. The Management Review Committee might decide to introduce emotional factors—that was its privilege—but it should start from a purely business basis. If IBM was to start a plant for other than business reasons, the decision should be made at the very top.

Acting on this advice, the Friedli committee quickly worked out a proposal for third-party operation. A year or two previously, the owner of a sheet metal working company had agreed, out of regard for Senator Kennedy, to rent a shop in Bedford-Stuyvesant where several black workers could be employed reconditioning IBM parts on contract. The committee suggested trying to persuade this man to take over the Nostrand Avenue building and enlarge his operation until in 1969 he had 300 workers. The 300 figure was something of an accident. It had been fixed upon when the consortium idea was being discussed (each of three companies was to have been responsible for 100 workers) and in the few days since the dropping of that idea, there had been no time to work out a rationale for a different figure. As Friedli and his assistants figured it, a plant of this scale, operated by a vendor, might begin to make a profit in its second year.

On March 29 Friedli put the third-party plan before Watson and the Management Review Committee. If a plant was to be in operation before the long, hot summer began, a decision would have to be made now.

Watson said that the committee had now made a decision. It liked the plan—*except for its third-party feature.* He had gradually come to the conclusion, which the committee now shared, that third-party plans were too conservative. The only reason for a consortium was to be able to lay the blame for failure on someone else. He had noted that other industrial companies had been taking third-party approaches, and he was afraid that if this became the general practice ghetto residents would be reinforced in the feeling that nobody was willing to bet on them. It was a mistake to try so hard to avoid risks. IBM was most likely to make a plant succeed if it knew that it had something to lose by failure. It would operate the plant directly because doing it that way would give the greatest probability of success.

"Will you run that proposition (the plan just submitted) with

'IBM' on the front door?" he asked Friedli. He would be glad to, Friedli said. But he was obliged to point out that under IBM management the plant was not likely to make a profit in its second year or even in its third. As a ball-park guess, it would cost the company $500,000 a year for several years. A vendor's costs would be less than IBM's, since it would not sponsor an employee's social club, put on a Christmas party with presents for the children, have a community relations manager or perhaps even a receptionist. A vendor would have one supervisor to every 40 employees, whereas IBM would have one to every 15. With IBM on the door, the plant would have to be a "real IBM place." Watson assured Friedli that he would not be surprised or upset at such large losses. But he wanted him to remember "to throw the book away"—to decide all questions on the basis of what the situation in Bedford-Stuyvesant called for, not on what was customary in IBM.

Under what circumstances, Friedli asked, would the company deem the venture a failure and decide to liquidate it? As far as he could see, Watson told him, the only thing that might cause the company to decide that would be a finding that employees, especially women, were not safe working there.

UNKNOWN QUANTITIES

IBM had never before located a plant in a big city. For a variety of reasons it had always chosen medium-sized cities, although medium-sized ones that drew upon the labor supply of a whole metropolitan area. Brooklyn, the head of the Systems Manufacturing Division later told an interviewer, was "an entirely different environment," an "unknown quantity."

One of the unknowns was the hard-core worker. In his presentation to the Management Review Committee, Carter explained that most ghetto residents were pretty much like other Americans. Hard-core workers were a minority. He described the problems that they might present to management under the following headings:

Background
    Police records
    Credit problems
    Broken families
    Health problems
    Alcohol and narcotics problems

Different Cultural Perceptions
Intrinsic value of work
Family and children
Masculinity syndrome

Lower-level Education
Dress
Attrition, lateness, and absenteeism
Unintentional vandalism
Lack of self-disciplined work procedures
Attitude toward money
Resort to physical violence

As if to underline the last item on this list, a 78-year-old man was murdered as he was walking from the site of the plant to a nearby subway station while the planning was still underway. This gave the Management Review Committee a chill of foreboding. Perhaps it was futile to try to build something in a community so disorganized. Was the ghetto some kind of quicksand into which anything that was built would sooner or later sink?

No one knew. Eugene Douglas, the production manager designate, and Henry Jackson, the personnel manager designate, had grown up in Negro neighborhoods but had spent most of their adult lives among whites. To them the Negro underclass was hardly less alien than it was to Friedli. Douglas had seen enough on assembly lines to know that black workers could be taught as readily as white ones; however, he did not claim to know how the conditions of ghetto life might affect the operation of a plant.

Their swing around the country had not given Friedli and his assistants much of an idea of what to expect in Bedford-Stuyvesant. Conditions were obviously very different from place to place. In Los Angeles, Aerojet-General's subsidiary, the Watts Corporation, had few lessons to teach them. It was essentially an on-the-job training program for hard-core workers; when a worker had been "trained," he got a job somewhere else—no one seemed to know where or at what pay. At the Eastman Kodak Company plant in Rochester, N.Y., Friedli was told that he would have a hard time recruiting workers. He did not take the warning very seriously, however, because he could see that the Rochester labor market, which Eastman-Kodak had long been drawing heavily upon, was much tighter than the Brooklyn one. In Brooklyn itself the reports were mixed and inconclusive. A chemical company had had very little trouble with crime or vandalism, but only a few of its 2,000 workers and none of its supervisors were black. The personnel manager of the Otis Elevator

Company was surprised at the sociological nature of the IBM questions. Seventy percent of Otis' labor force was black or Puerto Rican, and there had never been any noteworthy problems on that score. Production was good, and work habits, crime, and vandalism were not out of the ordinary. As for employee relations—there would be a dance that night to which employees of all races and nationality groups would come.

Friedli and his assistants found that the results of their inquiries were reassuring on the whole. They became convinced that they could hire ghetto residents in sufficient number and that they did not have to fear violence within the plant. Training would present some difficulties, but these could be overcome.

Despite this growing confidence, Friedli decided, and his assistants agreed, that it was essential to postpone hiring any workers who had very serious problems—the unmotivated, addicts, alcoholics, and so one—until after a work force that could meet minimum production requirements had been created and tested. He was aware that the Management Review Committee expected him to dig deep into the hard core, as Eastman Kodak, for example, was doing. He would dig eventually, but not right away. Eastman Kodak, he pointed out, was in an altogether different position than IBM: It was adding a small proportion of hard-core workers to the stable work force of a huge going concern, whereas IBM was starting from scratch. He had no objection to hiring persons who had had little schooling or even persons who had serious criminal records. He was determined, however, that his initial work force should consist only of those who were motivated to work and willing to accept discipline and training.

That he could find enough such persons in Bedford-Stuyvesant seemed pretty certain. IBM would offer pay and other incentives considerably more attractive than those offered by other employers in Brooklyn and—especially—in Bedford-Stuyvesant. For one thing, an IBM worker would receive a minimum of $84.80 for a 40-hour week—$2.12 an hour. This was more than it might seem at first, for the IBM worker would be on a salary, which meant that if for good cause such as illness in the family he missed a day's work, neither his pay nor his vacation time would be reduced. For another thing, the IBM employee would receive the unusually generous IBM insurance and other benefits. For a third thing, he would have a remarkable degree of job security: The company had not laid off anyone for lack of work for as long as anyone could remember. Finally, he would be treated with respect, given good opportunities to learn, and helped to rise on the basis of merit. Among the company's basic beliefs, respect for the individual stood first. That principle would work as well in Bedford-Stuyvesant as anywhere else, Friedli felt sure.

Friedli nevertheless instructed Iannone, the plant layout man, to proceed conservatively. Iannone guessed that absenteeism would run around 25 percent and that turnover in the first few months would be 100 percent. (The manager of a small factory in Brooklyn had told him that, in the course of the year, he had hired 45 workers to fill 15 jobs; since this was a 300 percent turnover it seemed conservative to expect 100 percent.) On the basis of what he had read—*Fortune* magazine was his main source—and what ghetto plant managers told him, he expected that many employees would have to be taught to use simple hand tools like soldering irons and some might even have to be taught the elements of personal hygiene.

The choice of a "product mission" was made with such limitations in mind. The product should be one that was simple to manufacture but not *so* simple that employees would learn nothing in the process. It should have few parts. It should not "tail-gate"—that is, require close integration with the production schedule of another plant. Power supplies (devices that modify incoming current to the requirements of computers) were probably too difficult and risky; assembling cables for computers would be safer. IBM's demand for cable assembly, Iannone found, would keep 418 persons busy; that was about the right number. The plant would begin in April with 50 directs, grow to 100 in the next three months, and then double in the next six months. If all went well, more workers would be employed later on.

When they considered how the building should be reconditioned, Friedli and Iannone remembered Watson's cautions against following the book and perhaps leaving a monument to their failure. They decided against putting in new level floors and against dropping the ceilings. Real Con had estimated that 30 footcandles of light would be enough, but Friedli and Iannone decided that the mood of the factory would be better with 70 footcandles. For the same reason, they ordered the walls painted in pastels, good quality floor tile installed in the toilets, and air conditioning.

When he heard that the building was to be air conditioned, Watson wanted to know why. (It was not the expense that bothered him; he wanted to make sure that IBM did not establish standards that other Brooklyn employers could not afford to meet; one of its main purposes, after all, was to establish standards that they *could* meet.) Friedli explained that in July and August the temperature in Brooklyn sometimes topped 100 degrees—enough to interfere very seriously with work. Office workers would insist on air conditioning, and, he reminded Watson, it was a principle with IBM that an advantage available to one set of employees be available to all at that location. Someone else made another point in defense of the air conditioning. "Supposing one of our employees goes up to the Endicott plant for training and then comes back here to a sleazy, non-air-conditioned building. Wouldn't that be bad?" Watson agreed that it would. It was essential that the Bedford-Stuyvesant workers realize that they were going to be treated like other members of the IBM family.

These matters having been decided, Real Con engaged a black architect from Hartford, Conn., to draw up plans for remodeling the building and a black contracting firm (one that had been brought into existence with a Restoration Corporation loan) to carry them out. It was understood that the contractor would use local sub-contractors to the greatest extent possible.

STAFFING THE PLANT

Friedli's principal assistants had been recruited very early in the planning process. In addition to Douglas, Iannone, and Jackson, they were Matthew Whitehead, a graduate of Loomis Academy, Tufts College, and the Howard University Law School, who had been with the company three years and was working in its Park Avenue office, and Eric J. Flood, a native of Ireland who had a master's degree in management from Columbia University and who in 10 years' service with IBM had risen to be administrative assistant to the divisional accountant. Whitehead was to be the plant's legal counsel, of course; Flood was to be its comptroller.

These assistants helped to recruit others. By the end of December 1968, there were 30 managers, of whom 15 were black. Only one, Edgar A. Fitt, the community relations director, came from Bedford-Stuyvesant. A native of Barbados, he had lived in Bedford-Stuyvesant for many years, commuting to the IBM office in White Plains. Another staff member from Bedford-Stuyvesant was Dolores Minott, a graduate of Howard University, who was staff psychologist and, informally, a link between the management and some of the politically active elements of the black community.

With a few exceptions, those who transferred to Bedford-Stuyvesant got promotions. Most of those who had not previously been managers got the increase that normally accompanies an unsolicited transfer. Those who had been managers were promoted one or two grades, and in most cases this meant substantially more money. It is unlikely that anyone sought transfer simply to increase his income, however. Certainly Friedli did not encourage anyone to do so. ("A good man," he told an interviewer, "takes a job because it is fun; you want the ones who *want* to do it.") Those who were eager to get ahead—and presumably most were—could in most cases have done so more comfortably by some other route; if they went to Bedford-Stuyvesant, it was at least partly because they wanted to take part in a struggle to solve an important social problem.

None of those who transferred settled in Bedford-Stuyvesant. Lack of suitable housing was one reason. Near the plant there were plenty of houses for sale, but they were very badly deteriorated, and the prices were high—$25,000 for what was essentially a shell. Fifteen minutes away, in Brooklyn Heights, there were fine old brownstones in good condition, but they cost from $75,000 to $100,000. Housing was by no means the only drawback: Bedford-Stuyvesant's schools were notoriously bad, and its crime rate notoriously high. Friedli came in from Rockland County, spending an hour commuting in the morning and an hour and a half in the afternoon. Douglas, whose son was in his last year of high school, went all the way to Poughkeepsie, a two-hour trip each way.

That the white managers did not live in Bedford-Stuyvesant did not surprise or interest the black community. The failure of any of the IBM blacks to live there occasioned some comment, however. The IBM people had associated with whites for so long, it was said, that they were now black only in a technical sense. Perhaps eventually they would rejoin the black community, but that was doubtful.

Presumably it would not matter much if the black managers did not identify with the community. If all went well, most of the managers who had transferred to Bedford-Stuyvesant—whites as well as blacks—would eventually transfer away, thus allowing Bedford-Stuyvesant residents who had risen through the ranks to take their places. No promises were made and no dates mentioned, but the idea gained currency that in two or three years the plant would be staffed with Bedford-Stuyvesant residents from top to bottom. In fact, it was most unlikely that this would happen since it would take at least five or six years for a man to learn what a production control manager, say, had to know in order to fit into the very complex IBM world of which the plant was a part. The plant could conceivably be all black in two or three years, but it could not be all Bedford-Stuyvesant in so short a time.

Friedli wanted to develop managerial talent from Bedford-Stuyvesant as fast as possible, however, and this influenced the personnel standards that he set. He had to have workers who could be promoted: Obviously there was no other way in which an all, or even predominantly, Bedford-Stuyvesant plant could be created. At the same time he could not neglect IBM's main purpose, which was to give jobs to the disadvantaged. The criteria of selection finally decided upon represented a balance between these two more or less conflicting goals. Preference was to be given to Bedford-Stuyvesant residents who had been unemployed for three months or more. But preference was also to be given to those who had "a desire to become part of something real," and no one was to be employed who did not give evidence of wanting to work. Men were to be preferred to women. One reason for this was that men would be readier to accept transfer to a plant in another city, and moving a certain number of people to other facilities was one of the company's objectives. The main reason, however, was that black people themselves wanted it that way. Employer prejudice had always been strongest against men, they said, with the result that women, "matriarchs," dominated Negro life, and men, having inferior jobs or none at all, were not respected and could not feel self-respect.

At first applications were not accepted from persons under the age of 18. Before long, however, it occurred to Friedli that in this he was unwittingly "following the book": A boy of 16 could do the work as well as anyone, and the usual argument against employing boys—that they should be in school—was not very strong in a community where seven out of ten high school students dropped out.

In evaluating applications, no importance was attached to lack of schooling. An employee had to be able to read and write (although not necessarily well enough to be able to fill out an application form; assistance was provided for that when necessary), but no one was disqualified for lack of a grade school education. Those who had missed out on schooling would have the chance to get the equivalent of a high school education after hours but at company expense.

A bad record did not disqualify an applicant either. At first the plant employed an investigating agency to check the employment, credit, and police records of those being seriously considered for jobs. This was standard practice in the company, and Friedli thought that if there was someone in the plant who had committed a serious crime he ought at least to know it. It soon became evident, however, that investigating agencies labored under extraordinary difficulties in Bedford-Stuyvesant; moreover, such scraps of information as they turned up were not really relevant. What the applicant had done in the past did not matter; what *did* matter was what, under new and much more favorable circumstances, he would do in the future. After a while the personnel officers stopped looking at the investigation reports. Soon afterward the company gave up the use of investigating agencies altogether.

Most applicants were interviewed twice over a two-week period. The first interview was conducted by a personnel officer who administered a dexterity test and screened out applicants who were clearly unsuitable. The reason for the dexterity test was to identify those who probably could not do the kind of work required no matter how hard they tried. ("We felt that these people did not need another failure.") Sixty-seven percent passed the dexterity test: This was exactly the percentage that passed in other plants.

Applicants who survived the initial screening were referred to whatever manager needed workers. Managers were told that in interviewing applicants they should try to decide whether the individual was capable of going beyond the particular job for which he was being considered. In another IBM plant an applicant would have been given a standard aptitude test; here a manager's judgment was enough.

Successful applicants were given physical examinations. If the individual was not a drug addict or an alcoholic and if he did not have an ailment, such as a weak heart or a hernia, that would interfere with his work, he was hired. Correctable defects would be taken care of later, the company paying about 75 percent of the cost. (When it was pointed out to him that hernias were usually correctable, Friedli agreed and checked to see if there was any reason why the policy in this matter should not be changed.)

As among applicants qualified for a particular job, choice was made on a first-come, first-served basis. Those who had no chance of being accepted were eventually sent letters thanking them for having applied and expressing regret that there was no job for them "at this time."

As of December 31, 1968, the plant had received 2,565 applications. Table 1, which is based on a random sample of those applications that were fully or almost fully executed, summarizes the characteristics of applicants for employment as directs. It will be noted that 60 percent of these applicants were women.

Applicants for secretarial and office positions were given standard performance tests. In general they did very poorly on these tests as compared with IBM personnel elsewhere. After Miss Minott, the staff psychologist, pointed out that the tests were culturally biased ("Why should a girl brought up in Bedford-Stuyvesant recognize words like *barrister* and *zealot?*"), no attention was paid to them.

THE ANNOUNCEMENT

At the beginning of April IBM was ready to announce its plans. Since one of the main purposes of the undertaking was to create

44

TABLE 1: APPLICANT CHARACTERISTICS, DECEMBER 31, 1968

	Males (n = 357)	Females (n = 551)
Average age	29	32
Percent married	47	38
Percent with children	54	60
Percent having been in prison	30	20
Percent unemployed six weeks or more before applying	60	67
Average base rate of pay on previous jobs *	$91	$71

* Many had been employed only a few weeks a year; union dues and hospital insurance charges reduced take-home pay in many cases.

interest on the part of whites and confidence on the part of blacks, it seemed like a good idea to make the announcement in a manner that would attract wide attention. Governor Rockefeller, Mayor Lindsay, and, of course, Senator Kennedy should be there, along with plenty of television and newspaper reporters. On reflection, however, it seemed that this was not such a good idea. After all, what was IBM doing that justified a big fuss? Hiring 300 people over a two-year period in a community the size of Kansas City or Cincinnati was not such a big thing. It would be best to come into the community quietly. Instead of putting on a big show, the company would invite about 75 community leaders to stop by for coffee on their way to work.

The making of the announcement was bound to raise some rather delicate problems of relationship with community leaders. The Kennedy-sponsored community planning body had the year before come under vehement attack from a coalition of militant women, youth leaders in the city-funded antipoverty agency, CORE leaders, and others. (It was this that had caused the creation of Restoration, a new corporation that included the young and the militant.) If in making its announcement, IBM gave the impression that it was hand in glove with the moderates, it might seem to be taking sides with them against their critics of the year before. On the other hand, not to acknowledge their help would be not to acknowledge any help at all. Eventually, it was decided that Franklin Thomas, the executive head of the old corporation and now of Restoration, would not sit on the platform. However, after the announcement had been made, he would be called upon first to say a few words.

The date for the announcement had been set when Dr. Martin Luther King was assassinated. This caused a two-week postponement. Bedford-Stuyvesant was too preoccupied with grief and anger to be asked for its attention.

When on April 17 the announcement finally was made, there were some tense moments, but all went well. After Thomas had replied to the announcement, which was made by the head of the Systems Division, the young leader of Brooklyn Youth Action rose to congratulate Restoration on having brought IBM to Bedford-Stuyvesant. Sonny Carson, the CORE leader, was not present (he had telephoned in advance to ask if the affair would be covered by the press) but he had sent his representative.

"I want to know in dollars and cents exactly how much you're bringing into this community," the CORE man said, without rising from his seat.

The biggest contribution would be through the payroll, the head of the Systems Division replied. The questioner was not satisfied and began again when a man behind him interrupted.

"At this meeting we stand up when we ask a question."
"Man," the CORE man said, "I don't stand up for nobody."
"Then shut up," the other man said.

That was the end of the opposition, if it was opposition.

Later a man got up to say that if the summer proved to be a long, hot one and some burning was done, the IBM building would not be touched. Anybody who tried to burn it would have to get past him.

FIRST RETURNS

The first directs—eight of them—punched the time clock for the first time on July 8. By the middle of September, 47 directs and 80 indirects were at work, and by the end of the year these numbers had increased to 87 and 108. Friedli and his assistants now spent much of their time orienting the workers. A new employee's first day was spent seeing the plant, meeting the managers, and hearing how his particular job fitted into the whole scheme of things. For the next week, an hour a day was devoted to explanations, often with slides, of the IBM health and insurance plans, IBM philosophy, and the rights and duties of employees. Each employee received a booklet containing further details about these matters. On the inside cover was a letter to Fellow IBM'er from Tom Watson, Jr. Watson also appeared in a moving picture to tell about the Three Basic Beliefs and the Speak Up program, by means of which any employee could carry a grievance all the way to him. These sessions concluded with a question period.

The booklet, slides, and movie were standard equipment in IBM. The daily talks by managers and question and answer periods were something new, an idea suggested by a manager who had come from a plant where there had recently been some racial trouble. After observing one of these sessions, the head of the SMD remarked that it might be a good idea to do the same thing in all plants.

By the middle of September, after two months of partial operation, Friedli and the other managers began to breathe more easily. So far, no calamity had befallen and none seemed likely.

Recruitment. It had become obvious at once that the plant would attract plenty of applicants, although perhaps not as many *men* as might be desired. Without a cent having been spent on advertising—the only publicity was a press release that made the New York *Daily News*, the *Amsterdam News,* and the news program of the Negro radio station—364 persons had applied for jobs within a few days. To be sure, fewer than one-third of these were men, and many of the men were either not employable or not promotable. In order to get a wider selection of men, Friedli relaxed the rule giving preference to the unemployed: Henceforth employed persons would be hired but (to avoid injuring other firms) an effort would be made not to take more than one employee from any company.

TABLE 2: CHARACTERISTICS OF THOSE HIRED

	Males (n = 65)	Females (n = 22)
Average age	30	37
Percent married	40	41
Percent with children	45	100
Percent having been in prison	19	0
Percent unemployed six weeks or more before applying	35	64
Average base rate of pay in previous job	$85	$70

As Table 2 shows, 73 percent of the directs were men. The applicants who got jobs were presumably the cream of those who applied.

In these first months the plant did not employ anyone who did not seem to want to work and who did not show promise of responding to training. A few of those employed were unpromising by some normal standpoints (one man, for example, had served a long term in prison), but even in these cases there was reason to expect good performance from them (the ex-convict had been a reliable worker in the same low-paying job for many years after his release). The term "hard core" had by now ceased to have any meaning. "There are two kinds of employees here," Friedli told an interviewer early in October, "the guy who does everything right: gets to work on time, follows instructions, learns—and the others, the guys who do nothing right. You can count the number of the others on the fingers of one hand."

By the end of the summer it appeared that a reasonable number of workers would eventually be capable of becoming managers. One man had already been promoted to department technician, the rank just below manager, and Douglas saw possibilities in several others.

Turnover and Absenteeism. As of December 31, only two employees had quit, one to take a college scholarship and the other, who had come into a small inheritance, to go into business for himself. Three had been fired. One of these was a drug addict; he was fired, Friedli told an interviewer, not for being an addict but "for failing to work with us on his problem." Another of those fired was a youth whose absenteeism was so frequent as to be practically continuous. The third was a man who needed medical assistance and refused to accept it.

In the first six months of operation the absenteeism rate was about normal for an IBM plant. Typically a plant runs at 90 percent utilization, a figure that includes vacation and sick leave as well as other absences. At Bedford-Stuyvesant the utilization rate was 92 percent until December, when the Hong Kong flu struck;[3] adjusted to take account of the less-than-normal accumulation of vacation and sick leave, this figure was approximately normal. The Bedford-Stuyvesant employees had more emergency situations requiring time off than did employees in other plants ("Some of these guys are going to a dentist for the first time in their lives"), but they

---

[3] During the flu epidemic, absenteeism shot up to 25 percent, which is about what it was in other IBM plants. As far as the managers could judge, the workers who reported sick really were sick.

were less likely than the other employees to miss work on account of political or church activities.

The low rates of turnover and absenteeism were to be explained in part by the patience that the managers showed. In another IBM plant a worker who frequently failed to show up on Monday morning would be fired; here the man's manager would go to his home and pull him out of bed. Sometimes workers were "fired" in a kind of morality play that was acted out for their benefit. A manager would affect to have come to the end of his patience. "You're fired!" he would say. Then he would add: "I've got to let Mr. Friedli review this, but I haven't any doubt that he will approve my decision." After letting a certain amount of time pass, the manager would go back to the man looking grim. "Mr. Friedli says that we've spent a lot of money on you and he's not about to throw in the towel. So you've got another chance."

Morale and Productivity. Anyone walking through the plant in its first six months would see that it was a "happy ship." The workers obviously liked the clean, colorful, air-conditioned building and, still more, the polite and considerate treatment they got from their bosses. They obviously wanted to do whatever was expected of them. Iannone soon saw that the assumptions on which he had based his planning were unduly pessimistic. The workers did more and better work than anyone had expected. To be sure, some of them had to be taught to use soldering irons; none, however, had to be taught the elements of personal hygiene. What held production back was lack of supplies: Expecting very little of the workers, the planners had not scheduled a large enough flow of material from the Poughkeepsie supply base.

At the end of the summer, Friedli, Douglas, and Iannone concluded that they had made a mistake in not taking on a more challenging product mission than cable assembly. Accordingly, they accepted a quota of 1,000 power supplies for November.

At the end of the year about half of the workers were attending night classes in basic arithmetic, English, and blueprint reading. The classes met at the plant twice a week for one and one-half hour sessions.

Crime, Vandalism, and Insubordination. Friedli had been warned to expect violence from the Bedford-Stuyvesant residents, those inside of the plant as well as those outside of it. If he was tempted to fill the plant with Pinkertons and undercover agents, he resisted the temptation: It would be disastrous, he knew, to let it appear that IBM was armed against its employees or against the black community. Accordingly, no cage was placed around the cashier; one guard, supplied by an agency, was posted near the front door during business hours. Later he was withdrawn and a buzzer system installed to enable the receptionist to call him and another guard from other entrances if necessary. Employees carried identification cards and wore name tags on the job; this was standard practice in IBM plants.

As of December 31 there had been practically no trouble from within. One worker pulled a knife on another; in another plant he would have been dismissed; here he was let off with a warning. Another worker came to work drunk and had to be sent home. There was no vandalism and no insubordination.

Crime in the neighborhood had been feared even more than crime in the plant. As it turned out in the first six months, there was very little of this either. One weekend several desks were rifled and personal belongings of small value were taken; money left in unlocked desks was very likely to be taken by members of the cleaning force. An employee's parked car was stolen. For reasons of their own, the police seemed to patrol the neighborhood more heavily after the plant began operating; this may have helped to keep crime down.

Special Costs. Hard-core workers, people had said, were constantly having their wages garnisheed, thus imposing an extra record-keeping cost on their employer. During the first six months of IBM's experience, no workers' wages were garnisheed. Requests for salary advances were somewhat more frequent than in other plants, but this was not a problem.

What *did* entail extra costs was being within New York City. The city's occupancy and sales taxes were more than trivial, and its building code was so unreasonably stringent as to add an estimated 10 percent ($100,000) to the cost of remodeling. To get permission from the city to pay employees by check (a precaution taken for their sake from fear of crime), six meetings with the New York City Department of Labor were necessary.

THE OUTLOOK FOR 1969

As the plant entered 1969 its principal problems, Friedli thought, were ones of management. In the production of power supplies, the plant was doing well. It had met its November and December quotas, the latter (because of the flu) by working overtime. At first it took Bedford-Stuyvesant five times as many hours as it did

Kingston to make a power supply. After two months, however, it took only twice as many. The workers were following an 85 percent learning curve, which was good. The curve had started from a high point, however, and it was questionable whether, when it flattened out, their productivity would equal Kingston's. Even if it did not, the plant might produce power supplies at a lower cost than Kingston. Kingston's labor and burden (overhead) rate was a third greater than Bedford-Stuyvesant's. This was partly because Bedford-Stuyvesant, being much smaller, had relatively few indirects adding their salaries to its burden rate (it used the medical staff at the company's Manhattan office and did not pay for it, for example) and partly because, being new, it had few workers who had reached the upper ranges of the pay scale. Having a burden rate that was one-third less gave it a great advantage over Kingston. If it got so that it made power supplies as fast as Kingston made them, its unit cost would be 65 percent less than Kingston's. Of course its advantage would diminish overtime, as more and more of its workers climbed the pay scale. But for several years to come, it would be in a favorable position.

If comparison was made not with Kingston but with vendors (and this was probably the relevant comparison, for IBM bought most of its power supplies), the advantage was overwhelmingly on the side of Bedford-Stuyvesant. The vendors' labor and burden rate was believed to be 25 percent less than Bedford-Stuyvesant's and their rate of production about the same. They, however, had to be paid a handling charge of 20 percent of the value of the parts that passed through their hands; the parts for a power supply being expensive this amounted to twice their unit manufacturing cost. Bedford-Stuyvesant, therefore, had a much bigger competitive advantage over them than over Kingston. Figured against what it would cost IBM to buy from vendors, Friedli expected to make a profit of $250,000 on power supplies in 1969.

With the plant's other product, cable assembly, the situation was by no means so good. The October, November, and December shipments had been missed. Missing them had not made much difference to the company—they were to have gone into shelf inventory anyway. From January on, however, the cables would be shipped to order, and any failure to meet schedules would be serious.

The trouble with the cable assembly operation did not lie with the workers, however. Hitherto, cable assembly had always been done by vendors; they had developed very sophisticated tools and methods for taking insulation off cable and for cutting it. By comparison the tools and methods that the Bedford-Stuyvesant plant worked out were crude and inefficient. "We were so concerned about orienting people," Friedli remarked wryly, "that we never learned how to do the technical part of the job." It would be necessary now to bring in specially qualified people from other plants to "method-ize" the operation and to develop proper tools for it. When this had been done, the plant would meet its schedules. It would never, however, have the advantage in cable assembly that it had in power supplies. The vendors' markup on cable assembly was nowhere near so great.

From a profit standpoint it would obviously be desirable to drop cable assembly altogether and to concentrate instead on power supplies or on something else that had a big vendor markup. Friedli had such possibilities very much in mind, but his freedom of action was not unlimited. For one thing, it was contrary to company policy to take work from vendors if doing so would seriously injure them: IBM could not depend upon them in the future if it precipitately took back from them anything that turned out to be profitable. So far, the Bedford-Stuyvesant plant had taken its power supply work only from the Kingston plant; how much more of it the Kingston plant could spare was not clear. For another thing, some of the plant's workers had acquired a good deal of skill in cable assembly. To drop the whole operation would discourage them and might even make them feel that they had failed.

The plant had another problem that might prove serious and that had nothing to do with the workers. The concrete floors of the building had been overloaded during its more than a half-century of service as a warehouse, it was discovered toward the end of 1968, and extensive repairs might be necessary. While the floors were under repair, production might be severely interfered with.

The principal problems of the plant—those it had had in 1968 and those it faced in 1969—were of the sort that might arise in any IBM plant. If there was any *special* problem, Friedli said, it was that the employees in general did not have "the same sense of the priority of the job" as other IBM workers. It was not that they were lazy or indifferent; with exceptions that could be counted on the fingers of one hand, they were eager to do what was asked of them.

"If they understand what is necessary to make this plant run," Friedli told an interviewer in the first days of 1969, "they're going to do. it. They're going to say to themselves: 'If that's what it takes to be competitive all right . . .'" As evidence of this he cited their behavior on the last workday before the Christmas holiday. This was a Friday, and it was absolutely crucial that the plant get a full day's production: Otherwise the month's quota would not be met. Knowing that the workers were bound to slack off in the afternoon as the holiday spirit rose in them, he asked them to come to work two hours early—at 6 a.m.—that day. All but four did so; the four who were late were the same four he had been counting on the fingers of one hand all along.

When he said that the employees lacked a sense of the priority of the job, Friedli meant that when there was a conflict between the demands of the job and the demands of something else, those of the job were likely to be ignored. The workers did not seem to see that it might sometimes be possible to arrange matters so that *both* the job *and* the competing value were served. A mother would stay home from work if her child did not feel well in the morning. That the child had first claim on the mother did not seem in the least odd to Friedli, of course; what *did* seem odd to him was that the mother never seemed to think of arranging matters so that the child would be taken care of without the job's being neglected. Why, for example, did she not have a relative or friend look in on the child from time to time and telephone her at the factory if it appeared that the illness might be serious? Again, if a man needed to go to the dentist, why did he take the whole day off? Once a manager asked a worker who had a morning appointment why he could not come to work afterward. He supposed he could, he said; apparently the idea had not occurred to him.

Friedli thought the workers gave the job a low priority because they had never had jobs on which anything much depended, either for them or for anyone else. Once it was made clear to them that the success of the plant depended upon each person's performing his assigned task they would see the necessity of giving the job a higher priority. "Each of us is important and will be missed," he told the employees when they assembled for an end-of-the-year celebration.

It was not just the attitude of the individual employee that needed changing, however. The institutions of the black community, which were the products of a long process of adaptation to reality, made it hard for the individual to change his ways. For example, a worker asked for time off to go to the dentist. "Why don't you see your dentist on Saturday?" the manager asked. "My dentist doesn't work on Saturday," the man answered. Thinking he might be mistaken or that perhaps he had been too shy to tell the dentist that his employer needed him during the week, the manager asked if he might call the dentist. By all means, the man said. The dentist, however, flatly refused. Friedli was astonished when he heard about this. *His* dentist always took him on Saturday.

Black managers, Friedli thought at first, were generally more successful than white ones in changing workers' attitudes; the whites seemed to be reluctant, if not downright unwilling, to scold black workers or even to have a heart-to-heart talk with them. Later he changed his mind when Douglas and other blacks pointed out to him that two of the white managers, men he had feared were too easygoing, were having extraordinary success in getting their men to work and in training them.

At the end-of-the-year assembly of employees, Friedli did his best to give the workers a feeling of pride in the plant and in what they had so far achieved together. They had, he told them, produced 2,251 power supplies and 3,140 cables. This was something to be proud of. But their real accomplishment lay in having shouted down the voices that had said it was foolish to start a plant in the inner city. There might be some difficulty in the next year because of the floors, he told them. But he was confident that in 1969 the plant would double the number of its employees, while at the same time increasing its production per man-hour. They would have to work as a team to do this. He hoped everyone would make suggestions. Everyone counted. Everyone was needed.

Two short films were shown. One, which had been made by a group of Bedford-Stuyvesant people who had been in a class at nearby Pratt Institute, was about the search for black identity. The other was one of the inspirational films made for use by big companies on such occasions. Its theme was commitment. A guitar-maker in a Spanish village labored lovingly over his work, selecting wood with the utmost care, sanding it, cutting it, inlaying it. . . . From him the camera moved at intervals to an office worker who, it appeared, was equally committed. When he picked up the telephone, the film said, he did so with the same commitment that the artisan felt in picking up a tool. At the end of the film, the guitar case snapped shut; then the office worker's briefcase snapped shut. Both snaps signified commitment.

After the film Friedli appeared with a guitar. It had been presented to the Bedford-Stuyvesant plant, he said, at a national meeting of IBM plant managers that he had just attended in Chicago, and it symbolized the whole company's awareness of the commitment that they, the employees had made. If he were to play something, he said, it would be "We Shall Overcome." Unfortunately, the guitar was new and had not been tuned; therefore he could not play just yet.

SIGNIFICANCE OF THE UNDERTAKING

It will be another two or three years before the Bedford-Stuyvesant plant can safely be called a success. Assuming that by then the workers are about as productive as workers elsewhere, what will be the significance of the undertaking?

Some other companies will doubtless be encouraged by IBM's example to establish plants in Bedford-Stuyvesant or other poverty areas. However, even if the productivity of labor in the IBM plant turns out to be fully equal to that of labor elsewhere, not all companies can expect the same success. IBM has several advantages over most employers. It can select a product mix from a very wide range of possibilities. Being nonunion it has unusual flexibility in hiring and promotion policies. Most important, perhaps, it has a *glamor*—perhaps the world is *charisma*—that attracts desirable employees to it. In the black community, where few people have jobs that give them prestige, this may be particularly important.

No matter how well ghetto labor produces, the disadvantages of an inner city location—especially high land costs and poor access to major transportation routes—will deter companies operating on a narrow profit margin or insensitive to the values of corporate citizenship from establishing plants in places like Bedford-Stuyvesant. That IBM can afford—indeed, perhaps for public relations reasons must afford—to take a somewhat lower profit for the sake of performing what it believes to be a public service is no indication that other, less favorably situated or less vulnerable companies will do the same.

Companies that build plants in the more advantageous locations on the fringe of the city may be encouraged by IBM's example to make more use of ghetto labor. It is questionable, however, whether IBM's experience in Bedford-Stuyvesant will have much bearing upon the situation of these companies. It may be that ghetto workers will not go outside of the ghetto for jobs. In Miss Minott's opinion, being in the very center of Bedford-Stuyvesant contributes greatly to IBM's success. "People wouldn't go to apply for jobs outside," she says, "because they would figure that it was a waste of time— they wouldn't get the jobs. Besides, they do not feel comfortable or secure where there are not many black faces." In her opinion, adding black workers to the predominantly white force of an existing plant would not, even for IBM, work nearly as well as starting a new, almost all black, plant. Having started it from scratch, the Bedford-Stuyvesant workers feel that it is theirs. If they had been introduced into the labor force of a white plant, this pride of possession would be lacking and in its place would be a certain resentment at having to adapt to a more or less alien and hostile environment.

Even if these factors should prove not very important (the locational disadvantage could be offset by government subsidies, of course) another feature of the situation would be. The supply of potentially good workers in the ghetto may be large, but it is certainly not unlimited. That IBM can find 300 does not mean that it or other companies could find 30,000 or perhaps even 3,000. Obviously, if the demand for ghetto labor continues to increase, a time will come when the quality of new recruits will be considerably below the present IBM standard.

IBM's success (if that is what it turns out to be) will have a value in showing that workers who have little schooling or job experience, whose style of life reflects a long history of poverty, and who lack confidence in themselves can in a few years and at moderate cost be given training, outlook, and habits that will enable them to perform adequately in a modern factory and in some instances to rise into managerial positions. No doubt this demonstration, along with other evidence, will cause a good many employers to see possibilities for the employment of ghetto workers that have hitherto been overlooked.

IBM's experience will not, however, show a way to employ what may be called "true hard-core," as opposed to "disadvantaged," workers—that is, alcoholics, drug addicts, persons who are deeply alienated or unmotivated, and hustlers who prefer a fast buck and action to any regular employment no matter how good. The true hard-core presents a problem altogether different from the one that IBM has tackled. That disadvantaged workers can be made productive does not mean that hard-core ones can.

This is not to say that the IBM plant will make *no* contribution to the problem represented by the true hard-core. It should make at least two contributions, each very important. For one thing, its trials and errors should help to make known what kinds of impediments to worker productivity are, and what kinds are not, removable and at what cost. In other words, it should help replace labels like disadvantaged and hard core, the tendency of which is to suggest sharp divisions where in fact there are none, with useful information about the world as it really is. What is the probability that a high school dropout who has shown no inclination to work or to accept any kind of discipline will, if offered a genuine opportunity, change his ways sufficiently in the course of a year so that it will be profitable to employ him? Questions like this may receive some answers in the Bedford-Stuyvesant plant.

The other contribution that the plant should make with respect to the hard-core is to discourage its formation. Presumably young Negroes turn to alcohol, dope, and other forms of escape because they see—or think they see—that their situation is hopeless. Insofar as it opens opportunities, the IBM plant will make it harder for them to think that. Even if he does not get a good job himself, the knowledge that others like him are getting them will give a Bedford-Stuyvesant youth some encouragement—enough, perhaps, to keep him afloat until help arrives.

Discussion

BY   SAR A. LEVITAN *

The creation of a separate office of minority enterprise in the Department of Commerce and a special White House assistant for the development of black capitalism are indications of the growing emphasis on programs for the economic development of central city ghettos. While the development process is complex, its viability hinges on being able to induce large manufacturing plants to locate in these areas. Alternative plans for attracting such plants have been proposed. These include the tax incentive approach offered by the late Robert F. Kennedy, which would subsidize the higher costs of ghetto operation, and the community self-determination plan, which would supplement tax benefits to firms which eventually sell their plants to locally owned community development corporations. Although these proposals contain specific tax benefit provisions, there is no way of predicting their impact, since very little is known about the differential costs of ghetto operation or the willingness of corporations to share any or all of these higher costs.

Professor Banfield's case study of the IBM plant in Bedford-Stuyvesant sheds some light on the issues involved in locating manufacturing plants in central cities. Generalizations on a single case study are exceedingly dangerous, particularly in IBM's case because of the following considerations:

1. Before deciding to locate a plant in Bedford-Stuyvesant, IBM executives visited plants operating in ghetto areas around the country for ideas on the specific problems they would encounter. They concluded that conditions varied so widely from place to place that little of practical applicability could be learned from the study of other projects. IBM officials recognized that difficulties en-

* Sar A. Levitan is research professor of Economics and director of the Center for Manpower Policy Studies, The George Washington University, Washington, D.C.

countered in finding qualified workers in Roxbury might not apply to Bedford-Stuyvesant, where the labor market was less tight. Similarly, land costs in Roxbury are much lower than in Bedford-Stuyvesant.

2. IBM profited from circumstances that cannot be duplicated today even within Bedford-Stuyvesant. There is no other building available in Bedford-Stuyvesant with as much floor space as IBM located, and it was able to lease the buildings at roughly half the going rate. IBM was also able to draw from a pool of qualified and highly motivated workers, which might quickly be exhausted by a few firms. At any rate, the next firm may have to settle for second best.

3. Finally, few companies and few industries share the peculiar structure of IBM and the computer industry. IBM judges its Bedford-Stuyvesant plant a success, not in relation to production costs in its other plants, but rather in relation to the higher costs which it pays to independent suppliers for components. In addition, IBM is a unique corporation in other ways, including its emphasis on a closely knit, achievement-oriented work force and its highly centralized executive structure. IBM's willingness to "go it alone" cannot be generalized; other large corporations, including Aerojet-General, Control Data Corporation, and Westinghouse, have taken advantage of available federal funds.

Despite these reservations, there are still some significant lessons to be learned from this case.

1. IBM's success raises questions about many common beliefs concerning ghetto operations. First, vandalism, arson, and theft have not been problems. Second, there was little difficulty in recruiting a work force, an indication that extensive outreach is sometimes unnecessary to attract workers to a ghetto plant if desirable employment is offered. Finally, the workers appear motivated and responsible. High rates of absenteeism and labor turnover have not been encountered.

2. The involvement of corporate executives in local development efforts may be of critical importance in attracting plants to the ghetto; IBM president, Thomas J. Watson's membership on the board of Bedford-Stuyvesant Development and Services Corporation was crucial in determining the choice of location. Studies indicate that the vast majority of location decisions are made at the top executive level in the corporation. Given stockholder approval of corporate involvement—a recent survey has found that 60 percent of stockholders favor more direct business involvement in social problems—the effort made depends to a large extent on the commitment and awareness of the chief executives.

3. The public relations aspect of involvement is of special significance. The appearance of social commitment was as important as the product of that commitment. It is doubtful that this effort, or any such effort, would be undertaken without the promise of favorable publicity. With this motivation, future effort may be limited by two factors. First, as more firms initiate projects, the publicity value will decrease. Second, the Bedford-Stuyvesant plant is a tenth the size of IBM's typical plant. If such a small project can be used to publicize corporate involvement, further efforts may be less pressing.

4. In the IBM experience, the role of the local development corporation was minimal. It is unlikely that large corporations would rely upon the staff of local development corporations for assistance on the business aspects of operation. The development corporations can provide assistance in outreach and with community relations problems, but these were not encountered by IBM.

In summary, the IBM case demonstrates that while some problems such as vandalism, theft, high turnover, and absenteeism are often overrated, the costs of hiring the disadvantaged are still substantial. While corporate commitment such as IBM's may be duplicated, its potential impact is limited. Substantial monetary incentives will be needed to attract large plants to ghetto areas on a meaningful scale.

3

196 Men Find a Chance

BY *THEODORE PURCELL* AND *ROSALIND WEBSTER* *

There were riots and frustration in Pittsburgh's Hill District last year. This essay is the story of how 196 men—mostly black—from the Hill District, Homewood, Braddock, Hazelwood, Turtle Creek, and East Pittsburgh have at last found a chance as men and as workers at the East Pittsburgh works of the Westinghouse Electric Corporation. These men are trainees of the Westinghouse Occupational Training School, a new, vestibule training program for the hard-core unemployed.

One hundred ninety-six men is less than one-tenth of 1 percent of the goal of 100,000 people that the National Alliance of Businessmen hopes to reclaim from the slums by the end of June 1969. But 196 men represents a beginning. The Westinghouse East Pittsburgh OTS experience, and others like it, could remain at the level of mere tokenism, or these programs could expand into a serious war against poverty and discrimination.

If success is any incentive for expansion, we have it here. Measuring success in quantitative terms may seem crass when the lives of people are involved, but the Westinghouse Occupational Training School is 90 to 95 percent successful, measuring by the number of its 196 recruits who remain in productive and responsible employment. This figure is higher than one estimated regional average of 80 percent for MA-3

---

* Theodore Purcell is a Jesuit priest and a Research Associate with the Cambridge Center for Social Studies. He was assisted in this research by Rosalind Webster. Fr. Purcell is currently directing a two-year Ford Foundation study of minority employment in the electrical industry.
,* Portions taken and adapted from "Wendell on the Hardcore World," Theodore Purcell and Rosalind Webster, *Harvard Business Review* (July-August 1969), pp. 118-129.

programs [1] and 67 percent for NAB programs in general.[2] As far as we can determine (although no overall plant statistics are available), if you measure success in terms of lack of absenteeism and tardiness, the Westinghouse OTS trainees compare favorably with other employees of the East Pittsburgh works. Comparable productivity figures are not available, but Westinghouse was sufficiently satisfied to apply for an MA-5 contract for East Pittsburgh into 1970. What is Westinghouse's program and why has it prospered?

THE WESTINGHOUSE OCCUPATIONAL TRAINING SCHOOL

In April 1968 the original plant of the Westinghouse Corporation at East Pittsburgh decided to set up an Occupational Training School on its plant site to select and prepare people from Pittsburgh's ghettos for productive jobs at the plant. With the consultation of the Westinghouse Learning Corporation, James Wallace, East Pittsburgh general manager, Donald Hiestand, manager of Industrial Relations and James Higinbotham, manager of Employment and Personnel Services, secured a U.S. Department of Labor MA-3 contract to finance a school to hire, train, and ultimately to place, 196 hard-core unemployed men during 1968 and 1969.

Purpose. Westinghouse East Pittsburgh management states the purpose of its new Occupational Training School as follows: (1) "To assist economically and socially disadvantaged persons in achieving educational and vocational skills in preparation for employment; (2) To place these individuals into permanent jobs in order to make them productive and responsible persons; and (3) to serve as an enlightened and guiding source in the community in eliminating the conditions that create poverty and social isolation."

The program's philosophy is that "each employee trainee must develop a concept of self-worth, since many of the participants have experienced failures many times. We believe that these employee-trainees will bring with them to the training program personal and social motives for self-improvement. . . . Personal characteristics such as self-confidence, acceptance of authority and

---

[1] Morris Rieger, manpower administrator of the U.S. Department of Labor for the Mideastern States of Region Three, reports on a department task force studying the first 700 to 750 trainees placed on jobs in four cities under the MA-3 contracts. By December 1, 1968, 80 percent of the people placed were still at work.

[2] Statement by Henry Ford II, *Wall Street Journal*, December 12, 1968, p. 1.

tolerance of self, as well as a fund of basic educational knowledge and skills, will be developed in an integrated way during the course of the program."

It is of major importance, that the program is concerned not only with *individual* trainees but with the significant effects that will result in the *communities* where the trainees live.

"They will be encouraged to help their fellows, both in the training program *and out of it*. This opportunity will measurably affect the depressing cycle of failure and frustration in which the unemployed live and attempt to solve their life problems."

Foreman Orientation. In July 1968 the OTS program was introduced to the foremen and supervisors of the East Pittsburgh plant in a half-day session of speeches, lectures, and films. Subjects covered were the magnitude of the racial-urban and ghetto problems, national and company policy, and problems of prejudice and community. The purpose and methods of the OTS program were explained by Richard R. Ross, the new director, and the cooperation of the supervisors was sought. The format for the day was largely supplied by the Westinghouse Learning Corporation.

Two weeks later the supervisors had follow-up sessions in smaller groups of 20. These were discussion groups on how to handle problems of the hard-core employee. "What do I do, if . . . ?"

What were the reactions of the foremen to the orientation? Foreman Jack Gillis [3] speaks for some when he describes one difficulty he faced for which the orientation program had not prepared him:

FOREMAN GILLIS: This fella more or less presents a little bit of a challenge to me. Not only his attendance is shaky . . . he'll go along pretty good, then he'll slack off. He'll miss, come in late, and I'll bring him right in here, and we'll sit down and we'll chat about the whole thing, and I'll emphasize his responsibility. Then it will pick up for a period of time; then he's right back into it. . . . He has an attitude problem also. Unfortunately, maybe I'm unprepared to handle some of these boys. I'm not familiar with their backgrounds. I don't know what real problems they have, and I don't know what my responsibility is to them.

WEBSTER (the interviewer):   Was there a foremen seminar that was held for a day?

---

[3] All names are fictitious, except for the OTS staff and Westinghouse top management.

GILLIS: Yes, several months back, a gang of us—whole darn division— went down to the auditorium in East Pittsburgh, and they told us there was going to be a program, and that they were going to get four weeks' instruction down here, and that after that they would be treated like any other employee. It all sounded real simple, and really I could have got as much out of it if they had sent me a note with three or four sentences on it.

WEBSTER: It wasn't very helpful?

GILLIS: No. Very little help at all. Just the fact that Westinghouse is going to be involved in this program and they wanted us to cooperate.

While reactions were undoubtedly mixed, some foremen were not greatly impressed with the orientation days. ("Here is just one more problem loaded onto my desk!") Westinghouse East Pittsburgh had had blacks and ghetto people in its employ for some time, and many of the problems presented were not unfamiliar, whereas the unfamiliar problems were probably unknown. Most persuasive in securing the cooperation of the foremen was the clear fact that Westinghouse top management, both at the corporate and at the plant level, wanted the OTS program to succeed.

Who are the OTS Trainees? The Westinghouse Occupational School contract stipulates that its funds are to be used to train for employment hard-core individuals. To be certified hard core, one must be poor, and either a high school dropout, under 22 or over 45, on welfare, a member of a minority group, or otherwise disadvantaged. The terms are broad, and the saying goes around Pittsburgh that anyone with a torn shirt can get certified at the Pennsylvania State Employment Service. Westinghouse imposes the additional requirement of a physical examination. Beyond this, the selection of trainees is the sole responsibility of OTS Director Richard R. Ross, and his judgment accounts in large part for the success of the program.

The original contract stipulated that candidates for the Westinghouse Occupational Training School could not be drug addicts or have felony records. These were viewed as problems too difficult to handle at the outset. Not long after the program was under way, Dick Ross felt ready to take on greater risks, and frequent exceptions were made to the initial ruling. Surprisingly, the risks proved to be worthwhile. Ex-convicts and ex-addicts have turned out to be some of his most motivated trainees.

The typical trainee is a young Negro man about 25 years old. He has been arrested and convicted of anything from petty theft to manslaughter. Although he has had two years of high school education, he has been out of work for nine months. At best he has been making only about $1.60 an hour at irregular jobs, such as landscaping laborer, dishwasher, or stockboy–not enough to support his four dependents. He is an outcast whom the white world hardly knows. He comes from a life of apathy, crime, anger, and especially hopelessness. He now has a job, a job involving a time clock, work on Monday morning, dealing sometimes with a foreman or fellow worker who dislikes him, but also a job supplying a substantial weekly pay check, the chance for promotion and for night school, and a job associating him with at least certain people at the Westinghouse plant who strongly want him to succeed.

If there is one truth that comes out of Table 1, it is that there are truly hard-core men in the Westinghouse OTS program, men who would never be given a chance by the average employment office for any kind of decent job. Compared with another study of two Lockheed programs at Marietta, Georgia, and Sunnyvale, California,[4] these OTS trainees are similar, but have more arrest and conviction records, have been unemployed longer, are more likely to be heads of households, and have more dependents. In a word, they have more problems.

Selecting the Trainees. Pasts of the trainees vary. What they have in common is the desire to work. OTS Director Ross, spends a great deal of time ascertaining this–listening, questioning. Ross makes every applicant aware that he must be willing to accept any position assigned to him, even sweeper or janitor; that no absence or tardiness is allowed; that the trainee is to be an example to his community; and that the success of the program is dependent upon the success of each individual. Mr. Ross's prime allegiance must be to the general success of the program, so he cannot afford to take needless risks. A risk, in Ross's judgment, is a man who does not really want to work or who is enmeshed in such serious problems that he is most unlikely to work steadily. Ross might be able to reform someone who is not yet truly motivated, but he feels the chances are slim and his time can be better used for others. As it is, the Westinghouse OTS is in the position of accepting only 17 percent of all those who have now begun to apply for the program. Is this really the hard-core Westinghouse OTS is training? Definitely, the trainees are all people who are unemploy-

---

4 James D. Hodgson and Marshall H. Brenner, "Successful Experience: Training Hard-core Unemployed," *Harvard Business Review* (September-October 1968), pp. 148–56. See also Allen R. Janger, "New Start–for the Harder Hard Core," *Conference Board Record*, VI, No. 2 (February 1969), pp. 10–19.

TABLE 1: CHARACTERISTICS OF THE TRAINEES AT THE WEST-INGHOUSE EAST PITTSBURGH OTS

(112 Persons from the start of OTS—July 1968 through November 12, 1968)

Total number of individuals who applied (in writing) to OTS	632
Total number of individuals accepted	112
Percent of applicants hired	17
Age span of trainees	18 to 44 years
Average age	25.7 years
Percent Negro	90
Percent male	100
Percent on welfare (Dept. of Public Assistance) when hired (almost none on Unemployment Insurance)	43
Percent of employee's dependents who were taken off public assistance when trainee entered OTS program	33
Percent with no employment since leaving school (2-16 months)	5
Percent with no employment since separation from military service	3
Percent having had at least one 3-month span of previous employment	93
Range of wages on part-time or temporary jobs	$ .75-$3.00 per hour
Average wages on last job before OTS	$1.60 per hour
Total previous unemployment span in months	0-84
Average number of months of unemployment between last job and OTS	9
Heads of households	66
Average number of dependents	4
Percent with records of one or more arrests	77.7
Percent with convictions (petty theft to manslaughter)	53
Average educational grade achievement	10 years
Span of educational grade achievement	4-12 years

able because they cannot meet customary employment requirements, that is, a high school diploma, absence of a police record, and so forth. In every other sense they are quite employable, being capable and motivated. What they need above all is an opportunity, a job. They are not the cream of the hard-core crop, in the traditional sense of having the best education, test scores, recommendations, and experience. They are instead the most desirous, the most ambitious.

Content of the Program. The Westinghouse OTS program consists primarily of motivational and sensitivity training. No formal training in work skills is provided. However, basic educational instruction in reading and arithmetic is offered. Since the educational levels of the trainees vary considerably, most of this learning is done independently. Each morning the trainee writes himself a "contract"—what material he hopes to cover, and what he hopes to learn for the day. Four weeks is hardly enough time to show much improvement, and this is not really the purpose of the course. No tests are administered to measure advances. The basic education courses are meant simply to refresh the trainee, to reaccustom him to studying, and to direct him to the proper source, should he become interested in earning a high school diploma.

Central to the four-week training program is instruction in the new world of work at Westinghouse. This learning is acquired through a variety of sources—a tour of the plant, guest speakers representing union and management, and feedback from previous trainees of the hard-core program.

For all the trainees, the opportunity to work, to begin immediately the first day as full and regular employees of Westinghouse at the rate of $2.645 an hour, with fringe benefits including life insurance and with full seniority is both a major achievement and a major incentive.

For a small minority, maybe 5 or 10 percent, the four weeks of training are mainly a means of learning and establishing a work routine that Westinghouse (or any corporation) demands—arriving on time, punching a time clock, getting to bed so as to be alert in the morning, figuring out transportation and carfare. For the majority the training period also provides a needed opportunity to talk out feelings and problems, to exchange ideas and experiences, and to receive a unique type of group support.

The typical training group is composed of 20 to 25 men, about two of whom are white. They range in age from 22 to 44, and their attitudes vary widely. The younger men are often cocky or militant, less able to realize the uniqueness of the opportunity now presented to them. Because of experience and failure, the older men are generally more ready to accommodate themselves to the discipline of an industrial society. In turn, the older men often find it more difficult to re-enter a modern, moving world. Talk and discussion force a man to think and articulate his ideas, relate to his peers, and adjust his attitudes to conform with reality. A great deal of time is spent simply talking and exchanging experiences. Gradually, a concurrence of opinions and attitudes is fashioned, and the men are ready for the plant.

Placement. The great majority of the trainees end up on unskilled jobs, as is indicated in Table 2.

TABLE 2: JOBS THE TRAINEES FOUND
(Groups 1 through 4)

By job (mostly unskilled)				By division	
Sweeper	35	Treat; dip;		Large Rotation	
Supplyman	13	insulate	2	Apparatus	37
Machine helper	7	Yardman	1	Switchgear	17
Coating machine	5	Shearman	1	Printing	5
Furnace helper	2	Material		Power Circuit	
Janitor	8	checker	1	Breaker	3
Molding machine	2	Drill press	2	Plant Services	12
Elevatorman	2	Material cutter		Transportation	8
		helper	1		
TOTAL			82	TOTAL	82

We emphasize that these first jobs are by no means dead-end jobs; there is a true opportunity for promotion. A number of men with outstanding mental and leadership abilities have been found. More than one ex-trainee is going to night school. Already 11.6 percent of the graduates have advanced beyond their first plant job at grade level 4, paying $2.765 an hour; one to semiskilled grade level 9, at $3.10 an hour. (See Table 3.)

Absenteeism and Tardiness. Table 4 shows a good record for the OTS trainees in terms of man-days absent or late. However, it shows a growing percentage of men involved in both tardiness and absences once they leave the protected environment of the school. This is understandable, for out in the plant the men no longer have the strong morale and *esprit de corps* of their OTS director and peers persuading them to make a perfect record.

During the entire training period, only three trainees had to be released; none quit. Once on the job, three of the OTS employees were released because of absenteeism (one was in jail at the time). Two

TABLE 3: PROMOTIONS OF OTS GRADUATES
(129 men, from August 1968 to February 28, 1969)

Number of graduates	From labor grade	To labor grade
1	7	8
1	4	9
1	4	8
3	4	7
8	4	6
1	4	5
15		

TABLE 4: ATTENDANCE AND PUNCTUALITY

	Four-week School Record as of December 31, 1968 112 Trainees	On-the-job Record as of November 30, 1968 84 placed on jobs
Men absent one day or more	21%	55%
Man-days absent out of total man-days	2%	7%
Men late one day or more	41%	62%
Man-days late out of total man-days	7%	2%
Men leaving shift early	12%	30%
Days when shift was left early out of total man-days	7/10%	1%

quit without notice. This adds up to the remarkable retention rate of 94 percent. In addition, two others had to take military leaves of absence.

WHY DOES THE PROGRAM SUCCEED?

Five factors appear to us as the main reasons why the Westinghouse East Pittsburgh Occupational Training School is succeeding.

1. *The commitment of management.* Donald Burnham, president of Westinghouse has taken a strong public stand both in theory and in action on the need for business to involve itself in the affairs of the ghetto and the city. Presently, he is head of the National Alliance of Businessmen's program for the Pittsburgh area. Burnham's stance has helped set up an affirmative action climate among Westinghouse East Pittsburgh managers that lets foremen, employees, and union representatives know that the company wants the Occupational Training School to work. As we said, top management's stance probably had more influence on effecting foremen cooperation than any talks on prejudice or discussions on how to deal with hard-core people.

2. *The dedication and ability of the OTS director and staff.* The devoted, intelligent hard work of OTS Director Richard Ross and his two staff men is another reason why the program is succeeding.

Mr. Ross brought an unusual background to his job. A graduate in social science of West Virginia State College, he had played professional football with the New York Titans and later had five years experience in social work, dealing with the poor and with retarded youths. East Pittsburgh was able to get him from the Westinghouse Learning Corporation, where he specialized in employee placement.

Ross combines the unusual talent of knowing the language and customs both of plant foremen and of the men of the ghetto. Moreover he is black. Ross and his staff work 15-hour days, far beyond the hours and confines of the OTS school itself, going to the ghettos, to the homes of the trainees, securing bail, arranging credit, fixing marriages, persuading, being tough when it is needed, encouraging, supporting and—more than anything else—believing in the integrity and possibilities of the men they select for the school.

3. *Careful and insightful selection.* As we said, Ross carefully screens candidates for the OTS school. In every case, he makes a visit to the candidate's home. Placement is never made on the basis of a mere application blank or a formal interview. Ross adds the intangible criteria of art and insight into the candidate's potential as a person. It is true that because of the growing reputation of Westing-

house OTS in the Pittsburgh ghettos, Ross now need take only seventeen out of every hundred people who would like to come. But he does not take just the cream of the crop. He takes high risk applicants, though not in numbers that would jeopardize the success of the program.

4. *The fact of having a certain job now.* The fact that a man from the ghetto, rejected nearly all of his life, can immediately become a full employee of Westinghouse once he is accepted for the program becomes a strong motivator for the hard-core person to stay and try to succeed. For most of the trainees, having a good job at good pay is the first breakthrough of their entire lives.

5. *A sensitive program fitted to the trainees' needs.* The Westinghouse Learning Corporation, as subcontractor for the OTS, was to supply a curriculum for the school. The curriculum was delayed two months, and meanwhile Ross, by trial and error, devised his own, perhaps a bit disorganized, breaking some of the rules of conventional teaching, but sensitized to the people Ross knew so well. His rather chaotic program developed so successfully that when the Westinghouse Learning format arrived, its traditional approach seemed too rigid and unrealistic.

School begins promptly at 7:30 a.m. and ends at 4:15 p.m. The trainees are expected to meet these deadlines . . . in fact, three offenses are grounds for suspension. But the intervening hours, from 7:30 to 4:15, are flexible and unstructured. The schedule adapts itself to the trainees—their attitudes, problems, questions, and attention spans.

There is no prescription for motivating and sensitizing hard-core trainees. Personalities and attitudes vary. Some are shy; some are cocky. Some need to be built up and encouraged; some need to be cut down. Problems also vary. Most of the trainees have one or more personal problems that will impinge on their work life—a housing problem, a marital problem, a psychological problem. There is no formula. The approach must be flexible and sensitive. Discussion, group interaction, personal counseling, and role playing are a few of the methods used.

A LOOK AT THE OTS

What goes on at the Occupational Training School is a kind of window to the world of the ghetto people as they come to the world of the plant. The middle-class white manager, labor leader, government officer, or college professor will need to look through that window and try to understand if he wishes to reach the black people of the ghetto, attract them, and help them (as well as himself) to build working relationships in the industrial plant.

The white manager or, for that matter, the Negro manager living in a middle-class culture will never understand the rejected hard-core black man coming to his plant merely by reading abstract propositions, executive summaries, or finely reasoned analyses. The white manager will learn only by confrontation, by hearing these people out with an effort at open ears, with neither rebuff nor sentimentality, and with enough humility to believe that he has something to learn as well as something to teach.

The authors think there is enough truth in McLuhan's "the *medium* is the message" to ask you to come with us through these pages to the rather dingy OTS meeting rooms on the third floor of the Apprentice Building of the Westinghouse East Pittsburgh works.

August 30, 1968. I walked into the training center at 1:00. They'd all just finished lunch and were about to begin class. Mr. Ross introduced me to the class, explained that in this room there was to be no smoking, that everyone was to address each other as Mr. ——, that he was in charge, and one must wait to be called on to speak. That's all the explanation I got and what followed was both bewildering and remarkable. Much of my bewilderment arose from not having been a regular participant in this classroom, I know, but the ensuing conversation moved so quickly and obliquely that it was all I could do to follow its winding and unstructured course.

Before I begin to relate this conversation, let me briefly describe the physical situation. There was a desk for the teacher, several long tables with chairs, a blackboard, and a makeshift lectern. Then, there were 17 trainees, 15 black and 2 white. Most of them were young, from 18 to 22, but there was one white-haired fellow, one bald, and another who spoke of his six-year-old child, so I figure that several of them were considerably older. They were all male.

This was the last day of the training program, and the class opened with a general discussion of what they'd learned from the training and what they were going to do Tuesday morning—the first day on the job. They were going into a variety of positions. All but two had been placed in jobs. Several had been to meet their foremen and get introduced to their jobs. One boy raved about his foreman, how he'd gone all the way for him, spending more than three hours with him explaining things. The question arose as to whether everyone had gotten the same warm reception from his foreman, or had expected the same reception. Why might he not get a warm reception from his foremen and co-workers? The students were well aware of problems and antipathies they might encounter in the plant (that did not at all relate to racial prejudice). The honesty and directness of the entire program were healthy and beneficial. The trainees understood the seniority system, union pressure for nepotism in hiring, the preferential treatment they were receiving compared to workers hired outside the program—and saw how these factors might work against them. Besides union and employee resentment, the fact that people are simply different and react differently was discussed. Although the training program was perhaps idyllic in its freedom and openness, the trainees were (rationally, if not emotionally) prepared for the industrial community.

Suddenly, this quite articulate balding fellow named Mr. Lucas, a trainee, was at the rostrum explaining what was needed in the Negro community. He had written down four points—leadership, recreation, education, and employment—and went on to explain his own participation in each of these areas. I figure this had been an assignment. The training program has a large and long-range goal, going far beyond employing one man at Westinghouse. These people realize, or are made to realize, their potential effect on the entire community.

Then Mr. Ross started tracing the course of a boy as he wandered through the ghetto—what he'd see (bars, vacant stores), what men would be his examples (pimps, hustlers). This was illustrated with a series of colored photographs. The question came up: "How many of you think you live in a ghetto?" A few reluctant hands were raised, and then all sorts of humorous hell broke loose between the faction from the Hill District and that from Homewood. The Hills boys didn't think they lived in a ghetto, but Mr. Ross reminded them of what they'd said just the other day about no police protection. Peace was obtained by sending a representative from the Hills to the rostrum to answer questions. Someone checked the dictionary for a definition of *ghetto*, and I guess the problem got resolved.

Then someone asked Mr. Ross why you can't call a pimp "a professional businessman." What he was getting at was, "why isn't a pimp a respected man of business?" Mr. Ross admitted to be caught, hung up on his white values. At this point, I'd forgotten I was a visitor and started waving my hand to get in my two cents. I think maybe I'd missed the whole direction of this conversation, because after I'd explained that no matter what one thinks about prostitution or drugs, good or bad, a pimp or a hustler is a middleman, making money off someone else's work. There was a pause. Then everybody started talking at once, and one boy asked me if I'd be a pimp, if I were a man, that is. The conversation was moving so fast, it could be only a yes or no answer, so I issued my expected no. Later, when we were all having a cigarette outside, I said that I didn't know what I'd do if I were broke and starving. If there were an option, as there is for me, then no, I wouldn't be a pimp.

Then we got into a general discussion of white values, how much of them we would buy. Most of us would buy some of them. The fact that illegitimate children are raised equally with legitimate children in the black community, while they're hidden and hushed up in the white community, was pointed out.

This is disjointed—but so was the conversation. There was another boy at the rostrum, talking about black history. He asked me if I knew what a Moorish-American was. I knew what an Afro-American was but not a Moorish one. Western Africa was settled by the Moors, so those Americans from that section of Africa are Moorish-Americans! He referred to whites as the "Europeans." It seems like everybody's hung up on terms, both for themselves and for others. Anyway, this boy and another boy who read a poem of his a bit later (about the ghetto being a prison without bars that must come down by violence now) were generally accepted as the most conscious and articulate of the group.

At about three o'clock, the group broke. We stood around and had a smoke, and then Mr. Ross asked me to interview someone—a trainee for the third program. He actually did the interviewing. He briefly asked the boy about his police record and employment record, then told him he wasn't much interested in his past, just whether he wanted to work. Mr. Ross made him aware that he was to accept any position given to him, including janitor; that he was to be an example to others; that no absence or tardiness was allowed—and he was hired, pending a physical and certification by the Pennsylvania Employment Service. I'm sure the boy knew what was expected of him right there at the start.

Then began a most informal discussion called "GGI" (Guided Group Interaction), a kind of group dynamics. It was held in another room, with smoking allowed, first-name basis, and no direct leadership—although Mr. Ross was certainly the guide. Tempers got pretty hot with nothing held sacred, but nobody got really miffed by the whole thing. Negroes are generally less self-deceived and hung up on their image; many a white would have dissolved under this honest scrutiny. Most of the conversation centered around being *programmed.* Generally *programmed* means spouting off unconsciously like a computer; specifically it means spouting off unconsciously the values of white society, in the case of a Negro, being an Uncle Tom. Mr. Ross was accused of being programmed, as were a few others. Ross admitted it, and this began another discussion of white values versus black.

We talked again about the pimp, what would you do if your daughter were a prostitute. Most of them didn't like the idea much but, if she were of age, it was her decision. We talked about why a prostitute needs a pimp—protection and so forth. Then we got onto violence as a means of securing civil rights. Mr. Ross agreed that violence had been necessary to achieve the progress made so far, but now that things were moving, more passive means should suffice. Several of the trainees were more militant than Mr. Ross. Then we talked about prejudice. Ross asked the white trainees if they were prejudiced, if relatives had taught them they were better than black men. The answer—yes. They were all very frank, and at the same time, very tolerant.

November 19, 1968. The fifth group was a bit larger than the second group—about 25 men, again two of whom were white. They were also a bit older than the last group and, as the discussion wore on, apparently more mature and accepting of the program. In the previous group, there were several quite militant trainees, and the discussion had centered mainly on black versus white values. The first thing I heard this time was a half-hour recording of a play written by the trainees on growing up in the ghetto. Each group (the trainees now work a great deal in small groups of five or six) had been responsible for a particular time span in the hero's life. The recording was pretty much as I expected: the broken home, bad examples presented to the child, the poor education of the adolescent—followed by dropping out of school, making it on the street, getting in trouble, prison and drugs. But then came the big surprise—it had a happy ending! The hero finds someone who believes in him and is willing to give him a chance, and life begins at 40! I couldn't believe the optimism was for real; couldn't help but feel they were putting me on, telling me what I wanted to hear. A discussion began on the tape and how the lives of individual trainees related to it. There was this universal feeling of optimism—that the training program had provided them with the opportunity of rebirth. I really felt that they were laying it on pretty thick for us, but three days later I was well convinced of their sincerity.

November 20, 1968. The previous day we had heard a rumor that one of the hard-core, now working on the night shift, had arrived drunk for work. The foreman had approached this Mr. Sinclair and asked him if he had a problem. Yes, he had a problem. He'd just cracked his wife over the head with a bottle, killing her, and then proceeded to shoot another man, I think, his father-in-law. Mr. Hiestand, manager of Industrial Relations, who was accustomed to such rumors, seemed rather unconcerned about the episode and quipped, "Well, Dick Ross has really succeeded in getting these people to work on time, no matter what!" The rumor had spread throughout the plant like wild fire. There are many nonbelievers, anxious to attack the hard-core program, and such incidents add fuel to the fire.

Dick Ross seemed a bit more concerned. He knew that Mr. Sinclair had been having severe problems with his wife during training and had once before threatened to kill her. Dick, on the pretext of inviting the trainees' wives in for the day, had previously managed to get Mr. and Mrs. Sinclair together to talk. They had been reconciled and returned home together.

I met Mrs. Sinclair that November afternoon; she was attractive and extremely charming. Mr. Sinclair loved her to distraction and was fiercely jealous of her associations with other men. No, Mrs. Sinclair wasn't dead—the story had been exaggerated—but the whole left side of her face was cut and bruised and swollen and stitched together. Dick instructed us to ignore the wound, which was rather difficult, and proceeded to ask her how she was. He had tried to get her a job a few months before, and he asked her if she had found work. Then, he asked her about her husband, how he liked his work, and what were a wife's duties to her husband. An unhappy home life affects a man's work life, and this is especially true for Mr. Sinclair. He always heads for the bar to drown his problems.

Mr. Sinclair arrived in the office a while later. He was a wiry little man, probably 40. He had spent years of his life as a sandhog, digging sewers in Washington and Baltimore and Boston. This was dangerous work and arriving in the open air at the end of a day was an unexpected pleasure. The sandhogs made good money, but they drank a lot of it away as if there really would be no tomorrow.

Mrs. Sinclair listened attentively as her husband spoke; she was very proud of him. But Mrs. Sinclair loved nice things, nice clothes, a nice home—and actually so did Mr. Sinclair. These things seemed to be a long time in coming, and it was hard to be patient for so long. Mr. and Mrs. Sinclair left together again, both realizing how important this job was to their future happiness, and how another marital disturbance might jeopardize that future.

November 21, 1968. Thursday is payday, so it was an appropriate time to discuss budgeting one's money. The trainees are paid $2.645 an hour, around $100 a week. It's easy to get taken in the ghetto. You may have been duped into buying diamonds or watches and learned a lesson, but there's always a new gimmick and always a chance you might make good. They sell water in expensive Parisian perfume bottles and Longene watches that, when you look closely, read Longreen and stop ticking two days later. One trainee got talked into giving his girl friend $75 for a new washing machine, leaving him a grand total of about $3 to last the week. Money flows fast in the ghetto. They call it "cop and go." They're trying to learn to "cop and lock."

The budgeting discussion was followed by instruction in opening and using a checking account. I've never thought of the hazards involved in a simple checking account. For example, some banks have blank deposit slips, which you don't sign; some smooth operator entered the bank and wrote his account number on all the blank deposit slips—and kept calling the bank to see how his account was soaring.

Dick then met with the six group leaders and I heard two amazing stories. Mr. Pratt was the first to speak. Pratt grew up in normal ghetto fashion, and by 15 he had started his bit—burglaries, robbing grocery stores. One night he broke into a little store, took the cash from the register and departed. An hour later he discovered he'd lost his wallet. And so it was time to leave the city and flee. He sped home and packed his bag—and discovered his wallet. Joy, relief, laughter. Pressure and relief. Pressure and relief. Mr. Pratt eventually got caught and put in reform school, and from reform school to the farm to the state penitentiary. Two years in jail, two months out, and back to jail. Pratt had spent a total of 17 of his 39 years in prison! On one of his brief vacations from prison, he'd staged a small robbery with a friend—which turned out to be a really small robbery, like $20. He was mad. The police started chasing him, but he was more mad than scared—mad that he was getting his clean clothes dirty.

Mr. Pratt talked about life in prison. A person gets tested in every new city, new neighborhood, and new situation—tested physically and psychologically. But in prison it's worse because you're so close and there's no escaping it. If you're a little guy, you've got to make a big buddy. And above all you've got to be ready to die to prove yourself. On one of Mr. Pratt's visits to a new prison, he encountered a particularly hostile fellow; so eventually they squared off and came to blows. The other fellow had a razor which he hooked behind Pratt's ear. Pratt dipped his finger in the other guy's eye. The guards came and ended the fight. Pratt had one ear flapping in the breeze, but he'd proved himself—in that jail at least. But there were always new jails.

Around 1962, while he was filling out a two-year term on the farm, he got summoned on another charge and sentenced to "60 years and one dark day." He'd become rather used to his two-year stays, but 60 years was something else. Six months later, his case was reviewed, and the 60-year sentence was reduced to 3! Pratt gladly packed his bag and moved from farm to "pen"—for what, in comparison, was only a brief stay. Pressure and relief. Pressure and relief and real soul laughter.

Mr. Pratt was sincere and emotional. He really never spoke a complete sentence—every other phrase was *you know* or *you know what I mean?*—and damned if they didn't know exactly what he meant! He'd been the full gamut and knew what was happening. It took Pratt 17 years to learn that you just can't make it that way. He tells them, and they listen. If anyone can learn from another's experience, they will learn from Pratt.

Mitchell [5] learned faster—one three-year term in the penitentiary and he knew he couldn't knock the system. Tom Mitchell's mother died when he was two, and he was raised by his sister, who was 17 years his elder. Somewhere in his teens, this sister and her husband got involved in pushing drugs. She didn't want Tom to get involved, but he soon sat down with the family to divide the bags into caps. Tom soon learned to look out for Tom, and he'd brush some weed on the floor, scoop it up—enough to make some fifty caps. So he had his own little dope hustle, a girl who left $40 on the table every morning, and some other profitable little side racket. Life was pretty nice, and he started moving around, usually running when things got too hot, to Buffalo where he really started making big money in dope, and then back to Pittsburgh, where he immediately hooked onto the big system. He was making something like $3,000 a week, and thinking nothing of blowing $500 a day. He had clothes—expensive clothes—11 suits and 20 pairs of shoes. He'd buy a pair of shoes and then go buy a $175 suit to match the shoes.

He also got himself hooked on heroin. One night he borrowed a friend's car and took himself and a girl and a bag out to the woods, and they split the bag. He was so high he couldn't get the needle out of his arm, and this girl had to get home. Somehow, he got her there, dropped her off, and proceeded toward his own place. Suddenly he found himself on the wrong side of the street with a car approaching not four inches away. His jaw was ripped open, the car demolished, but he wasn't feeling a thing, he was so high. He staggered out of the car, and some people grabbed him and got him to the hospital . . . where they immediately pumped him full of more dope to relieve the pain that he was already far from feeling. They released him, and Mitchell returned to find his own relief from pain. Eventually, the racket was busted, and 11 men were arrested at once and sentenced to three years in the penitentiary.

---

[5] See the Appendix for the interview with Tom Mitchell.

Mitchell was huge and impressive and intelligent. He'd been a rather successful drug pusher and was seeking the straight life. He'd been an addict and had cut the habit loose six years before. Mitchell was leader of the entire training group. The trainees listened to him and many followed his lead.

One aspect of the training program is called "Guided Group Interaction." The group is guided by one of its members, who holds the rostrum. Topics for discussion center on attitudes toward self, toward others, toward work, toward society. The topic is sometimes introduced by way of a film or visual aid that helps to provoke discussion.

"Willie Catches On" was a rather simplistic film on prejudice. It told how the seeds of prejudice were sown in a young boy's mind when his parents drop idle comments about Jews and Niggers, when his teacher makes oversimplifications about races for lack of time, until the point where Willie scratches the names of Weinstein and Marumba arbitrarily off his fraternity rushing list.

The film was followed by a lengthy discussion on prejudice. Mr. Wayre took over the rostrum and directed the discussion. He asked Mr. Martignetti, one of the two white trainees in the group, whether he had been brought up thinking that he was superior to black people. The answer, yes. Mr. Wayre then asked Mr. Martignetti if he'd learned anything and changed his opinion about blacks during the training program. The answer was again yes. Now, two months from now, if he saw Mr. Hamill (a militant black with an enormous Afro haircut seated beside him) walking in the rain, would he pick him up? Yes. Would he pick him up if his wife and mother-in-law were in the car? A more reserved yes; but no, if his father-in-law were there too. Why? Well, his father-in-law didn't like Negroes too much.

Now it was time to pick on Mr. Hamill. Would Hamill pick Martignetti up? Yes. Would Hamill pick Martignetti up if he had three Black Panthers in the car? No. Why? "Cuz he knew they didn't like whites." Now Hamill turned to Martignetti and asked him if he'd get in if he knew he had three Black Panthers in the car. The answer: "No, would you get in if I had three Ku Klux Klanners?" The conversation goes back and forth and round and round, but it is open and honest and much comes out.

November 22, 1968. The morning began with a session in role playing. It soon became apparent that the trainees were not only sensitive to the problems of others but also cognizant of the many forces at work for and against their entry into the world of work at Westinghouse. Had I not been present for the previous three days, I

would have been sure that the play presented to me was the result
of many hours rehearsal.

Dick Ross set up the plot, selected the leading characters, and
then disappeared. The little drama took shape, broadened to include
some 15 characters and a number of subplots, and continued for
more than an hour. Essentially, the situation was as follows: Mr.
Ross brings three hard-core trainees to meet their new foreman
(white). The foreman tells them about the three openings he has,
two as machinists and one as sweeper. He welcomes them, knowing
that the top brass in the company are anxious to see the hard-core
program succeed.

Now three white employees working in the area obviously over-
hear this conversation. (Three black trainees, by the way, are playing the three white employees.) One of these three whites is a
sweeper and has been a sweeper for 30 years. He resents having one
of these black hard core moving into a job level above him, but obviously to have remained a sweeper for 30 years, he must be rather
incompetent.

The three hard-core trainees exit, and the white sweeper approaches his two buddies, in the hope of getting their assistance in
attacking this grave injustice being wrought upon him. He'd been
with the company 30 years, and the idea that some no-good nigger,
fresh off the street, was going to move into a position he wanted was
just not right. The sweeper got sympathy from his two buddies. Because of their higher job rank they were less threatened, but they
were not anxious to work side by side with black men. The three
of them decided to approach the foreman. Now the foreman was
caught in the middle. He owed allegiance both to the company,
which was pushing the program and to his gang, who were opposing
it. This foreman was a cagey fellow, and he was ready when his
three gangmen approached. It seems that the three had poor attendance records lately, and their production was lower than it
ought to be. Before they could get a word out, he had placed them
all in a defensive position. They departed but the situation was far
from settled.

The three returned at lunch time, and the tables were turned.
After all, the foreman was also their buddy, who had grown up in
the union with them, lived around the corner, and certainly understood the problems of the working man. Besides they knew he
wouldn't want Mr. —— to know he'd been fooling around with his
wife, and they really didn't want to bring the union into this. So
the foreman was in a bind. He managed to wriggle out for the mo-
ment, but they'd see him again after work.

Meanwhile, the foreman was not idle and got on the phone to Mr.

—— and asked him if he'd be free to come over around 4:15. The sweeper was pretty busy too, and he got hold of his union steward. After all, this sweeper had been in the union for a long time and had some seniority, and the union had to fight for its people. Now the work day ended and the three white men showed up and so did Mr. ——, which threw a wet blanket on their outcries. But the foreman knew he wasn't safe yet. There was this little threat of blackmail they certainly would use if things didn't start going their way. Now the foreman took Mr. —— aside. It seems that there was still another job opening higher up, actually probably too hard a job for the sweeper. He'd probably fail quickly at it, but he wouldn't really be jeopardizing production much, at least for a few days, and he'd be appeased. . . .

This little drama could have gone on and on, the characters had so completely involved themselves in their roles, but there were other things to do.

REACTIONS TO THE OCCUPATIONAL
TRAINING SCHOOL PROGRAM

What are the reactions of the union, the blue-collar Westinghouse employees and the first-line supervisors to the Westinghouse OTS program? Of course the program is new, reactions are changing, and we cannot claim to have made a scientific sample of the foremen. As for the work force, we know of them only through the foremen. But after many conversations with the trainees, general management, and foremen, we think we can give insights that are generally valid.

Unemployment in the Pittsburgh area is relatively high. There are many regularly qualified people seeking work. On the other hand, employment at Westinghouse East Pittsburgh had dropped in recent years from 28,000 in the forties to 12,000 at present. Because of seniority provisions, it is natural that the work force is old. Furthermore, the plant had traditionally been a family plant, with sons and daughters, nephews and nieces, of employees having top priority for job openings.

Westinghouse East Pittsburgh only started hiring again in numbers in about 1965. At that time, the work force was networked with family relationships. To get away from excessive family relationships and also to upgrade the quality of the work force, Westinghouse East Pittsburgh established, in 1965, a high school diploma requirement and also certain entrance tests, such as the Wonderlic. In vain,

Local 601 protested the requirements, which they held were irrelevant to job performance.

When the company waived the high school and test requirements in 1968 exclusively for the hard-core unemployed OTS trainees, it is not surprising that Local 601 again protested. The local distributed handbills entitled, "Union Protest Dual Hiring Standards." Although not opposed to the hard-core program as such, the union could see no reason for retaining the requirements at all.

The regular work force at Westinghouse also has reservations and resentments concerning the hard-core program, some of them understandable. Dropping the requirements of a high school diploma, successful test scores, and the absence of a criminal record as criteria for employment for the hard core quite obviously represented a double standard.

Negroes have been employed at Westinghouse East Pittsburgh since World War II, though not in large numbers. Today they represent about 5 percent of the work force, a percentage lower than the average in the Pittsburgh area. Some white hostility is based on prejudice and not backlash. There have been a few incidents of cross burnings and wall scribblings, "Niggers go home." The rest of the resentment is due to the inability or unwillingness of the white employees to see a need for some preferential treatment for blacks, at least in hiring and in vestibule training.

The best way to get the very human reactions of both foremen and blue-collar workers to the OTS program will be to listen to a cross section of four of the foremen we interviewed. Foreman Gillis gives his reaction to the Sinclair episode we mentioned earlier. Sinclair was one of his employees.

GILLIS: Well, I had one incident. One of our boys from the hard-core program come in here one evening and was visibly under the influence of alcohol or some type of intoxicant; he was very unsteady on his feet. I was notified . . . that he was coming in. And he come in, and he was staggering around. And he took off his clothing, and his clothes were all disarrayed, and there was blood on his shirt. And I went out and I said, "Well, Roy, have you been drinking?" And he said, "Well, yes I have. I have troubles, you know." And I said, "Is there anything I can help you with?" Well, he hesitated about discussing anything with me because I was right out here with the group. So I took him aside and said, "Look, Roy, if there's anything I can help you with, let's hear." Well, he said he's been having troubles at home; he and his wife weren't getting along. As a matter of fact, he just got done shooting his brother-in-law.

This takes you back. And, gosh, what is my job? Yes, I'm a foreman, yes. But I'm not equipped to handle a lot of this when they catch you flat-footed. He went through a story about, he evidently was waving a pistol around at home. And his wife and his brother-in-law took it away from him. And he got a shotgun and shot his brother-in-law and hit his wife with a hammer. I was flabbergasted. What do you do, you know? Is he telling me the truth? Is he fabricating something in his mind because of the condition he's in? I didn't know. Like I said, he was unfit for work. So I told him I couldn't put him to work in his condition and advised him that if what he told me was true he'd better go see a policeman. After some conversation with him, he finally agreed that the best thing he could do was go see a policeman. . . . Well, I tell you, I've only been a supervisor since May of '67, and my training period was approximately six months, so really I've only had a section of my own since last September. Boy, it's been a broadening experience!

I took him over here to put his outer wraps on, and, gosh, what's he pull out of the top of the locker but a big woman's purse. And there's a woman's blonde wig in it, falls out on the floor, and he picks it up and shoves it in his pocket. Off we go down the aisle. And he's still talking about shooting somebody. Man, I don't know if this guy's got a revolver on him. . . .

WEBSTER: Did a lot of people hear this?

GILLIS: Unfortunately, evidently on his way up the aisle, he had stopped and talked with several of the other fellas about it and had told them a similar story, not exactly what he told me. Afterwards I went back and tried to piece together. . . . Here was an unfortunate incident. Although the fella himself, as far as a worker was concerned, was average, he applied himself probably as far as most of our OTS boys. He was a little better. He wasn't afraid to go in and hustle and sweat a little bit and get a little bit dirty, do his share of the load and maybe a little bit more.

So, in a way, I was a little sorry to see him go. [Sinclair was being transferred, not because of this incident, to another department.] But, unfortunately, when he did come in, he had talked to so many people the story got around. He was very desirable up until this point. He had missed a couple of days or was late on occasion with what I felt was good reason. . . . It did create some excitement over the group. They thought, "If a guy comes in and is mad at me, he's going to pull out a gun and shoot me or something. All these hard-core guys are the same; they're all a bunch of gangsters."

Responses of the foremen to the program have been varied. Most reactions are lukewarm, neither favorable nor unfavorable. The foremen we interviewed found that they had to spend more time counseling the hard core than their regular employees. However, all said that they would give the same time and advice to any of their workers. Preferential treatment is over, and the hard core, like all employees, are subject to company rules and regulations and are expected to meet company standards.

Some of the foremen, probably a minority, actually prefer the hard-core trainees, as men doing twice the work of regular employees. Foreman Tom Hennessey makes the point that, unfortunately but typically, the trainee's fresh enthusiasm for hard work may soon get dampened by established employees who do not want to be shown up.

Here are the comments of Foreman Hennessey, along with the comments of Mr. Ross, and the interviewer.

FOREMAN HENNESSEY: You have to watch that Carl [a trainee] doesn't get brainwashed by the other people that we have too.

WEBSTER: Brainwashed by whom?

HENNESSEY: Other employees. Some of them, you might say they're. . . .

ROSS: Be sure you get this. This is something that goes all the way.

HENNESSEY: Hard core, but we've had people in here all along who are in just the same situation, and these people, they've set their standards and so on, and maybe they're a little reluctant to see someone here getting a little better break than they will, you know. There might be a little backlash.

WEBSTER: But how would Carl get brainwashed, I don't understand?

HENNESSEY: Well, I say get brainwashed. When Carl first come out here, he went to his machine and he'd go to work. Now maybe a fellow'd say, "Well, look, you're making us look bad. Take a little break now and then." I just had a talk with Carl. Didn't put out quite as much as I thought he should last month; I didn't say anything to him, I just let him go ahead. But at the end of the month, I showed him what he'd done this month and what he'd done last month. . . .

WEBSTER: And it was because people had talked to him?

HENNESSEY: I can't say that. But I feel it was. So I told him, "Carl, you're on your own, you know what you can do." This is where one of our big problems is.

ROSS: If he were on incentive, it would be a different story. I worried about that, that's one of the major problems of training men. He goes out, he really improves in motivation and wants to work. But there are certain places where you only do so much. Would you agree?

HENNESSEY: This is true. This is true in the shop.

WEBSTER: You've got to get along with your fellow workers as well as your boss. . . .

ROSS: So, if you work a little bit too hard . . . you know . . . this has happened . . . some of the fellas have told our trainees, "Go, go take a break, go to sleep, you know, go hide." And they don't know how to absorb this.

HENNESSEY: . . . . There's a limit to what you can force em to do. You can't stand over one man all the time, because the men are not going to stand over him all day. Some of them come along and they say you're discriminating. . . . Actually, what I'd be trying to do would be get Carl to do what he's supposed to do and help him. Because if I help him, I'm helping myself. The same thing with Richard, I've put a lot of time into Richard. I've worked hard with him and I feel like I've accomplished something. Right now, he'll stay away but he'll be disciplined. And I'll come up and, what I tell him to do, he'll do, regardless whether I tell him to jump off the building.

I don't think Richard ever had anybody in his life who he could put any faith or any trust in. I think from the time that he's been a kid what he's had, he's had to hang on for himself. I don't think anyone was ever willing to help him or talk to him. . . .

One day, I know he'd come in here, and he said, (and I believe he was telling me the truth) he didn't have but about an hour's sleep that whole night because he couldn't get into his bed. He tried to sleep in a chair and then when he did get to bed about six o'clock in the morning, he slept. And, as a result, he was late getting here. And I was giving him heck about coming in late, you know. This is the thing you've got to impress on them . . . they're never going to get out of the hole and they're never going to better themself. . . . The only way they're going to get money is by coming in and working. . . .

ROSS: How about Carl? What's his record? How many times has Carl been late since he's been here?

HENNESSEY: Ah, I'd say about five, six times. And the reason he is late is he comes from Belchertown, I believe it is. And I don't know but I think he has to catch two or three buses. This is why he's late. Now Richard, we had quite an interesting time with him. He comes in, couldn't get here on time, so we even bought him an alarm clock. This is when I first put my foot down. This is when

I first started to have a little faith in Richard. He came in and he said to me, he said to me, he'd like to borrow, he'd like to get an alarm clock. I said, "All right, you see me after lunch." I said, "You need the money to get it?" "No," he says, "I've got enough money to get it." He bought the alarm clock and then he brought it in and he says, "Now, you see if this works."

WEBSTER: Did you prepare the rest of the people who work here at all for these people who were coming in?

HENNESSEY: No. No. You can't do that. Cuz the minute you say to the other people, "Now, this is a hard-core fella that we're bringing in here. . . . The more you can have the other people forget about it and treat him as another employee, another person, the better off. . . .

WEBSTER: Have you had any problems with the other people?

HENNESSEY: Yes, we've had problems with the other people. There's going to be people who's going to resent. And one of the reasons: Some of the people had the idea that these people were here and the government was paying their wages. And this wasn't true. But this was something, the government was paying their wages; as a result, they were getting special privileges.

WEBSTER: You mean they were getting more money?

HENNESSEY: Well, maybe they were getting a subsidiary payment or something like that.

Foreman Walter J. Gedrin of the Switchgear Division, Assembly Section, is rather favorable to the OTS program. About the hard-core trainee he has received he says:

I have just one so far, and he has been with me for a good piece of time, and I have a lot of trouble with absenteeism. All good excuses I would say . . . all legitimate excuses. . . . He has not been the Sunday afternoon football player, or whatever it might be, to get himself mixed up. . . . He had a baby not too long ago. In the past couple of months this baby has had problems, so emergency calls to rush her back to the hospital. His wife is in the hospital now. Like I said, he had quite a few good excuses. I hope he gets straightened out pretty soon, because even those become too much.

Gedrin brings up an important point that the white community often forgets.

It is surprising the fear some of them have that somebody hates them so bad that they are going to drop a whole load of steel on them and squash them flat. . . . They have an idea that there is a tremendous hatred perhaps. And I am going out there as a hook-on and these cranemen don't like me, and he's going to swing that load and wipe me out. As if this is an everyday occurrence with bodies laying all over the place! And this is all ridiculous.

Foreman Bill McGuire in the Transportation Division received two of the hard-core trainees, and he is generally dissatisfied with them though not dissatisfied with the total program. About one of his men he says:

This was the way he started out. He was very slow. If I told him to sweep between those two electric lines down there and when he was finished, look across the aisle and see if that needed sweeping, he would sweep between those two lines and take a long time doing it. And then he'd sort of stand there and look across the aisle and just wouldn't make up his mind whether he even wanted to go over and see if it needed being swept or not. He had the attitude that he was on a menial task. And apparently this is a prevalent thought, with a few of them anyhow. And in one of our conversations, he remarked to myself and the general foreman, he said, "Well, my friends tell me that I'm on the lowest job in Westinghouse."

McGuire makes the important point that the foremen are not being pressured into giving preferential treatment to the hard-core people they get.

This would have really irked me if I said well, look, I want this man fired [and] he would come to me and says, "Well, now, you don't fire this guy, the government's behind this program, and Mr. Burnham's behind it, and you don't want to get yourself trouble." If they were to try to put me on the spot by saying, "Look, pal, you're going to swing alone on this," I would have been, I would have washed my hands of the whole deal, right then and there! As it is, I've gone along with them, and I'll say this for Mr. Ross and Mr. Justus, they have been fair with me, in the sense that they told me that you're the foreman, you're the boss; what *you* tell us is what we will do. You want the man dismissed from the company, we'll even write the letter for you. You won't have to write it, we'll write it on your recommendation. For this I respect them. At least, they're not trying to push something down my throat and make it look to me like we're going to put you out on a limb, you know. If the program doesn't work, we're going to say it's guys like you that won't make it work. This I don't think they'll do.

However, McGuire goes on to say:

My boss is on me, and the workers are watching this; the old hands, they're watching this like a hawk. They want to see how I'm going to handle this situation because they have the attitude that these guys are getting preferential treatment, and it's tough to break this notion out of their heads right now. . . .

Preferential treatment in hiring, as McGuire brings out, is hard for the white blue-collar workers to accept.

So they seem to look at these guys as if the company's just dumped them on them. And they're afraid that they're going to get good jobs one of these days and knock these old guys out of a job. This is one of their thoughts. One of their prime complaints is that they can't get their sons in here, and I've had this the last couple of days. Men have come to me and have said, "Is it okay if I go down the employment office for a couple of minutes?" Okay, just don't make a day of it. And they come back with a very disgusted look on their face. What's your problem? "Well, I went down to employment, I wanted to get an application for my boy, and they tell me they're not hiring. Yet all I see is these hard cores coming in by the dozens! The company's not hiring? What's the deal! I've been thirty years in this shop. How come I can't get my boy a job? And yet they'll go out and recruit, actually go out on the streets and bring these people in and give them jobs. My boy will push a broom!" This is their attitude. "You know, he isn't proud, he'll push a broom. Give him a chance behind the gate." So, a little bit of resentment from the people. . . .

Finally, McGuire brings out an issue that may occur in some plants, the matter of the Negroes tending to congregate together.

PURCELL (the interviewer): How do they get along with the whites and vice versa, Bill?

McGUIRE: Well, here again is something I don't like and it's prevalent in the shop. It's there's definite segregation by choice—by choice

—I don't think they make too many attempts to get friendly with the white workers. They'll congregate together. This is the problem I have had prior to the occupational training started here. Four out of five of my laborers were Negroes and I was constantly breaking up little conferences. I had a bad egg working for me, a real troublemaker, and he was one of the main causes of these conferences; he was called on the carpet several times. But they do seem to congregate; I don't think that they make any attempt. And in the same respect, I don't think the white workers make any attempt.

PURCELL: Congregate on the floor? On the job?

McGUIRE: Not too much during working hours, but before the shift starts, at lunch time, they'll go be together. When I come out of the cafeteria (our cafeteria happens to be located right at the end of our aisle), and I'll come out about five after twelve or so, and out of the ones that we have in the Machine Section right at the start of the aisle in the subassembly further up, there's probably maybe eight to ten of them working these sections on both incentive and laboring; and they'll be six or seven of them, and they'll all be in one little group. And that way you get the feeling: What are you guys plotting out? I think there's a natural reaction that's due to the social environment as it is and the trouble that constantly runs in the cities. The workers always when they see more than two of them congregating together, right away they take the attitude that these guys are hatching something up. So we do have a little bit of a problem.

One conclusion comes out of these foremen interviews—the need for special counseling and help for the often very legitimate problems that hard-core people continue to have in the plant. We see much of this support coming from foremen who are concerned and a great deal of it coming from Mr. Ross and his associates in the Occupational Training School. The incidents that we have given must not obscure the fact that many of the hard-core people have had no dramatic incidents or problems in the plant and have been adequately received.

WHAT OF THE FUTURE?

The success of the Westinghouse OTS program must be related to its costs, $375,691, or about $1,900 for each trainee. As far as we can determine, these costs are mostly paid for by the federal government, though there are some direct and some hidden costs paid for by Westinghouse. Some of the direct costs are represented by the cost of renovating and renting the training facility. Hidden costs are represented by the extensive use of time for the OTS by such managers as James Higinbotham, manager of Employment and Personnel Services, for the foremen orientation days programs, and for whatever time the foremen have to spend on extra counseling for the hard-core employees. The OTS costs, however, compare favorably with the NAB average of $2,900 per man on the job.[6] Another report [7] puts the range of costs from $2,000 to $5,000 or more. The Westinghouse costs seem small compared with the minimum welfare costs of each of the trainees of $1,000 per year for the rest of their lives. There are problems lying ahead for expanding programs like this, but they are not primarily financial.

Industries, such as steel, with declining blue-collar employment and few new hires cannot easily undertake hard-core programs. Such programs will require plants that are at least stable in employment. Westinghouse East Pittsburgh faced the possibility of cutbacks because three departments were being moved out and there was a ten-day wildcat strike affecting part of the plant. Fourteen OTS men were laid off. Within three months Westinghouse recalled every man. All but two came back; one was in jail and the other had a good job. During the layoff, Ross helped the ex-trainees on temporary jobs, credit, bail, housing, even marital adjustment, keeping them from falling back into ghetto anonymity and despair.

Should programs of this kind be expanded into many other plants and companies? We think that they should be. But each plan will need to be tailored to the special local plant conditions. Two major problems are these: First, the need to secure competent and dedicated men to direct and staff the program. Such men, like Richard Ross, must know how to reach both the people of the ghetto and the people of the plant. They will need to give much of themselves, at all hours of the day and night, for the sake of the men in the program. Men like these are not easy to find. Second, there will be the continual need to convince the local unions and especially the blue-collar work force and the first-line supervisors that preferential treatment, at least for hiring standards and vestibule training, is necessary and justified.

In 1968 and 1969, nearly 196 hard-core persons will have been

---

[6] *Time* (November 22, 1968), p. 16.

[7] Samuel M. Burt and Herbert E. Striner, "Toward Greater Industry and Government Involvement in Manpower Development." Staff paper of the Upjohn Institute for Employment Research, Kalamazoo, Michigan, September 1968, p. 6.

hired by Westinghouse East Pittsburgh. Because of the commitment of top management, the devotion and ability of Richard Ross and his staff, the motivation of the trainees themselves, and the preparation provided them, 95 percent will remain in company employ. Given the bootstraps, these people have managed to pull themselves up. They have been helped to help themselves. One hundred ninety-six men have found a chance.

APPENDIX: INTERVIEW WITH TOM MITCHELL

MITCHELL: . . . . like my childhood, it wasn't what you would call bad. My environment was more of a middle-class environment, like I lived in a low-rent housing project. And everybody in there had a sense of pride to an extent, you know, and the children that I grew up with, we were active in sports. In the basketball season we played basketball and we played football and we swam; we had baseball diamonds. So it was really a real active thing.

Then, I don't know, when I got in grammar school I started drinking like my sister. Well, my mother died when I was two years old. My father went in the hospital when I was around thirteen, and he died in the hospital. He never came home again. He had diabetes, tuberculosis . . . it was a list of things. They had to amputate my father's leg, and he never came home no more than for a weekend or something, you know, and I stayed with my sister. My sister reared me, her and her husband. And I got in the habit where, they kept whiskey around the house. The environment in school . . . the school was a ghetto school that I went to, an old school that had been there maybe seventy-five years before I got into the school, you know. It was outdated, and outmoded, and then it was in a ghetto neighborhood and the majority of the pupils were from the ghetto area. And I went to this school. This was where my friends went to school, you know, and we got to where we started drinking in the class. We'd bring little medicine bottles, like cough syrup, in. It could be wine or whiskey or whatever we could get. We'd drink it in school. It was just a lot of fun, nobody meaning, you know, any harm. And like my grades were good, I could understand. . . . And from this drinking, one of our friends, his brother was using drugs, he used to steal the caps and bring them to school, and we'd store them, you know, and hide. But it wasn't a thing where anybody got hooked up or anything like this, and I started into high school.

PURCELL: Kind of starts off like a little game?

MITCHELL: Like a game, that's all it was, have some fun. I didn't know. Like Halloween we'd get drunk and go out and mark up the windows . . . and so I went into high school, and when I went to high school, I went to Rindge Vocational High, this's very high academic standings, you know. It's aviation mechanic I was studying for, and it was a different environment altogether. This field was away from the ghetto completely; 90 percent of the students were white, you know. I had a different environment. But even there I had like leadership qualities, you know, like in my class, like I became a leader in my class. The little white boys, they followed me and they followed my lead, you know; I set the pace, they'd follow my lead. Then, I don't know, I got involved with the girls—that was another thing. Now this side-tracked me from school again. I'd get out and get to running with the girls and everything . . . and ah, I wind up knocking a girl up, you know, and we get married. Well, I figured this was a mistake. Now I know it was a mistake.

PURCELL: How old were you then, Tom?

MITCHELL: Seventeen, going on eighteen. We get married. Then right away we start having differences; I get to messing around again with stuff, narcotics, and I pick up a pistol and I go in and rob a liquor store.

PURCELL: What were you on? Marijuana? Heroin?

MITCHELL: Heroin. Marijuana isn't habit forming. This is something that nobody can control, see, and it's something that's hard to explain because if you haven't experienced it, I can't tell you how bad it is, like, I can know how bad it is, in here. I know how bad it is, I know how I did. But if you haven't experienced it, nobody can tell you how bad it is; you can't imagine how bad it is. Well, anyway, I got to messing around again, and I wind up going to jail. I took up a pistol and went in and robbed a liquor store, and I think we got six hundred dollars, me and two more guys, we got six hundred dollars, and run through that little six hundred dollars in a day or two, and me and my wife were buggin'.

PURCELL: Well, that heroin costs dough.

MITCHELL: Oh, yeah. Well, then it was only $2.50 a cap. They had little number five caps; you see them, the smallest caps, number five, $2.50 a cap, and I didn't have no heavy habit then, just a small habit, and then I didn't have the habit long. I went to jail before I really got strung up, before I got a real big habit. I was in jail, so that saved me that time. This was in '53, I went to jail, I come out in '55. Me and my wife we bug again, we bug again. I wind up going back for parole violation. So now I get out in '58, and I still got these ideas, you know, making the big money, making the fast money. By this time now my sister and her old man, they're into this narcotic traffic too.

So my wife and I, we go to buggin' again, and I get into a different bag now. I start gambling now. And I was on parole so I had to work, but I was gambling; I got obsessed with gambling. I started going into crap joints and a couple times I went in with maybe ten dollars, and twenty minutes later I got two hundred dollars, you know, and it hooked me up. It was almost as bad as a narcotic addict, and I couldn't stay out of those crap joints, you know. I couldn't wait. Like payday come, I'd get my pay at twelve o'clock, I'm going home at one o'clock. Yeah, I'm running the crap game, I'm the bag man, and I get a girl, she's giving me thirty or forty dollars, and then the money I'm making from the dope; I'm making money all around. It looked like everything I touched turned to money.

PURCELL: It seemed like it was going pretty well.

MITCHELL: Everything was going beautifully; I bought plenty of clothes, a lot of clothes, anything; it was just going real nice. And then one of the guys I had dealing for me got busted, he got busted with a outfit—that's a spike and a needle—and all this time now, I hadn't been messing around, I had snorted two or three times. But when the stuff would come in, I'd take a little snort to see if it was any good, you know, that's all; but I wasn't messing around myself. I stayed away from it from '53 to around 1960 when I came to Pittsburgh.

I came to Pittsburgh in '59, when this guy signed a statement on me. I caught a plane the next day, I left there, I weren't taking no chances on going back to jail there, you know. I say, if they get me, they've got to come and git me wherever they git me. So I went onto Pittsburgh and right away I got accepted into the same trend, the same vein of life, you know. I got accepted by all the dope pushers, the dope fiends, I got drawn right into that crowd. They looked at me, yeah, well come on. You're accepted right away, you know, and the same thing started in Pittsburgh. I started dealing here. But this time I started messing around a little more, you know. I get a girl; she's a dope fiend. And every time I see her, she'd be like saving me some, and "Well, baby, I saved you some, come on," and I get to popping in my arm again; popping in my arm again before you know it, and then I'm dealing too. I got all the stuff that I want, you know; I can get high any time I want to. I've got enough stuff to take care of my habit and her habit and maybe three or four other people, you know, and I suppose I never really realized how bad it was, until I got busted. And after they busted everybody out there, they cut it all off. Then it dawns on me how really strung out I am, you know. Like a bag of stuff ain't nothing now, for me; I've got to have two or three bags, just, just to be all right.

PURCELL: It's getting bigger and bigger.

MITCHELL: Yes. So then that's when I decided again that I had to cut this loose. Like it's no place to go, if you use the stuff. I see guys now that I know, and see em and you can see death on em. Maybe, I don't know if you've seen this, but you can see death on em. They just have a look like they're dead, like all they got to do is just lie down and die. And you know that drug is doing it to them; they just have that look about em. And this is the way I was getting; I had lost weight. I could take the seat of my pants and grab them like this, and pull the seat of my pants all the way around in front of me, that's how, you know, I'm just melting away to nothing. And I thought well, this ain't for me, you know. Cut it loose, I'm with that, you know. And from then on, I just started.

PURCELL: You cut it loose. That's a big move, a big step.

MITCHELL: This is the only real accomplishment that I feel I've made, you know.

PURCELL: Well, how did it go after that, then, Tom?

MITCHELL: Well, I was almost bust; I was on my way to jail when I started to kick. So by the time I was got to jail, by the time they got my sentence and everything, I had kicked. And I went on, I went to Lewisburg, and I went in industry there and saved up some money, you know. And then they sent me and put me in a vocational training program—barbering—I went through there and I came out. And I haven't been into anything since.

I came back, I went to Buffalo, and I decide to come back to Pittsburgh, to come back here. And I went to work in a barber-shop down there, and that's where I've been, up until this time, until I got into this program. I've only been back here about a year, a little over a year. I came back, August of last year. So I was looking, like I say, I was looking, I had been down there. I had signed up at a couple of employment offices down on Penn Avenue, down on Fifth, one in Homewood, ah, Oakland.

I've been out to American Bridge, every place that I heard that they were doing anything. I would take time off, you know, and go see about it, go put in a application anyway.

PURCELL: Didn't get anything to go through?

MITCHELL: No, didn't get anything.

PURCELL: Why not, do you think, Tom?

MITCHELL: Well, they'd say they'd take my application. They would get in touch with me if anything comes up. But then, see I wasn't lying about my record, for one thing, and this was really the handicap.

PURCELL: That prison record you mean?

MITCHELL: Yes, my prison record, and the fact that I, you know, I told the truth. . . .

PURCELL: That you'd been on heroin?

MITCHELL: . . . about the narcotics thing. Well, that's the worse thing in the world to expose to the public, you know; the first thing they say, "narcotics, oh, can't be trusted, he's through," you know, so. . . .

PURCELL: So then you heard about here?

MITCHELL: One of the fellows he come by this shop and he told me he had just got hired; he's starting out here at Westinghouse. He was in this program here, and he told me that Mr. Ross was the man to see, you know. And he told me, well, tomorrow morning I'll be out there. And I got in my father-in-law's car the next morning and I come on out here and talked to Mr. Ross, and he said, well, he's going to give me a chance, you know, and I've done my best ever since.

PURCELL: He believed in you.

MITCHELL: That's the first person, the first person, you know, that just accept me at my word, when I told him about I was hooked, and what I had went through, about being in jail, about my record and everything. And I told him that I hadn't used no stuff in six years and that all I wanted was a chance. Somebody had to give me a chance, somewhere. Yeah, and I told him, well, like, if you don't give me no job, this doesn't mean that I'm going back to narcotics, you know, because I'm not going to be. I'm not going to let you or nobody turn me around to this point where I go back to this. So if I don't get a job here, well, I'll just go someplace else. I'll just keep on looking. But he said, "All right, I'll take a chance on you." And he's given me a job, and I intend to do everything I can to prove to him that he didn't make a mistake, and to help the program. Because I know there is a lot of other people out there, you know, that would really appreciate this.

PURCELL: Why does the program go well?

MITCHELL: Everybody put a lot of interest in it. See, that's the main thing. He has made everybody realize that this is an opportunity for em, you know. This is a one chance in a million and you have an opportunity, you know. Now it's up to you. If you're not interested in it, why bother with it, why block it for somebody else, keep somebody else out? And everybody has got this interest in it and that's what makes it good. Everybody wants to succeed in this, and that's the main thing, getting the desire. Let people know that we do have another chance, you know. See. Because it's other guys out there that have records. Maybe not like mine, but they have records. They've been in the penitentiary, and they've been slapped down, you know. They go lookin' for a job, and they get slapped down and get back into the involvement again.

And he has shown us that we do have a chance, you know, that we have a chance. And that's what's making it work. . . .

I'm really devoted to the program, and everybody here is devoted, everybody here. Like some of the dudes when they first, when the program first started on, they had, like I said, militant attitudes, you know. Attitudes that if you say something to me, you're picking on me, so. But they're coming out of this, you know; they're all adjusted. And they see the importance of the program, and they're like me and Wayre and the group leaders. We try to talk to the dudes, you know, every chance we get. And try to make them see that we're older, and the things that these younger boys got to go through, a lot of the things we've been through already, you know. And we try to make them see that if you don't do something now. . . .

PURCELL: Why does it help?

MITCHELL: Well, it lets you get some of that inner tension off. And you see I feel that anything I've done, I don't have to be ashamed of, because this is something that I've done coming up, this is something. Maybe it was just because I didn't know any better, you know, so why should I be ashamed . . . ? So, it eases some of this tension off, to get it out in the open; you know, it does. I know a lot of things that I could talk about here that I couldn't talk about at home, you know, things that I've done.

PURCELL: Is that so?

MITCHELL: Sure, at a time, not now, you know. Because now I can talk about anything I want to, you know. I tell my wife what I want to tell her, you know. If she likes it, all right; if she don't, well, you accept it anyway, because I'm going to be the man in the family.

PURCELL: So it releases some of the tension, gets it out, outside.

MITCHELL: It gets it out. But I really feel that this is the best thing that ever happened to me, you know. This is the best thing right here, besides me kicking my habit. Besides that, besides that, this is the best thing that happened to me, you know, to get into this program. And I'm going to do my best at it.

Discussion

BY *DONALD J. WHITE* *

The Westinghouse program has focused upon the truly hard core. The program consists primarily of motivational and sensitivity training, with basic instruction in reading and arithmetic, where needed. Candidates are prepared for the "world of work at Westinghouse," moving into jobs they can do—even menial—but with genuine opportunity for advancement.

The discussion of this case opened with brief comments from four of the principals involved in the study. Father Theodore Purcell, S.J., stressed the critical difficulty of recruiting staff people who could relate adequately to the disadvantaged covered by such programs—and he pointed out the problem of managing workers from the ghetto after they had gone through the "vestibule"; Rosalind Webster underscored the necessity to accept the double standard, for at least a few weeks after hiring, if programs like that at Westinghouse are to succeed. She emphasized the necessity for industry to explicate the double standard, not to attempt to camouflage it; stressing that it has prevailed commonly for years among the actually employed among alcoholics and others with special employment problems. Richard Ross, director of the Westinghouse East Pittsburgh Occupational Training Center, emphasized two points. First, that the merits of the present program include the indirect benefit of improving the capacity generally of foremen to manage effectively and, second, that much remains to be done. For example, the rule under present policies that no one who leaves the program

---

* Donald J. White is professor of economics at Boston College.

may be rehired is open to serious question. James Higinbotham, Westinghouse manager of Employment and Personnel Services, stressed the great need to provide the anchor points which would give the candidate the security feeling essential to permanent rehabilitation.

The discussion participants in the two sessions reacted vibrantly to the above comments, and to the case itself. They added a number of independent observations that are summarized below.

   a. The modification of formal hiring requirements—such as high school diplomas—should be extended to the general class of applicants so that emphasis can be placed upon relating qualifications to the job structure.
   b. Foremen need special training for dealing with the disadvantaged, and they can be brought more successfully into the process by being integrated into the hiring process.
   c. Better results can be obtained by integrating vestibule training of the Westinghouse type with formal job training to facilitate upward mobility. Reference was made to results of the Doeringer Study of ABCD (Boston) in 1968,[1] which showed that good earnings and earnings expectancy are key factors in insuring success in rehabilitating the disadvantaged.
   d. The key role of top management, support and leadership, was stressed. In Westinghouse, although top management did not dictate, its public espousal of efforts to aid the disadvantaged provided motive force. The company president was both a source of inspiration and a strong support.
   e. Scarcity of job opportunities handicaps efforts to aid the disadvantaged in a given plant. This was a restraining influence at East Pittsburgh, and it set up tensions between the union and the rehabilitation effort.
   f. Managements that are convinced of the propriety of implementing programs for the disadvantaged should press ahead, because "behavior follows reality, and managements which are trying to do the right thing in the present social environment can count on necessary changes in attitudes if they have the courage of their convictions."
   g. The key factors in the Westinghouse success were the willingness to take risks, to stick with the program in the face of criticism, and the willingness of the program director to become totally involved—even to the point of spending considerable time in researching the potential candidates through home visits and personal guidance.

---

[1] See Chapter 9.

h. Reaching and rehabilitating the disadvantaged is costly in both human and material terms, but the returns justify the effort.

There are no panaceas in this area, but it seems clear, from both the case write-up and the discussion, that the Westinghouse East Pittsburgh Vestibule Training program has served as an effective "decompression chamber," through which men who were almost unemployable have been able to move successfully into the mainstream of industrial life at a cost that society, and those immediately involved, can afford. The program would seem worthy of further elaboration in other precincts.

4

Employing the High School Dropout: Preparing for the New Work Force

BY   *ALLEN R. JANGER* *

Employing the high school dropout is a complex process. Equitable Life Assurance Society has learned, in the four experimental programs it has completed since 1962, that the dropout goes through many steps on his way from the economic margins of society into the mainstream of regular employment. To establish the environment in which he can make this passage—or will want to make it—requires planning and adaptation of personnel procedures. Also needed is the involvement of a broad slice of company management and supervision. Managers and supervisors have been introduced to the world of minority groups in a vital and comprehensive way, a not inconsiderable benefit, since conditions in the New York labor market have placed a large and increasing number of people from the disadvantaged minorities into Equitable's home office.

Of course, little of this was known in 1962 when the company initiated its employment program for unqualified high school dropouts. The company's management and Personnel Department were unaware of the dimensions of the hard-core problem or that a special program was needed. As the company's senior personnel executives look back, they see much of the impetus stemming from James F. Oates, Equi-

* Allen R. Janger is a senior research specialist with the National Industrial Conference Board, New York, New York.

From *Managing Programs to Employ the Disadvantaged*, by Allen R. Janger, National Industrial Conference Board, 1969. Reprinted with permission.

table's chairman of the board and chief executive officer, who was serving at the time as a member of President Kennedy's Committee on Youth Employment. Looking towards the future, that committee stated:

> We face an unprecedented growth in the number of young people and a substantial reduction in the number of jobs traditionally open to youth.

Unemployment among the country's youth (16-21 years of age and not in school) was averaging about four times the overall rate, as it still is—with high school dropouts the chief sufferers. Not only was unemployment highest among the dropouts but the longer they were out of work, the harder it became for them to get jobs. The committee saw a potentially chronic problem:

> Among these [unemployed] are tomorrow's castoffs and chronic dependents, those who will live in poverty of body and mind, and who will bring up their children in their own image.

THE PROBLEM

Equitable hires large numbers of high school graduates every summer, primarily for entry-level clerical positions. The hiring pool from which the graduates are drawn has been changing: A higher percentage of high school graduates now goes on to college; military service has been cutting into the number that remains. One study estimated that one out of every four people between the ages of 16 and 19 who entered the U.S. work force in 1968 would be nonwhite.

Within the city of New York, Equitable's main home office recruiting ground, about 50 percent of high school seniors come from minorities generally considered to be educationally disadvantaged.

The result, an Equitable personnel executive reports, is that:

> We are reaching a point where the quality of the youngster at the lower end of our acceptance scale seems too low to meet our standards for routine clerical work; and where there seems to be too few of the youngsters at the upper end of the scale who might have potential for eventual promotion to technician and supervisory jobs at middle levels. The problem is complicated by the racial tensions of the country which involve all of us and all of our supervisors in a deeply emotional way. We are not a world apart from our city. Our air conditioners do not filter out

fear and belligerence and frustration. We all feel it in ourselves and in others.

Responding to this mix of moral and environmental imperatives, Equitable developed, over the years, a broad range of programs and procedures designed to employ and upgrade Negroes, Mexican-Americans, and Puerto Ricans. The dropout program is one.

THE PLAN

Toward the end of 1962 the company's personnel staff noticed that its salary grade 1 entry jobs had much higher turnover than higher grades. More to the point, employees in these positions were turning over at a much higher rate than other recruits of the same age and length of service. The jobs called for limited skills—mailboys, stockroom, and custodial duties, as well as jobs involving transfer of figures from one document to another with, in some cases, simple computations along the way—and the personnel people theorized that selection standards for them were too high. Possibly Equitable might gain greater stability in these jobs by filling them with high school dropouts.

It was never assumed that the dropouts would remain permanently in the entry-level jobs for which they would be hired, nor did Equitable see itself as undertaking a lifetime commitment to employ them. The program was "an attempt to provide an experience from which these youngsters could gain a degree of self-confidence, see new alternatives, and begin to shape and determine their own lives." Equitable was committing itself to social rehabilitation as well as economic employment.

The Qualified and Unqualified. There were originally two parts to Equitable's dropout program, one for "qualified," the other for "unqualified" dropouts. This division arose because the company had had prior experience with hiring dropouts—occasionally, in times of manpower shortage when high school graduates had not been available, Equitable had waived its diploma requirement when a dropout was otherwise qualified for company employment. What distinguished the new qualified dropout program from earlier practice was that hiring was put on a regular—and more sizable—basis, and some systematic attention was given to finding out what sorts of jobs the dropouts might most profitably fill.

The program for qualified dropouts ended after three years. The qualified dropout did not make a more "stable" employee than the high school graduate. But, on the other hand, he was by no means a poorer employee than the fellow with a diploma. Performance, promotability, disciplinary matters, and turnover were about the same for both groups. To give equal pay for what was now regarded as equal work performance, salary policy was changed to permit qualified dropouts to earn as much as high school graduates.

But the second part of the program, for unqualified dropouts, was *terra incognita* for Equitable. These young people were Equitable's unemployables, their hard core. They generally were not able to pass the company's verbal and numerical tests, did poorly at the entrance interview, and possibly had minor police records. Further, some had been identified by community agencies as "employment problems."

While the first group—the qualified dropouts—had come through usual recruitment channels, the unqualified were recruited and initially screened by neighborhood community centers of the New York State Employment Service. (Later programs would use the city of New York's Jobs in Neighborhoods (JOIN) program and its successor, the Manpower and Career Development Agency for unqualified recruits.) It was presumed that the young applicants would have some minimum skills which could be used in white-collar work and some desire to work in an office.

Under its agreement with the Employment Service (substantially the same as in later editions of the program), Equitable agreed to hire half the number of people referred. Equitable interviewers would seek to identify in their hard-core applicant the motivation and potential that might make it possible for him to succeed at Equitable. The applicant would be tested, but results were not binding. Married men were not considered for employment in this program. Also, because of the large number of young people at Equitable (70 percent are young female clerical workers), prospective trainees were also disqualified if they had a record of narcotics or sexual offenses.

If Equitable subsequently wanted to dismiss one of these dropouts, it agreed to notify the Employment Service at least a month in advance. During this grace period, someone from the community center would try to improve the employee's performance by counseling. But if this was unsuccessful, the Service would attempt to place the young man in a more suitable job.

Unlike the qualified group, the unqualified dropouts presented many problems. The group was split into roughly 70 percent Negro and 30 percent Spanish-American. Unlike earlier members of minority groups whom Equitable had hired, the dropouts' education, experience, attitudes, and expectations were so different from those of Equitable's managers and supervisors that problems of communication and understanding quickly arose. Bridging the gap, many of the managers and personnel staff found they were learning along with the dropouts. They were learning, of course, what would work and what wouldn't; but also as they learned about the world and problems of the hard-core dropout, they found that their own expectations and approach changed, not only in dealings with dropouts, but with members of minority groups in general. What Equitable learned about employing hard-core dropouts—and how it learned—serve as the focus of this report.

PHASE 1—TREATING THEM THE SAME

Equitable hired its first group of 20 male unqualified, non-high school graduates late in 1962 and early 1963, starting with the operational assumption that there was no basic difference between these hard-core employees and anybody else hired for entry-level jobs. Most were 16 and 17 years of age (see Table 1 for the ages of the trainees in each of the four programs). Supervisors were briefed on the experiment but were instructed that no special consideration was to be given to the trainees; they were not to be identified as

TABLE 1: AGE AND SEX OF TRAINEES IN EACH PROGRAM

	Trainees in Program	16	17	18	19	20-22	Data not available
Trainees in age group	123	14	35	23	17	19	15
First program (1962-1963)	20	11	7	—	—	—	2
Second program (1964-1965)	24	1	10	2	5	4	2
Third program (1965-1966)							
Males	24	—	8	7	3	5	1
Females	15	1	2	3	3	4	2
Fourth program (1966-1967)							
Males	20	—	4	8	2	2	4
Females	20	1	4	3	4	4	4

"experimental" or in any way set apart in their work groups. Organizationally, the program was not given special emphasis: No one person within the personnel staff, for example, was made responsible for coordination of the program.

Within six months, 45 percent of the young men were gone. For the year, turnover stood at 70 percent—more than three times that of the company as a whole. Lateness and absence were the customary reasons given when dropouts were dismissed, and, while these are the most frequent reasons for which Equitable dismisses people from entry-level jobs in any case, the dropouts had a much higher dismissal rate than other employees. With one or two exceptions, the work of the dropouts was appraised by their supervisors as "generally marginal."

Numbers tell only part of the story, however. Equitable's managers had also had a series of experiences that convinced them the dropouts differed from other employees. "It didn't take long for us to learn that dropouts lived in a world outside our experience," Equitable's manpower vice president observes:

> Within a month of hiring one of our first dropouts, the man disappeared. He did not appear at work. People who answered his telephone number said they did not know him. A letter sent to him was returned as undeliverable. His parents could not be located. Initially, no one in his neighborhood could be foun who would admit that they knew where or who he was. At last an address was given to the investigator—an address that turned out to belong to a local hospital. We found him there dying of cancer.

For Equitable's management this episode was a forceful and sobering introduction to the life of the disadvantaged. Other incidents indicated that the dropouts operated on a different and puzzling wavelength when he came—or didn't come—to work.

> Day after day, X came in late. When asked about it, he was always apologetic. It really seemed to bother him. But he kept coming in late.
>
> Although the company provides time off with pay for death in the family, a supervisor who gets three requests for such time off from one employee within a short time is suspicious—and the work of his section suffers. As a supervisor reported: "First it was a cousin who was killed in Vietnam, then it was his uncle, and two weeks later he said his brother died. We called the hospital

where he said he had died, and they said no one of that name had died there."

Y asked the Personnel Department for a transfer, saying the work was too difficult for him. His supervisor was surprised; he said Y had been performing very well, and that he would talk to him to find out the precise nature of the difficulty. The following week Y was intermittently absent because of severe nosebleeds. The next Monday, he called in to resign, saying that he could not perform the mathematical calculations in his work. Offered a transfer, Y resigned two days later.

Initially, the main result of examining these episodes may have been managerial confusion. The usual methods of establishing supervisor-subordinate communication and understanding did not seem to work. Few of the supervisors had gotten to know any of the dropouts very well. Routine analysis by the personnel staff gave only limited indications of what might be done to make future programs more successful.

PHASE 2—MODIFYING THE PROGRAM

On the basis of what it knew, what it extrapolated from university and government studies of the dropout, and what it felt it had still to learn, Equitable established a second program. A major modification in the new program was to extend the dropout's initiation period from the usual six months to one year. Equitable felt the dropout needed more time to learn his job duties, to become oriented to work discipline, to acclimate himself to work rules, and, above all, to settle down to getting to work regularly and on time.

Another major modification was that dropouts were no longer considered part of the regular complement of the unit to which each belonged. As an extra man or "overhire" relative to the regular staffing of the unit, his productivity—or lack of it—did not affect the overall production of the unit. This step was taken to gain supervisory acceptance of the dropouts, and to avoid penalizing those who took dropouts into their units. It was also a signal to the supervisors of the degree to which top management was committed to the success of the program.

A third significant modification was the introduction of a full-time counselor to help the supervisors and to give the dropouts counseling, orientation, and help with personal problems. As co-ordinator of the program, the counselor also took on key responsibilities for listening to the dropouts and the supervisors; in effect, he became the mechanism through which Equitable could gain a greater understanding of the dropout's employment problems.

Aside from these alterations, the program remained more or less unchanged until 1965, when women were added. The final major problem change was made in 1966 when, after three years of experience, basic education courses were added.

Some Results. Overall, Equitable had employed 123 hard-core dropouts by the end of 1967. (Toward the middle of 1968, Equitable started new programs, which are discussed later in this paper. These programs employed 51 men and women, bringing Equitable's hard-core total to 174. But since these programs are still in progress, no attempt has been made to analyze them here.) In his evaluation of the programs, Equitable's chief executive called them a "mixed bag" of success and failure. As Equitable's vice president for manpower notes: "We have learned a lot, we have made progress, we are still making progress." In its four years, Equitable has not been able to reduce the employment of the hard core to an exact science, and a certain amount of managerial ambivalence is probably inevitable. Personal involvement with individual trainees has on occasion been close, and executives have experienced moments of both deep satisfaction and disappointment. There are a number of trainees who have done well at the company and left for better things. But far more common is the trainee who does well for many months and then seems to lose interest or to develop overwhelming personal problems that lead him to quit or be dismissed. Even the trainee who does well may ultimately leave for a job that is no better—and may be worse—than the one he is leaving.

Equitable evidently has not been able to transform the lives of the bulk of its trainees. But there is evidence that their work experience at Equitable was a "step up" for the trainees in the programs. For the majority, Equitable was their first regular job. (See Table 2 for the trainees' work history.) More than one-third of the trainees for whom information is available listed no previous jobs on their applications. Almost an additional third listed only one job. Of those who had worked, about 45 percent had spent no more than two months on their last job, and only four (or about 6 percent) had been on the job longer than a year. About 60 percent of the dropouts had been out of work for more than three months before coming to Equitable.

The previous job experiences that could be listed—even by the 20 and 21 year olds—were of the order of delivery boy in a drug store or grocery, dishwasher or counterman, sweeper in an apparel factory, or helper on a delivery truck. Women cited baby-sitting and cleaning experience. This, of course, was the best of their work experience; the casual day jobs and the "hustle," by which many

TABLE 2(a): WORK HISTORY OF TRAINEES IN EACH PROGRAM

	Trainees	First Pro-gram	Second Pro-gram	Third Pro-gram	Fourth Pro-gram
Trainees in the program	123	20	24	39	40
Trainees for whom data are available	108	18	22	36	32
Number of previous jobs					
No jobs and/or time in-dicated	39	7	5	16	11
One job	34	5	8	12	9
Two jobs	24	5	5	6	8
Three or more jobs	11	1	4	2	4
Time worked in last job *					
No jobs and/or time in-dicated	40	7	5	17	11
Two months (or less)	31	5	9	9	8
Four months	17	5	2	5	5
Six months	8	—	1	2	5
Eight months	2	—	2	—	—
Twelve months	6	1	2	2	1
More than one year	4	—	1	1	2
Time out of work since last job †					
Not known	2	1	—	—	1
No time out (working or in school)	15	6	3	4	2
One month (or less)	17	5	1	7	4
Three months	23	3	7	4	9
Six months	10	2	3	4	1
Eight months	10	—	2	5	3
Twelve months	17	1	5	6	5
More than one year	14	—	1	6	7

* Does not include experience in prevocational training or work experience projects.
† Where the trainee came to Equitable from a training program, the table indicates time spent out of work before entering training.

TABLE 2(b): WORK HISTORY OF TRAINEES BY AGE AT TIME OF HIRE

	Trainees	16 Years	17 Years	18 Years	19 Years	20-22 Years
Trainees in the program	123	—	—	—	—	—
Trainees for whom data are available	108	14	35	23	17	19
Number of previous jobs						
No jobs and/or time indicated	39	9	15	9	5	1
One job	34	3	12	6	7	6
Two jobs	24	2	6	6	1	9
Three or more jobs	11	—	2	2	4	3
Time worked in last job *						
No jobs and/or time indicated	40	9	15	10	5	1
Two months (or less)	31	2	10	8	4	7
Four months	17	2	7	2	3	3
Six months	8	—	—	3	2	3
Eight months	2	—	—	—	2	—
Twelve months	6	1	1	—	1	3
More than one year	4	—	2	—	—	2
Time out of work since last job †						
Not known	2	—	1	1	—	—
No time out (working or in school)	15	4	6	3	—	2
One month (or less)	17	5	5	2	2	3
Three months	23	3	9	5	3	3
Six months	10	1	4	1	2	2
Eight months	10	1	5	1	2	1
Twelve months	17	—	5	4	6	2
More than one year	14	—	—	6	2	6

* Does not include experience in prevocational training or work experience projects.
† Where the trainee came to Equitable from a training program, the table indicates time spent out of work before entering training.

TABLE 2(c): WORK HISTORY OF TRAINEES BY SEX

	Trainees	Male	Female
Trainees in the program	123	88	35
Trainees for whom data are available	108	79	29
Number of previous jobs			
No jobs and/or time indicated	39	24	15
One job	34	25	8
Two jobs	24	20	4
Three or more jobs	11	9	2
Time worked in last job *			
No jobs and/or time indicated	40	25	15
Two months (or less)	31	24	7
Four months	17	16	1
Six months	8	4	4
Eight months	2	2	—
Twelve months	6	4	2
More than one year	4	4	—
Time out of work since last job †			
Not known	2	2	—
No time out (working or in school)	15	12	3
One month (or less)	17	13	4
Three months	23	18	5
Six months	10	9	1
Eight months	10	6	4
Twelve months	17	9	8
More than one year	14	10	4

* Does not include experience in prevocational training or work experience projects.
† Where the trainee came to Equitable from a training program, the table indicates time spent out of work before entering training.

ghetto dwellers survive obviously do not get mentioned on application forms.

Equitable's trainees evidently stepped up in other ways when they came to the company.

Higher pay. Some of the trainees did not indicate on their applications what salaries they had earned at their previous jobs, possibly because their earnings were irregular, or varied from week to week. But of those who did indicate previous salaries, more than three-fifths earned more by coming to Equitable than they had on their previous jobs. (See Table 3.)

More stable employment. If Equitable's unqualified dropouts did not stay on the job as long as regular hires, they did tend to stay longer than they had on their previous jobs. Approximately 45 percent of those trainees who indicated work experience on their application form had worked two months or less on their last job. However, the median employee stayed at Equitable about eight months. Only about 18 percent of the trainees had stayed so long on their previous jobs. (See Table 2(a).)

Of course, hard-core dropout turnover is relatively high. Annual turnover for the four programs averages 67 percent, probably not significantly lower than the 70 percent posted by the first program, and more than three times the annual turnover rate experienced by Equitable as a whole. (See Table 4.) Of course, it is expected that young people may change jobs a number of times in the years following graduation from high school. But the dropouts seem to change jobs faster than their peers. Turnover for the dropouts ran at more than twice the rates of the regular male hires of the same age, occupations, and length of service.

By 1966, however, Equitable's work force was going through drastic changes. Where 50 percent of Equitable's high school re-

TABLE 3: SALARY OF TRAINEES IN LAST PREVIOUS JOBS *

	Trainees	First Pro- gram	Second Pro- gram	Third Pro- gram	Fourth Pro- gram
Trainees in program	123	20	24	39	40
Trainees for which data are available	108	18	22	36	32
No previous jobs	39	7	5	16	11
Previous jobs but salary not given	16	1	1	7	7
Salary $10-$25 weekly	7	3	—	2	2
Salary $26-$50 weekly	23	4	10	4	5
Salary $51 weekly—Equi- table hiring rate	10	2	1	3	4
Salary—above hiring rate	13	1	5	4	3

* Salaries earned during prevocational training or work experience projects are not included.

TABLE 4: TURNOVER RATES FOR UNQUALIFIED AND REGULAR HIRES BY SEX

Employee Group	FIRST PROGRAM 1962 — 1963		SECOND PROGRAM 1964 — 1965		THIRD PROGRAM 1966	FOURTH PROGRAM 1967
Male unqualified hires	70%		67%		75%	60%
All Equitable males	18.8%	14.4%	18.8%	19.1%	21.1%	22.3%
Males one year of service	31.8	26.3	29.4	31.2	124.8	76.1
Males 16-19 years of age	23.2	27.7	44.6	49.1	98.4	71.3
Males in general clerical occupations	—	—	36.6	39.5	69.4	47.3
Salary grade 1 *	42.3	—	—	—	72.2	55.4
Female unquali- fied hires	—	—	—	—	45%	75%
All Equitable females	—	—	—	—	29.5	24.6
Females one year of service	—	—	—	—	83.1	50.7
Females 16-19 years of age	—	—	—	—	55.4	33.4
Females in general clerical occupations	—	—	—	—	32.4	24.9
Salary grade 1 *	—	—	—	—	72.2	55.4

* Information is for both males and females in aggregate, except for 1962 where rates were not computed separately for each sex.

cruits had come from Manhattan public high schools in 1963, Manhattan's share rose to 80 percent by 1966. Where public high schools from disadvantaged neighborhoods placed one out of five applicants at Equitable in 1964, they were able to place one out of 3.7 applicants by 1966. All told, these schools were able to place more than three times as many of their people with Equitable as they had only two years earlier. Eleven percent of the 1964 high school hires had come from disadvantaged minorities. By 1966, however, the proportion had risen to 37 percent and by 1967 it would rise to 45 percent. Still Equitable could not fill its 1966 job requisitions and had to call back 200 people it had rejected on the first go round.

Accompanying these "dramatic" changes in work force were equally dramatic rises in turnover. (See Table 4.) Turnover doubled for teen-age male employees and quadrupled for men with one year of service. Against turnover rates of 100 percent or more, the dropout programs' turnover rate of 75 percent suddenly did not look so bad to Equitable executives. The rate of the new women's program (45 percent) looked especially impressive to Equitable executives.

The dropout turnover rate was all the more impressive to Equitable management because the dropouts of 1966 were more unqualified than those of 1962 and 1963. Poverty programs were digging deeper into the city's disadvantaged population for recruits, and for the first time, dropouts were applying to Equitable who had come through prevocational training or work experience projects. Three-quarters of the men and half the women in the third program came through such training, and about half of them indicated no other work experience when they applied. An indication of the role played by the poverty programs is the relative "unemployability" of this "trained" group. Most of them had been out of work for eight months or more before entering training, while only one in ten of the people from earlier programs had been out of work so long.

The third program also included more people at the low end of the educational spectrum. (See Table 5.) Eight, or more than 20

TABLE 5: YEARS OF HIGH SCHOOL COMPLETED

	Trainees	First Program	Second Program	Third Program	Fourth Program
Trainees in program	123	20	24	39	40
Trainees for whom data are available	108	18	22	36	32
Less than one year	12	1	—	8	3
One year	34	7	5	9	13
Two years	43	8	8	15	12
Three years	17	2	9	3	3
Four years but did not graduate	2	—	—	1	1

percent, had not completed a year of high school, while this was true of only one earlier trainee.

The characteristic trainee of the first two programs was 16 or 17 years of age and less than a month out of high school. The men and women of the third program, however, were older—almost three-quarters were 18 to 22 years of age—and most had been out of work for six months or longer. Despite their relative youth, well over half the first program people had had previous jobs before coming to Equitable, and all had been employed for two months or longer on their last job. In contrast, almost half of those in the third program listed no previous employment on their application forms, and the median individual in the program had spent less than one month at his last job. The company's rationale was explained by a recruiter: "As we have learned more about the unqualified dropout, as our supervisors have learned to handle them more effectively, we have been digging deeper into the hard-core group; we are taking people with poor motivation and people with chips on their shoulder whom we would not have touched before. Our hard-core dropouts of 1962 would not be considered hard-core today; most would be normal hires."

Despite the changes in program and quality of its recruits the differences between Equitable's regular hires and its hard-core drop-outs—both culturally and in terms of work performance—were seen to be lessening. The training, counseling, and supervisory insights and techniques that had been developed with relative success for the dropouts took on new significance. They were now seen in the context of their possible application to Equitable's new work force.

The company hesitates to summarize what it has learned beyond concrete results. However, several major themes show up in the development of the Equitable program:

> —Equitable's method has been essentially pragmatic. The program began with the working assumption that the dropout was no different from the graduate. For the first year, nothing was changed or done on the assumption or anticipation that the dropout was different and required different treatment. Since then, changes have been made as need for them arose, often on an individual basis, sometimes programwide. An important element in this approach is a method for establishing communication between trainee, supervisor, counselor, and management.
>
> —As the company has learned more about its dropouts, the program has grown increasingly structured. Equitable simply hired its first dropouts, for example, but now dropouts are re-

cruited for a special program, at the end of which they may or may not be retained. Within this structure, the dropout may be given a special employment status, whereby particular needs may be met without raising questions of preferential treatment.

—In testing what would and wouldn't work with its dropouts, Equitable found it needed skills and services that it didn't possess. Increasingly, the company has gone outside to supplement its training and counseling expertise.

UNDERSTANDING THE DROPOUT

The bare bones of the program change, of course, tell only a small part of the story. Behind its evolution was a growing understanding of the dropout and what Equitable and he could do for each other.

The counselor—and particularly the first counselor—is credited with a key role in giving Equitable its picture of the ghetto-bred dropout. A theological student who had taken a year off to do field work, the first counselor was notable for his social conscience, psychological insight, and ability to relate to the organization. A co-worker recalls: "I never saw anyone angry with him as a person, even if they disagreed with him. He was a good listener, one of the best nondirective counselors I have ever known." Later counselors were selected for similar qualities. But they weren't alone in providing insights about the dropout; a large portion of Equitable's management, supervisors, and staff were involved.

In this part of the program, Equitable was interested in trying to go behind work habits to get at the sources of dropout motivation—or lack of it.

A Low Tolerance for Boredom. Grossly oversimplified: Equitable believes that the main reason its dropouts fail is because they don't see much point in succeeding. When they do succeed, it is basically because they personally see some point to their working.

There were, of course, occasional dropouts who turned out to be physically or mentally unable to do their jobs. Cases of emotional maladjustments also appeared. But the dropouts rarely left or were dismissed because they couldn't do the work. Motivational factors emerged as central. An indication of their significance was the fact that 20 percent of the dropouts had IQs of 120 or higher.

An Equitable report notes: "This lack of difference [in ability between dropout and graduate] seems to reinforce the notion that what the high school graduate brings to a job is 'stick-to-itiveness'

114

rather than [superior] intellectual ability, curiosity, or academic achievement."

Explaining this conclusion, Equitable's personnel executives point out that when the counselors discussed lateness and absence with the dropouts, the word *boring* occurred again and again. They were *bored* with their jobs, their supervisors *bored* them, their life was *boring*. They quit because they couldn't stand the *boredom*. Of course, others were also bored; Equitable's high school graduates can find entry-level jobs boring. But bored or not, minority and non-minority graduates alike did not quit in nearly the same numbers.

The dropouts, in Equitable's view, could not tolerate this boredom. Their life was centered in the here and now. "He doesn't look forward even to tomorrow morning," a counselor noted of one of his charges. Pleasant working conditions, pleasant associates on the job were necessities. The dropout saw little reason to defer his satisfactions; in many cases it was evidently impossible for him to do so. This seemed so basic that an Equitable personnel research analyst went so far as to hypothesize:

> The chief difference between the dropouts and the recent high school graduates employed by Equitable, lies in a different ability to tolerate boredom. Those who graduated from high school probably found much of their education boring, but were able to stick it out. The dropout was not.

"Bad Luck." Why couldn't they stick it out? Equitable's analysis (backed up by other research) points to several factors in the dropouts' background. Many of the dropouts didn't see much point to planning for the future. Many viewed their lives as one long bad luck story. They had had the bad luck to be born into minority groups, and often had been born to broken or unstable families. They were born poor; to go to poor schools; to live in violent, dangerous neighborhoods. What happened to them did not seem the result of their own efforts or lack of them, but of blind fortune. As one dropout received the word of his dismissal, his counselor noted, "His attitude was one of resignation to his fate. It was as though he was an impartial witness to his own destiny."

The dropouts were not necessarily without aspirations. Among the interests a dropout might list on his application form were such pursuits as singing and English history, collecting snakes, playing the violin, working with children, poetry, mathematics. But these aspirations belonged mainly to the realm of dreams and wishes. Rarely had the dropout done much to develop his interests. Where he had ambitions, usually no attempt had been made to realize them. Luck, not action, was viewed as needed to change his fate, and without it, his condition seemed inevitable and unchangeable.

Dropouts expected to fail at Equitable because they felt they had failed in the past. Usually they had failed—or been failed—in their relationships with their families, particularly their fathers, and they had failed in school. Many had been in trouble with the police and other public agencies. Among some, feelings of inferiority and anxiety impaired their ability to work with white people. The result, as one counselor noted, was that "even those who have had moderate success on the job often quit or wished to." Anxiety could become so severe that the dropout developed nervous ailments. A trainee who did not call his supervisor when he was ill reported, "I forgot in the morning. Then later on I was afraid."

The dropouts did not necessarily lack pride. "LF came in today to say goodbye," reads a counselor's report. "He resigned because he felt he was taking advantage of M (his supervisor), who was covering some of his absences. He is pretty dejected now. He feels he has failed several things and doesn't want to be a burden to anyone. He doesn't want to go back to JOIN because he doesn't want to bother them."

Family and Friends. As Equitable sees it, family and friends usually contributed to the dropout's failure. In most cases, they did not value work achievement or advancement and had no better understanding of the world of work than the dropouts themselves did. Typically, no one awakened the youngsters in the morning to go to work—or had, earlier, to go to school. Some hadn't been taught basic habits of cleanliness and self-discipline. A majority of the dropouts came from homes without fathers. When a father was present, he was often a negative influence, and not a satisfactory model after whom a son might pattern himself.

When the family was strong, it was likely to be organized like the large farm family of an earlier era, with sisters, grandmothers, cousins, and aunts all making demands on the dropout's time. Equitable's personnel staff found, for example, that on occasion when a dropout claimed his repeated absences were due to deaths in the family, sick relatives who had to be cared for, or a grandmother in trouble in North Carolina, he was telling the literal truth.

The Ghetto. The living conditions in which the minority group dropouts lived also raised barriers to achievement. Equitable's counselors found their trainees living in noisy, crowded housing, with one bathroom shared by several families. Merely going to sleep early or waking up and getting ready for work were tasks much more difficult for the slum dropout than for his middle-class counterpart. Calling up one's supervisor to report an absence might be a task of major proportions:

> One morning PK awoke with flu. There was no telephone in PK's house. When he had been ill in the past, his mother had used a neighbor's telephone to call her son's supervisor. But this morning the neighbor was not home. The temperature was below freezing, and PK's mother, who did not have a coat, refused to go outside to the candy store several blocks away to make the call.

Discussion with the counselors discloses that often dropouts did not eat properly. In winter, apartments might not be heated. Pipes frequently froze. While dropouts may not have suffered from incapacitating ailments, physical examinations showed a prevalence of dental ailments and many trainees who seemed to lack stamina. Histories of major illness and injury were common. "I was in the hospital for six months for kidney trouble," one reported. Another could not come to work one morning because "I was stabbed."

For the first two years after entering the company, Equitable's hard core used Medical Department services at a rate about double that of other employees hired at the same time for the same type of jobs. Apart from the dental problems mentioned above, the hard core tend also to suffer from a greater prevalence of gastrointestinal upsets and upper respiratory infections commonly associated with anxiety. After about two years, these ailments tend to disappear, and the hard-core employee uses the Medical Department no more than his peers.

Equitable's Medical Department asserts that the needs of the new work force are changing its function from a referral to a treatment center. It is not that today's minority poor work force uses medical facilities more than the minority poor work forces of several years ago. Indeed, Equitable's older employees—relatively few of whom are members of minority groups—are still the department's prime users. But where in the past Equitable's Medical Department had mainly sent sick employees to their neighborhood doctors for treatment, they have found there are often no local medical facilities to which minority employees can be sent.

Past experience with immigrant groups has led some observers to note that the hope of getting out of a ghetto can operate as a powerful incentive to achievement. But evidently the dropouts usually didn't have this much hope. The ghetto operated mainly as a deterrent to successful employment at Equitable.

As Equitable gained a more comprehensive picture of the dropouts, both counselors and supervisors were able to develop their particular roles to more nearly fit the dropouts' needs.

The counselor was the man who listened to the dropouts, heard their problems, analyzed their behavior, and, in turn, interpreted to management, but he was more than management's "ear." He was also the voice through which Equitable oriented the dropouts and the supporting arm that helped them understand and cope with the world of work.

The counselor explained Equitable's policies and procedures to the dropout. For example, dropouts often ran afoul of work rules that required them to work close to their desks or in their own sections. The counselor could discuss the rules with a dropout, explaining the reasons for them, and if a trainee just could not sit still seven hours a day, arrangements might be made to transfer him to a more active job, if one were available.

Equitable's personnel procedures in some cases needed interpretation so as not to interfere with the objectives of the hard-core employment program. For instance, the procedure for paid absence needed modification in order to allow a dropout to take his evening school examinations.

Possibly the counselor's most important role, however, was to provide the dropout with the added support he needed to help him mature as an individual. In the early days of the program, counselors often went beyond the employment counseling usually given to Equitable employees:

> I explained the company's policy on absence. We talked about what it meant in terms of review, promotion, increases, and transfers anywhere in the white-collar world. I told him that the doctor's excuse was our attempt to check up, but more, it was a way for him to keep track of himself. At 20 years of age, he had to begin checking up on himself if he were to spend 45 more years in the work force. Any time he wasn't feeling well he should come in to see our doctor. He would save money, [protect his] health, and show his supervisor that he was really committed to the job.

A major objective of counseling in the earlier stages of the program was to encourage the dropouts to complete their schooling.

> C has matured and wants to continue along with Equitable as far as he can go. He has completed 3½ years of schooling, and I suggested that he finish that half year and look into tuition refund courses in the actuarial area; he has a very high math aptitude. I think he will contact either the Board of Education about home correspondence courses or Mr. B about what must be done.

Since basic education courses have been added, there is now no need for the counselor to steer dropouts into remedial education programs. Recently, counselors have taken a subtler, more indirect approach to counseling, which they feel gets better results than "sermonizing." One says, "I try to put a guy in a situation where he'll come away wanting something and thinking maybe if he works for it he can have it. Any method will serve. Perhaps I'll invite him to lunch with some of our Negro executives. He'll laugh and tell me, 'You trying to pull something? I can't make it like these cats; they're college graduates.' But maybe he can see himself someday, somewhere between them and where he is now."

When female dropouts were added to the program in 1965, a second counselor was added—a woman member of the employment staff who performed counseling duties as a part-time responsibility. In June 1966 the duties of the male counselor were taken over by a member of the employment staff, in addition to his regular duties.

Unlike the first incumbents, the two present counselors are Negro. Even the most sensitive of the white counselors noticed problems in understanding and rapport. While able to predict fairly accurately whether a dropout would succeed or fail, the white counselor was not always able to dig beneath the surface. The present male counselors believe that Negro trainees "won't level" with a white counselor, and Equitable's manpower vice president echoes this assessment: "The barrier is just too high now. They won't believe anyone but another black man; it's got to be Negro-to-Negro."

Equitable executives also cite additional reasons for having Negro counselors. The black counselor is much easier for the dropouts to identify with. Especially for dropouts with no fathers at home, the counselor provides a male figure against whom the young men can measure themselves.

Supervisory Support. Strong counseling is considered important in rehabilitating Equitable's dropouts. But the supervisor's role may be still more critical. The supervisor spends more time with the dropout than does any other member of Equitable's management. He is responsible for the dropout's on-the-job training. Behavioral scientists have found that much of any employee's attitude toward work, the

119

company, and his job is formed by the nature of his relationship to his supervisor. Equitable found that dropouts need especially strong supervisory support.

From the second year's program onward, special emphasis was placed on the supervisor's training role. With experience, many of the supervisors have learned to adapt their old training methods. For example, a recent progress report notes that a number have learned "to rely less upon exclusive rapid oral and written instruction and more upon demonstration associated with practice routines and cases and close verification with immediate feedback of errors to improve understanding." These techniques have proven useful not only for dropout trainees but for beginning employees generally.

At first, the supervisor's responsibility was limited to on-the-job training to prepare the dropouts for entry-level general clerical positions in one year. As the company learned more about the dropouts' motivational problems, however, training for promotion became an integral part of the dropout program. By the third year, supervisors were made responsible for preparing the dropout for at least one promotion in two years. Supervisors knew from previous experience that their own progress at Equitable was intimately linked to their ability to fulfill training and development responsibilities.

Equitable's management feels that its supervisors, in most cases, brought considerable good will and common sense to their tasks. Supervisors went to considerable lengths to understand the dropouts and their problems. Within the constraints created by fear of establishing double standards, supervisors were often flexible in applying work rules. Leeway was given on lateness and absence in the dropouts' early days on the job, often with good results. "It is interesting to note," reports a counselor, "that EJ was extremely liberal in recording attendance. If there was an excuse, no record was noted. I think this has encouraged better performance."

Generally the counselors have come away believing that the dropouts wanted more rather than less support and leadership. The young men remembered even small instances of friendliness or encouragement long after receiving them. Six months after their induction, the trainees would recall their supervisor's simple courtesies during orientation: "He wished me luck"; "He smiled at me"; "He offered me a chair." A supervisor who "gave me a book on annuities to read up on" was remembered. One who offered "congratulations on your diploma" was felt to have an important motivating effect on the dropout.

Negative supervisory attitudes also had a strong effect. Attitude surveys showed that when a supervisor thought a job menial, boring, or unnecessary, the dropout usually did too.

Close supervision was sometimes resented, especially when it reflected a supervisor's lack of trust. But the trainees more often felt they were supervised too lightly. "No one explained the rules or showed me around," said one. Another "wanted to be pushed and prodded." A third felt he didn't see his supervisor enough. The most favorable comments were aroused by supervisors whom the young men perceived as strict but fair. "Mr. J is strict, but he can really handle people."

The counselors make repeated references to how far supervisors have extended themselves to make the program and the dropout succeed. Yet keeping the supervisor's support of the program has not been something that Equitable's management could or did leave to chance.

Equitable is not aware of any outspoken anti-Negro sentiments but is fairly certain that such attitudes do exist here and there in the supervisory force. Some supervisors view the presence of dropouts in their units as a downgrading of their importance or standing in the company. Early in the program some supervisors made no secret of the fact that they wanted no dropouts in their units. Others, while accepting dropouts, gave them little support and did not seem terribly surprised or unhappy when they failed.

Equitable recognizes that even with the best will in the world, some supervisors would find the dropout a frustrating and disillusioning experience. The management didn't feel that a supervisor should have to bear the experience alone; encouragement or specialized assistance should be available when needed. Especially when the program was beginning, the counselor was supportive of the supervisory groups as well as the dropouts. His original responsibilities included, for example, a charge "to help supervisors with special problems relating to this group, to allay any anxiety they might feel about dealing with these employees, and to educate them not to evaluate them solely as producers." Through the counselor, the supervisor could draw upon the entire personnel staff, if need be, to help with his problems. An evaluation of the program notes: "The supervisor who took advantage of the opportunity to discuss a case with the counselor contributed more to the program than one who acted first and reported later."

Members of the personnel staff at Equitable do not feel there is a policy of preferential treatment for dropouts or for minority group employees. In reporting a recent meeting, a personnel executive noted, "A number of supervisors pointed out the importance of understanding the handicaps of some of these youngsters, and of adjustment of training techniques and even of methods of supervision to their special needs, but this was not seen as the application of a double standard or as a failure to maintain firm discipline. . . ." Meeting the special needs of the hard core is not viewed by Equitable as maintaining a double standard because—as a nonunion company—it is not contractually bound to a set of work rules and disciplinary procedures. It lacks a double standard because—in the words of one of its executives—"We don't have a single standard, we try to understand and deal with our employees as much as possible in terms of individual and group needs." Nevertheless, the company does have standards, and as a personnel executive puts it, "little can be gained for the company or our minority employees by avoiding sanctions where individuals, after correction, do not measure up to acceptable standards."

The company has established standards of office behavior and decorum. But as the nature of its work force has changed, Equitable has found many of its traditional standards under pressure. Supervisors have come to accept a far more "colorful" vocabulary from the employees, even the women employees. What might have been regarded as insubordinate behavior in its traditional work force, Equitable supervisors have come to regard as a kind of playfulness: "These kids are used to noise and color, all sorts of stimuli, coming at them from all directions, all the time. They are used to responding to these stimuli, talking, laughing, moving around. I don't know how long we're going to be successful in keeping them at their desks doing routine tasks seven hours a day in a quiet office."

But if Equitable considers adjusting the work environment for the dropout, it has learned the hard way that the dropouts may bring their burdens of despair and alienation into that environment, sometimes with devastating results.

> In one department, where eight of these young women were placed under a young male supervisor, friction with non-dropout girls developed immediately. The dropout girls complained of not having desk jobs; they picked quarrels with the other girls, swore, and threatened the supervisor. The supervisor was especially able. But if *he* made headway with one of them, the others accused her of being with him, instead of with "us." . . . The lesson that it is necessary to disperse dropout employees throughout the organization has been learned.

As time goes on, the supervisors rely less and less on the counselor. Experience with dropouts and with minority group employees has made it possible for first-line supervisors to handle many dropout problems that formerly went to the counselors, one of whom notes that he now deals with "only the most serious of the dropouts' problems. Usually, these are of a personal nature, like garnishments." As mentioned earlier, dropout counseling has become a part-time duty.

But if direct counseling support to the supervisors has declined, meetings between groups of supervisors and members of the personnel staff have become more frequent. The meetings are purposely kept small to give the supervisors a chance to exchange information and to air their problems. A common topic at these meetings is some aspect of how to avoid the double standard. Many supervisors lack the knowledge and sensitivity to know when to be lenient with the trainees and when they should be firm. They can draw on the personnel staff and other supervisors during the meetings for guidance and information. At the meetings, supervisors and personnel staff reach agreements on how to handle common supervisory problems. Otherwise, differing practices arising in the different departments could erode acceptable standards. An indication of the importance accorded these meetings is that in the past six months alone, more than 14 were held, enough to include all company supervisors, each chaired by Equitable's vice president for manpower. Recently, the company has considered bringing outside supervisors, sociologists, and psychologists into these sessions.

BASIC EDUCATION

In the first year's program the dropout was given no special status, and the results were considered very poor. In the second year's program, counseling was added, and a special role was delineated for the supervisor. The third year further emphasized the supervisor's role, as the relationship between motivation and promotability was better understood. But it soon became clear that the program as it stood still wasn't enough.

The male counselor for the third year's group summed up the problem this way: "A fellow comes to us with either high hopes or a cynical attitude about the opportunity we are offering. The types of work initially assigned and the fact that the people they are competing with are better prepared for advancement dampens hope or renews cynicism."

Equitable's management ultimately concluded that the dropouts needed more orientation and preparation if they were to do their jobs properly. Viewing the program from the perspective of 1968, one executive observed that lack of basic education was almost an insurmountable motivational handicap to satisfactory performance and to promotability. The company had encouraged the dropouts to attend night school and to work towards their diplomas or equivalency certificates, and a few did. But most trainees had already experienced too much classroom failure and boredom to return willingly to a conventional classroom. So Equitable turned to the Board for Fundamental Education.

BFE is a nonprofit organization "to improve the education of those not prepared by pre-job schooling for advanced work assignments." The target at Equitable was the New York State high school equivalency examination.

As Equitable sees it, its BFE courses were different from the conventional school in a number of important regards:

1. Company training rooms were used—not "classrooms."
2. The two instructors were Negroes specially trained by BFE to give the course; neither was a teacher by profession.
3. Classwork was closely related to the kind of work dropouts did, or would get if promoted.
4. The course was adult education; all students were addressed as Mr. and treated as adults.
5. The approach put emphasis on "de-brainwashing," attempting to change attitudes of racial inferiority and failure.

The course was given two hours a night, four nights a week, to 20 young men, who were asked to carry the course work in addition to full-time jobs in Equitable offices. The goal was a high school equivalency diploma after 62 weeks. Only three of the men actually reached high school equivalency. But executives in charge of the program noted signs of progress. Turnover among those attending classes dipped well below the corresponding figure for male high school graduates and was lower than for any other group of male dropouts. Moreover, many of the young men, although they did not receive diplomas for various reasons, improved their performance and potential enough to be considered much more desirable employees.

The results of the basic education approach looked still more impressive when contrasted with the conventional skills training course set up for another group of dropouts. Concurrent with BFE effort, 20 girls were given typing instruction to bring them up to Equitable's minimum standards. This, according to Equitable, was "our worst failure so far." Like the men, the women attended classes after work, but a similar course was being given to non-dropouts on company time; the women felt discriminated against. This was further accentuated by the fact that almost half the class came from the clique situation previously described, where the dropouts felt their co-workers were being favored. Also, while the men's instructors were Negro, and their program was specially geared for minority-group dropouts, the women's teacher was white; she taught in the city school system, working part-time for Equitable, and she used conventional teaching methods. The counselor's report noted: "Although Miss Z is an excellent teacher, I do know that some of the girls feel that she is just another high school teacher who could not understand them or their plight."

THE 1968 PROGRAMS

Equitable's management has continued to put still more emphasis on basic education in more recent programs. In mid-1968 a fifth group was started off on a program that combined work and a regular schedule of remedial study. The work—5 1/5 hours a day—was designed to give experience leading to an entry-level job at the end of a year. The study—2 hours per day—leads to a high school equivalency diploma. Class size does not exceed 12 trainees per instructor. The men and women are paid at the same rate and receive the same benefits as any other regular part-time employee.

The work-study program is being conducted jointly with the Manpower and Career Development Agency of the City of New York. MCDA supplies teachers and curricular materials; Equitable provides classrooms, administrative services, and counseling assistance. The cost per employee is expected to be about half that of last year's program.

With this program Equitable is attempting to mesh trainee abilities more squarely than in the past with its needs as an employer. More women are being trained (24 women to 12 men) because Equitable has more jobs for them. As in the past there were few rigid selection standards. But a floor was set on reading skills below which applicants were not accepted. A six-month review was designed into the program at which performance would be reviewed, pay raises given where merited, and—a new departure—trainees dismissed if performance were poor. Married men and unwed mothers, neither of whom were eligible for the first program have been eligible since the third program and, having turned in good performances, are now viewed as desirable employees.

High school equivalency, while still a major objective, has been somewhat de-emphasized. At the end of a year, any trainee whose work performance and abilities appear sufficient to cover an entry-level job will be offered one, whether or not the trainee has reached high school equivalency. The program staff felt that basic education

125

was, of course, necessary but that high school equivalency may be more appropriate to college preparation than to a job at Equitable. It was also noted that while more than half of the men from the fourth program stayed through to the completion of the nine months' BFE course in May 1967, the eight who failed their equivalency examination left Equitable by the end of the summer, despite the fact that they were otherwise adequate workers. For those who passed, Equitable executives felt "there is not enough tangible and immediate reward for the trainees. We must face the realities of promotion opportunity in a company that is not growing rapidly."

Course work and objectives are even more closely related to the job in a skills training course that began on November 4th, 1968. Over a period of up to 16 weeks, 15 women trainees are spending half the day in the classroom and half in on-the-job training. Classroom training is conducted by Equitable employees. Each day two hours are devoted to a remedial education program developed around materials in arithmetic and language skills prepared by MIND, Inc. of Greenwich, Connecticut, and daily typing classes are held for an hour. The rest of the day is spent in on-the-job training in a typing pool operated by the corporate personnel staff; here the women do real work assigned by two supervisors from Equitable's home office central typing pool. The women move ahead at their own pace in the program, and as they complete the course and as jobs open up, they go into permanent positions at the home office.

The program is designed to lighten the training load the hard-core individual imposes on the supervisor. "By the time a woman finishes the course she should have fairly desirable skills," a director of the program observes. Hopefully, the new program will alleviate some of the continuing supervisory objections to the hard-core training programs.

The emphasis on job-related typing skills should also make the trainees more promotable. "We noticed that typing is at the center of a cluster of related jobs in our company," an executive observes. With solid typing skills, a woman can go up a number of promotional ladders." And the men are not to be neglected in these skills training programs. Another job cluster with attendant promotional possibilities has been identified centering around certain basic computational skills. A course is soon to be offered to teach these skills to young men.

The new program would also eliminate some of the shortcomings of the overhire system. "The overhire method is logical for us," an Equitable executive observes, "because we often 'stockpile' people for whom we will not have positions for several weeks or months." Overhires are generally viewed by supervisors as extra help. But

126

they can also be viewed as extra trouble. Some supervisors have not welcomed them, especially during recent periods of heavy turnover when a relatively large number of replacements had to be trained. Some supervisors, because they did not regard the trainees as their own, did not feel a commitment to do as well with their overhires as with their regular subordinates. Working conditions could also be uncertain for the trainees. There might not be enough desks to go around, and as overhires the hard-core trainees might not have a settled work location. They might even be transferred from position to position in the early weeks on the job. The new programs are designed to make working conditions more settled and to put early training and orientation on the job under more systematic control.

Discussion

BY   *CHARLES A. MYERS* [*]

The Equitable Life Assurance Society of the United States is the only firm represented in this symposium which has attempted to provide white-collar jobs with promotional ladders for high school dropouts. The full report indicates the successive programs that Equitable has undertaken to utilize a part of the labor force with which it had little prior experience. Management has learned a great deal in the process, but even now, it does not claim to have solved the problem of employing the disadvantaged.

In reviewing this case, I have been impressed with the following points, which may have applicability beyond this particular experience.

1. Management adopted a pragmatic approach, moving from a program with no outside support to the latest one which recognizes that the company does not have all the skills necessary to prepare the more disadvantaged employees for productive employment. Recent programs have drawn upon outside private and public training resources, such as the Board of Fundamental Education, the Manpower and Career Development Agency of the City of New York, MIND, Inc. (for remedial education), and the U.S. Department of

---

[*] Charles A. Myers is professor of industrial relations and director of the Industrial Relations Section, Massachusetts Institute of Technology.

Labor for financial support through an MA-4 contract. The case thus represents a movement toward a significant degree of private and public cooperation in dealing with a problem which was beyond the private resources which the company had, or felt it could commit.

2. As its accustomed supply of high school graduates proved inadequate to its needs, the hiring of high school dropouts was probably in the company's self-interest. But it cannot be said that the dropouts proved to be as good candidates for employment as the high school graduates, who brought to the job " 'stick-to-itiveness' rather than superior intellectual ability, curiosity, or academic achievement." The dropouts tended to be easily bored with work. Their lives had always centered in the present, and their deprived home background did little to encourage sticking to a job. This was reflected in higher turnover rates for dropouts in the earlier programs. As the labor market tightened, turnover rates for all newly hired employees increased, narrowing the differential between dropouts and graduates. This narrowing may also have reflected the company's growing experience in developing and training the dropout group.

3. The supervisors at Equitable, who were friendly, supportive, and flexible in applying work rules in the beginning and who provided demonstration methods of on-the-job training, were vital to the success of the program. The role of the counselors, very important in the early programs, became less central as supervisors developed skills in handling the problems they faced. Supervisory conferences were helpful in further spreading this experience.

4. While the company has insisted there is no double standard, the fact is that supervisors were more flexible with dropouts in applying work rules on lateness and absenteeism during the first days on the job. There was also more acceptance of the tendency of the new employees to walk around, "use colorful language," and even engage in some playfulness—all quite different from the normal pattern of orderly office work. Clearly, supervisors and managers had to tolerate this behavior until the new recruits became accustomed to the expected standards. That not all supervisors bore up under this experience is seen in the factual statement that the new pre-employment programs for basic education will "alleviate some of the continuing supervisory objections to the hard-core training programs."

5. Costs are now shared with the federal government. While the company has an MA-4 contract providing for approximately $1,600 a year per hard-core unemployed youth hired, it is also contributing an estimated $100,000 per year in training efforts, training staff, extra supervisory time, and other costs. The federal subsidy goes to

pre-employment basic and remedial education, and other pre-employment orientation and training.

6. On-the-job training for entry jobs is viewed as leading to higher skilled jobs after some experience—from general clerical to typing pool and typist jobs for the girls; and from messenger to analyst jobs for the men. But these in turn require more training and self-study, which not all will achieve. Meanwhile, others hired without the hard-core designation are being trained and advanced as they qualify. Thus, the attention drawn to the specific group overlooks the normal effort most managements make in hiring, training, and promoting many whose qualifications are perhaps only somewhat better than the target group, in the period of generally tight labor supply.

5

The Cooperative Steel Industry
Education Program

BY *JOHN SCOTT MC CAULEY* *

Under a pilot program sponsored jointly by the federal government, the United Steelworkers of America, and the nation's ten major steel companies, approximately 4,100 steelworkers have attended classes in basic elementary education. The classes began in September 1967, and are conducted by a private nonprofit organization, the Board for Fundamental Education. Many minority group members participated. By the beginning of the program's second year, some of the workers had advanced to courses at the high school level. This paper describes the development of the project and discusses some of the problems encountered and accomplishments achieved during the program's first year of operation.

The Cooperative Steel Industry Education program was designed to meet the needs of steelworkers with limited education, many of whom had entered the industry during the severe labor shortage that prevailed during World War II. Some plants had employed large numbers of workers who spoke little English. The Inland Steel Company, for example, hired over 1,000 Mexican Americans who did not speak English. Moreover, recent manpower shortages have caused some steel companies to lower their hiring standards and employ workers deficient in basic education.

Many steelworkers with limited education found themselves locked into the labor pool or other jobs at the bottom of

---

* John Scott McCauley is with the U.S. Training and Employment Service, Manpower Administration, U.S. Department of Labor.

the career ladder. In fact, convinced of their inability to advance, some had signed waivers giving up their rights to be considered for more responsible jobs. Embarrassment over their inability to read or write may have led them to avoid work assignments that might further expose their educational inadequacy. Lacking the basic educational skills required for admission to company-sponsored apprenticeship or other training programs that might open the way to higher skilled jobs, these workers were ill prepared to adjust to the technological changes that were occurring in the steel industry.

Another aspect of the situation was what the reactions of long-service workers with limited education might be to efforts by the steel industry to recruit from the hard-core unemployed. It is understandable that employees who had worked in the industry for a long time with little or no advancement up the career ladder might oppose recruitment of "outsiders" and resent special help given new recruits to assist them in adjusting to jobs. Management officials and labor leaders agreed that giving present employees opportunities to improve their education would help make them more receptive to working with recruits from the ranks of the unemployed.

The lack of basic educational skills also had a serious impact upon the lives of the workers outside the steel mills. Those who were unable to read or write had experienced the humiliation that often arose from situations in which they found themselves expected to do both. They were unable to help their children with their school work, and often had to rely on other members of the family to handle simple business transactions.

Both the companies and the union were concerned about the problem. Many grievances and operating difficulties resulted when senior employees were denied advancement because of educational deficiencies. The 1965 collective bargaining agreement between the ten major companies and the union included the following clause:

> In order to serve the basic educational needs of employees and thereby enhance their qualifications for job opportunities on new and improved facilities and enable employees, including those on layoff, to improve their capacities for advancement or re-employment with the Company, the Companies and the Union, together with various agencies of the United States Government, have been and will continue to actively explore the development of certain training programs under the Manpower Development and Training Act of 1962 (MDTA) and other applicable laws.

At the same time, officials of the Departments of Labor and Health Education and Welfare had become interested in developing a pilot project to demonstrate what could be done to help workers who, because of the lack of education, had become trapped at the bottom of a career ladder. These agencies agreed to assist the steel industry in planning and developing a pilot project in two geographic areas. Approximately one million dollars was provided under the Manpower Development and Training Act to cover the cost of instruction for a 14-month period, under a contract to be administered by the U.S. Office of Education.

It was anticipated that if the pilot project proved to be successful, the companies would consider the feasibility of conducting this type of program in other steel plants throughout the country.

PLANNING THE PROJECT

Prior to getting the project under way, a series of discussion was held by representatives of the steel companies, the union, the U.S. Department of Labor, and the U.S. Office of Education. Mr. I. W. Abel, president of the United Steelworkers of America, and Mr. Elliot Bredhoff, special counsel for the union, participated in these meetings. Mr. William G. Caples, vice president of Inland Steel,[1] and Mr. H. C. Lumb, vice president of Republic Steel, represented the coordinating committee of the ten major steel companies. Dr. Howard Matthews represented the U.S. Office of Education. These meetings were chaired by the author of this paper.

There was general agreement that many workers in the industry needed additional education, but there was some skepticism regarding the willingness of workers in the lower labor grades to participate. It was recognized that it would be reasonable to expect promotional opportunities would eventually be made available to many graduates of the program. However, it was felt it would not be feasible to guarantee promotions to employees successfully completing the program, since it was not possible for any given company to determine its manpower needs in each job classification six months in advance.

The participants in these meetings agreed that the program should be designed to demonstrate that when a steelworker has expanded his academic base significantly, "he will be enabled to perform his present job more efficiently, be used more effectively in a higher job classification to the extent that such becomes available, successfully participate in available in-plant job training programs, and be flexible and competitive in the modern industrial situation, which involves

---

[1] Now president of Kenyon College, Gambier, Ohio.

132

new processes and equipment necessitated by modern technology." [2]

There was considerable discussion about what could be done to make the classes as attractive as possible to the workers. Although it was not feasible to arrange for classes to be held on company time, the companies provided classrooms on company premises in locations as convenient as possible. Because of the number and variety of shifts worked in many steel plants, it was arranged to hold classes at several times during the day and night. This gave most workers an opportunity to attend classes immediately before or immediately after their shift. It was agreed that participation would be completely voluntary.

The policy of encouraging workers to attend classes on their own time without any promise of promotion is quite different from the policy followed in some other educational training programs that have been established for employed workers. For example, the upgrading demonstration program funded by the Manpower Administration with the Skill Achievement Institute provides for an outside training organization to give free upgrading training in specific work skills and human relations, but only where the employer agrees to identify the higher level jobs available to the workers and to promote graduated workers to such jobs with a pay increase. The employer also agrees to have the training take place on company time and premises (with such extras as company-provided coffee and cake to indicate to the workers the company's strong interest and support for the program).

Because of the urgent need for educational programs in steel companies in the Baltimore and Chicago-Gary steel producing areas, it was decided to conduct the pilot program at these two locations. The Armco Plant and Bethlehem's Sparrows Point Plant in the Baltimore area were selected for the project, while the mills participating in the Chicago-Gary area included Inland, Youngstown Sheet and Tube, Republic, Midwest, and the South, Gary, and Gary Sheet and Tin Works of the U.S. Steel Corporation.

Both the companies and the union were in favor of having the experimental training conducted by the Board for Fundamental Education (BFE). This is a private nonprofit agency founded by Dr. Cleo W. Blackburn, former president of Jarvis Christian College. It was brought into being to help solve the housing, health, employment, and education problems of the disadvantaged. BFE is still active in all of these areas, but in recent years it has placed increased emphasis on helping undereducated persons to improve their basic word and

---

[2] *Cooperative Steel Project,* Board for Fundamental Education Report Number 1 (Indianapolis, Indiana, January 8, 1968), p. 3.

number skills. The agency was chartered by the Congress of the United States in 1954.

Following a visit to BFE headquarters in Indianapolis, Indiana, by members of the study group, it was decided that the agency should be invited to develop a contract proposal. Plans were made for a curriculum that would include two levels of instruction:

I. A basic level for individuals performing below the 4.5 grade level in both word meaning and arithmetic, as measured by the Stanford Achievement Test. Training objectives would include:
   A. A sight vocabulary of 3,000 basic words
   B. The ability to add, subtract, multiply, and divide
   C. An acceptable form of English usage which would permit the individual to write a communicative letter
II. An advanced level designed for individuals performing between the 4.5 and 8.0 grade levels in both word meaning and arithmetic computation. Trainees would be graduated from the advanced course when they had achieved a test score of at least the 8.0 grade level in both word meaning and arithmetic. Training objectives for the advanced course would include:
   A. A 7,000 to 10,000 word sight vocabulary
   B. Reading comprehension
   C. Inductive and deductive reasoning skill
   D. A functional use of fractions, decimals, percents, weights and measures, and graphs
   E. A knowledge of acceptable English usage
   F. A knowledge of the principles of science
   G. An introduction to U.S. history

Curriculum materials used by the Board for Fundamental Education included: *System for Success,* Books 1 and 2, supplemented by the *Reader's Digest Science Series,* and *Documents of Freedom. System for Success* was written by BFE project director, Dr. R. Lee Henney, while he was working with male inmates in an Indiana reformatory.

LABOR-MANAGEMENT PARTICIPATION

Emphasis was placed on obtaining the understanding and support of management and labor officials at every level. An initial briefing session for key officials in May 1967 was co-chaired by Mr. R. Conrad Cooper, executive vice president of U.S. Steel, and Mr. I. W. Abel. This meeting was attended by representatives of participating companies and by the district directors of the United Steelworkers of America, who were the chairmen of the contract negotiating committees. Dr. Henney described the plans that BFE had developed for operating the program. He explained that classes would be held two hours a day, three days a week. Although each course was scheduled to run twenty weeks, classes would be continued until all of the participants had an opportunity to complete the program successfully.

To aid in launching the program, a joint committee was appointed composed of Mr. W. G. Caples; Mr. Warren Shaver, administrative vice president of U.S. Steel; Mr. Elliot Bredhoff; and Mr. Ben Fischer, director, Contract Administration Department, United Steelworkers of America. The committee established trainee quotas for each of the participating plants, drew up procedures for implementing the program, and arranged for the company and the union to designate a coordinator for the program, in each plant.

Meetings of key officials were then held at each of the participating plants. These meetings usually were attended by members of the personnel and training staffs of each plant and also by a representative from corporate headquarters. The local unions were represented at these sessions in most instances by the president of the local and the local union coordinator for the project. Moreover, the educational officers of the district office of the United Steelworkers attended the sessions, along with the district staff representative.

To assure that the program was understood at every level of supervision and local union officialdom, briefing sessions were held by BFE staff members for a total of 3,926 supervisory personnel and union representatives. By helping to prevent misunderstandings and encourage cooperation, these meetings contributed greatly to the ultimate success of the program. The active role played by the union in getting the program under way did a great deal to erase doubts the workers may have had about management's motives in sponsoring the classes.

At each briefing session the supervisory personnel and union representatives were requested to submit to their coordinators lists of potential candidates for the first phase of the program. Some workers volunteered, and their names were added to the lists. In subsequent phases of the program, there was greater emphasis on encouraging workers to volunteer.

The guidelines that had been developed for the selection of trainees indicated that, in general, a participant should be a reliable worker who is cooperative with his peers and supervisors, who could do his present job better if his education were greater, or who has the potential of being utilized at a higher job classification when such an opening becomes available.[3] Also to be included were persons who spoke a language other than English and needed to improve their ability to speak and write English. Employees with longer service were given priority.

The company and union representatives were asked to discuss the matter with the individuals who had been nominated. From the lists that had been submitted, the coordinators made rosters of employees they felt should be invited to learn about the program at a series of employee clinics, to be conducted by the staff of the Board for Fundamental Education.

THE ENROLLMENT PROCESS

Approximately 510 employee clinics were held during regular working hours to explain the nature and operation of the program. To encourage attendance at these sessions, the employee clinics were usually held in the production departments on company time. Included in the employee clinics was a brief discussion of the overall employment situation in the industry. Stress was placed on the need for education in order to advance; however, it was emphasized that the company would not make commitments to change the job assignment or increase the pay of employees participating in the program. Following this presentation each employee was given an opportunity to ask questions about the program and to indicate his interest in the course. Of 4,306 employees attending the clinics during the first year of the program's operation, 3,845 (89.3 percent) expressed a desire to participate.

Workers who indicated that they wanted to participate were immediately given the Word Meaning and Arithmetic Computation subtests of the Stanford Achievement Test to determine where they should start in the education process. It was explained that since the program would be at the elementary level, anyone demonstrating skill above the 8th grade level would not be included. Only 322 (8 percent) of those tested, scored too high for inclusion.

Although the original plan called for only two levels of instruction, it was later decided to modify this approach when a considerable number scored above the 8th grade level in language ability but

---

[3] *Cooperative Steel Project,* Report Number 1, Board for Fundamental Education (Indianapolis, Indiana, October 15, 1967), p. 44.

scored far below that level in arithmetic. To meet the needs of this group, it was decided to organize special mathematics classes in each of the mills.

Of the 3,523 workers assigned to the program, approximately 21 percent did not attend a single class. Some of these workers may have been unduly sensitive about their inability to read, write, and do simple arithmetic problems and possibly were reluctant to expose their inadequacies. When asked at the employee clinic if they wished to participate, they may have felt that they should say yes because everyone else in the room was saying yes.

In light of this development, some changes were made in the format of the employee clinics at the beginning of the second phase of the program. For example, instead of having foremen and union officials nominate workers to attend the clinics, emphasis at Inland Steel was placed on self-selection. Posters and items in the company newspaper called attention to the employee clinics. Rather than have these sessions in the production departments, they were held at the training facility that had been established at the mill. Although the new arrangement did not permit workers to attend clinics during their regular shift, the company continued the policy of paying workers for time spent at the clinics.

In appraising the reactions of workers who had participated in the clinics, it is important to keep in mind that seniority was a factor in nominating workers for the program. Senior employees were given priority, partly because many of them were eligible for promotion if they could improve their basic education. Of course, those who were close to retirement could not be expected to place very much value on a possible promotion that might result from completing the educational program. Moreover, older workers in the steel industry generally have accumulated enough seniority to be eligible for lengthy vacations, which may last as long as 13 weeks. Vacation plans caused some workers to reject or postpone the opportunity to participate in the educational program.

OPERATION OF THE PROGRAM

Classes were conducted in an informal manner in very plain surroundings. Anything that might resemble a classroom atmosphere was carefully avoided. Work tables were usually arranged in a circle, rather than in the rows typical of most classrooms. Workers were encouraged to help each other, and a strong group spirit usually resulted. A more outgoing student was occasionally assigned to work with a passive one.

The instructors, many of whom were members of minority groups, were generally successful in reaching and motivating the trainees, and the workers felt comfortable with them. The instructors worked hard and demonstrated keen interest in helping the trainees improve their educational skills. They concentrated on leading the students rather than driving them. BFE was prepared to remove inadequate teachers; however, it was necessary to release only three of the fifty-two employed.

Some of the instructors were not college graduates, although all had had at least a year or two of college. They were each given three days of instructor training. At weekly staff meetings they exchanged ideas with other BFE instructors in the same geographic area. In addition to those employed in the steel industry program, instructors assigned to other BFE projects participated in these meetings.

Of the 2,762 workers who attended at least one class during the first year, 1,726 (62 percent) were graduated. A much lower proportion of the older participants completed the program. For example, only 25 percent of those 60 years of age and over, and 31 perecent of those in the 55–59 age group satisfactorily completed the training, as indicated in Table 1.

Although statistics are not available on reasons for failing to complete the program, it is known that some workers left because of illness, their own or that of a member of the family. Others left because they found the classes were interfering too much with a second job.

TABLE 1: COMPLETION RATE BY AGE IN THE STEEL INDUSTRY EDUCATION PROGRAM *

YEARS OF AGE	NUMBER ATTENDING	NUMBER GRADUATED	PERCENT
Total	1,602	1,000	62.4
Under 30	143	73	51.0
30-34	169	101	59.8
35-39	327	229	70.0
40-44	343	252	73.5
45-49	281	189	67.3
50-54	187	112	61.0
55-59	99	31	31.3
60 and over	53	13	24.5

* Based upon data on employees of Inland, Bethlehem, and Armco during the first year of the pilot project.

Still others may have left because of kidding by fellow workers. "Are you a kindergarten dropout?" some of the participants were asked. To help combat this situation, company officials emphasized to foremen the importance that management attached to the program. The union also re-emphasized its support. The fact that the vice president of a local union was attending classes was a helpful factor at one mill.

Transportation difficulties within the plant were sometimes given as the reason for dropping out during the first phase of the program. Although the companies made a special effort to provide classroom space at centralized locations, this was very difficult because of the wide dispersal of buildings in large steel plants. Some workers found it hard to get to and from their work stations and classes, especially during the winter months.

A great deal of overtime work became available during the second phase of the program, as other industries began to store up steel in anticipation of a possible strike. Many workers felt that they could not afford to pass up the opportunity for overtime earnings and stopped going to classes.

During the first phase of the program, some companies relied on BFE to keep records of class attendance and to follow up on absences and dropouts. In an effort to reduce the number of dropouts, the companies and the union kept a closer eye on the operation of the program during the second phase. For example, at Inland and Bethlehem, full-time staff members were assigned to monitor the program. When it was found that a worker was missing classes, an inquiry was sent to the man's foreman to find out the reason. Foremen were also helpful in taking care of many personal problems associated with the job. When family problems were indicated, a BFE staff member or a union official visited the worker's home after working hours. These measures succeeded in persuading many of the absentees to return to classes.

RESULTS OF THE PROGRAM

Some program accomplishments became apparent during the first few weeks that classes were in session. Dr. Henney related an incident about the steelworker in the special math course who brought a problem to the class during the third week. The worker was building a patio and sidewalk in his backyard and needed a load of concrete to complete the job. He had called the material yard, given the measurements to a clerk over the telephone, and asked him to figure how much he would need. The clerk said he could not figure the exact amount but would estimate that about seven cubic yards would be needed. Not satisfied with the clerk's answer, the steelworker brought the problem to class. The instructor explained to him how to figure cubic yards, and he came up with an answer of 5.9 cubic yards. The steelworker obtained permission to leave the class long enough to call the material yard to change his order. At the next meeting of the class, he brought back a favorable report. "I had only a handful of concrete left over," he said, "and I saved nineteen dollars."

To measure academic improvement accomplished during the program, BFE tested participants with the same form of the Stanford Achievement Test that had been administered during the employee clinics. The 646 employees who were graduated from the basic course had a mean postinstructional reading level of 6.0 grades, as compared with a preinstructional reading level of 3.2—an increase of 2.8 grade levels. In computational skills the basic group attained a mean postinstructional grade level of 5.9 as compared with an entry level of 3.3—an improvement of 2.6 grades.

The 729 employees who completed the advanced course attained a mean postinstructional reading level of 9.6 grades, as compared with an entry level of 6.2—an improvement of 3.4 grade levels. An even greater increase was achieved by this group in computational skills. They attained a mean postinstructional level of 10.1—a 4.5 grade increase over their preinstructional mark of 5.6.

The 351 special math graduates had a mean postinstructional grade level in computation skills of 10.9, as compared with an entry level of 6.3 grades, for an increase of 4.6 grades. As indicated above, the special math classes were organized for workers needing instruction in this subject but who scored above the cutoff mark that had been established in terms of reading skills. Their mean preinstructional reading level was 9.1 grades. No postinstructional test in reading was given to participants in the special math course.[4]

Company-administered tests have supported the results obtained by BFE. Although some of the improvements reported by BFE may reflect increased skill in taking tests, there is no evidence indicating that this was a significant factor.

The mills held individual graduation ceremonies at the end of each phase of the program. Officials of management and labor participated, and many of the graduates brought their families. Most of the trainees regarded the graduation as a significant milestone in

---

[4] For more detailed data on test results, see *Final Report on the Cooperative Steel Project*, Board for Fundamental Education (Indianapolis, Indiana, September 1, 1968), p. 26.

their lives. The companies provided a buffet lunch to help celebrate the occasion. A national press briefing was held in Chicago to mark the completion of the first phase. Participants in the briefing included Mr. I. W. Abel, president of the United Steelworkers of America, Mr. R. Conrad Cooper, executive vice president of U.S. Steel, and officials of BFE, the U.S. Office of Education, and the U.S. Training and Employment Service.

Although it is too early to appraise the full impact of the program upon the careers of the participants, some of the steelworkers who completed the program have already been promoted to better-paying jobs. For example, Tom Jones had worked in one of the mills for 23 years as a laborer. He enrolled in the basic course in September 1967. Although he began a ten-week vacation two months later, Mr. Jones continued to attend classes regularly. In mid-January of 1968, two weeks after he returned to his job, Mr. Jones received the good news that he had been promoted from laborer to clerk.

Supervisors also report that program participants have displayed greater interest and capability in their present jobs. For example, foremen at Inland Steel rated a sample group of graduates significantly higher than a control group of nonparticipants in regard to attitude toward work, understanding of verbal orders, job performance, and promotability. An unsolicited endorsement of the program was given by a senior melter foreman at Inland Steel in explaining how a new production record had been achieved in the Basic Oxygen Furnace Shop. He said that participation in the education program by crew members had resulted in improved performance in the shop. He noted that the courses in basic communications and mathematics had paid off for them on the job as well as in their off-work activities.[5]

There is also evidence that skill and confidence gained from the program have enriched the lives of the workers and improved their ability to handle family responsibilities. For example, a graduate of the program at the Bethlehem mill at Sparrows Point, Maryland, proudly told his instructor that he had ordered some new carpeting for his home and did not have to ask his wife to calculate the amount needed.

An important by-product of the program was a project under the Manpower Development and Training Act to train unemployed workers for entry-level jobs in the steel industry. This program was established to improve the employability of persons who had applied

---

[5] *The Inland Steel Maker*, Vol. 14, No. 26 (Inland Steel Company, East Chicago, Indiana), p. 3.

for work but had been rejected because of their limited education. Basic education classes for these workers were organized by the Public Employment Service and the public schools of South Chicago, Illinois, and Gary and East Chicago, Indiana. At Gary, classes were held in the union hall. Of approximately 250 workers enrolled, about 180 had completed the program, about 50 had dropped out, and about 20 were still attending classes on March 15, 1969. By that date over 90 of those who completed the program had been employed by the steel industry.

The 1968 collective bargaining agreement contains the following provision:

> For the past three years the Companies and the Union have been jointly involved with a pilot training program for adult basic education in the Chicago and Baltimore areas, under the Manpower Development and Training Act (MDTA). It is agreed that these efforts have been sufficiently beneficial to warrant continuation of this type of program for further exploratory development under MDTA, other applicable laws, and through other mutually agreed upon means.

As the end of the second phase approached, it was agreed that the pilot project should be expanded and continued for another year. The companies felt they had not yet had sufficient experience to enable them to judge the feasibility of extending the program throughout the industry. They wanted to see how it would work in other locations. Furthermore, both the union and the companies wished to expand the project to include courses at the high school level. Accordingly, the contract with BFE was extended to November 1969, at a cost to the federal government of approximately $900,000.

Under the provisions of the extended contract, basic and advanced courses have been started at Armco Steel in Houston, Texas; Bethlehem Steel in Lackawanna, New York; National Steel in Ecorse, Michigan; U.S. Steel in Fairchild, Alabama; U.S. Steel in Lorain, Ohio; and Youngstown Sheet and Tube in Youngstown, Ohio. Special math classes were organized in Houston and Lackawanna. Meanwhile, high school-level courses were started in the plants that had participated in the pilot project during the first year. At most of these plants the basic and advanced courses were repeated. At the end of January 1969, a total of 387 workers were enrolled in high school level courses, 350 were in the basic course, 555 in the advanced course, and 49 in special math classes.

Experience gained from the second year of the program, when added to the first year's experience, should provide a sound basis for appraising the feasibility of extending the program throughout the steel industry. The results of the pilot project should also be of interest to management and labor officials in other industries, particularly those having recently hired disadvantaged workers whose basic educational skills will need to be strengthened to enable them to move up the job ladder. Moreover, the experience obtained from extending the project to the high school level may give management, labor, and government a new vision of what can be accomplished by working together to improve the skills and knowledge of employed workers.

Discussion

BY   *E. ROBERT LIVERNASH* *

The pilot educational program sponsored jointly by ten major steel companies, the Steelworkers Union, and the federal government has clearly been an important experiment. As it happens, the discussion of this program here at the conference benefited greatly, in addition to Mr. McCauley's paper, from personal observations by Mr. Robert A. Graney of Inland Steel, whose enthusiasm for the program served to emphasize the fundamental contribution made to the lives of participating Inland employees, perhaps particularly to a group of Mexican-American employees who for years had been locked into labor pool jobs and low-status positions, both in the plant and community, by deficiencies in basic education. The remarkable achievements in reading, writing, and computation made by these employees primarily serve as the basis for the following three comments.

First, increased attention to aid the disadvantaged must be given to removing hindrances which block promotion. Primary attention up to this point in time has been given to providing employment opportunities and obviously much remains to be done in this regard. But, just as obviously, problems of major proportion are becoming more and more apparent because of frustrated promotional aspirations. A balanced effort is required. This would seem to imply

---

* E. Robert Livernash is Albert J. Weatherhead, Jr., Professor of Business Administration at the Graduate School of Business Administration, Harvard University.

renewed review of job requirements (a) to remove artificial and unnecessary required qualifications, (b) to establish realistic and operational standards for promotion to protect both employee and company, and, finally, (c) to devise the best possible training programs to supplement the normal on-the-job learning process. Also required is continuous review of promotion sequences and seniority practices which may be needlessly restrictive. Clearly, enlarged employment opportunities must be matched by enhanced efforts to provide normal promotion opportunities.

Second, the program appeared to be associated with a high degree of achievement motivation. Many variables no doubt were involved, but there were some interesting contributing circumstances which may provide guides in other situations. The training was voluntary, so that those content with their present pay and conditions would not participate. More speculative, but also more intriguing, was the seeming close connection, at Inland at least, between the training, the promotion hurdle, and subsequent job performance. The bottom job on lines of promotion sought by these employees required passing qualification tests. The tests were based upon computational, verbal, and written operating requirements of the jobs. The tests were thus built from very specific actual requirements of the jobs. Passing the tests rested upon mastery of the skills taught in the training program. The program supplied a missing link which may well have stimulated a real desire to achieve. If such visible and meaningful connections could be created elsewhere for training programs, similar results might follow.

Third, and finally, the training methods and circumstances, coupled with the points noted above, achieved most impressive results. In what was in fact a very small number of hours, the average grade level of some taking the training was raised from roughly zero to four and, for others, from four to eight. Results were real and were checked by more than one method. The materials used in teaching, the informal methods and classroom attitudes, the personal involvement and interest of those teaching, and other conditions combined to produce these impressive results. Experimentation in educational methods, personnel, and conditions made its own most substantial contribution. From all these points of view this pilot educational program warrants attention and investigation.

6

General Electric —
Woodland Job Center

BY   *PETER J. SIRIS* *

INTRODUCTION

This case traces the conceptualization and implementation
of the Woodland Job Center. Created in 1968 in Cleveland
by the General Electric Company, the school system, and
the business community, the center was a complex and
highly innovative project developed to recruit and train the
hard-core unemployed for jobs in industry. Conceptually,
the program at the Woodland Center was to provide a unique
interaction between business and education. The business
community was to provide skills training in real production
shops, and the school system was to supply academic and
social training, specifically tailored to the needs of the job,
in an environment that did not carry the stigma of a school.
The object of the shop program was to motivate workers by
providing individualized training for a particular job. By
uniting the work-training ability of business and the educational competence of the school system, it was hoped that
the shop program would break the school dropout-unem-
ployment-poverty cycle.

---

* This case, General Electric—Woodland Job Center, IM 1926, was prepared by Peter J. Siris, Research Assistant, under the direction of Professor
Richard S. Rosenbloom as the basis for class discussion rather than to illustrate either effective or ineffective administration. It was prepared under
the auspices of the Program on Business Leadership and Urban Problems,
Harvard University, Graduate School of Business Administration.
The case was written with the collaboration of Jeanne Deschamps, an edi-
torial assistant at Harvard Business School.

145

The conceptualization of the program was excellent, but its complex and innovative nature made it difficult to implement. Lengthy negotiations with many private businesses and government agencies were required. Problems with funding arose because the program did not meet the requirements of any existing training program. Funding was finally obtained by dividing the Woodland Project into two parts: the original shop program and a new program that satisfied the regulations of the MA-3 and the National Alliance of Businessmen. Only the latter program received federal funds, and even this funding did not provide for renovation or capital equipment.

Further delays and modifications were caused by the complexities of coordination, recruiting difficulties, and necessary adjustments during the early months of the program. Almost one year passed between the program's conceptualization and its implementation, and the final product differed significantly from the original plan.

As the problems of implementation are described in the body of this case, the reader may begin to assume that an exposé is in progress. Such is anything but the case. The Woodland Center was created and implemented by highly enlightened leaders from business, education, and government who were willing to cooperate and to modify their interests in an effort to create a successful program. Despite the problems and the delays, each of the participants continued to work to implement the original shop concept, and as a result a program was finally established. Without the affirmative actions of everyone involved, the program would have become a second-rate alternative. This case demonstrates why the innovative solutions that are so often needed are so rarely attempted.

The Setting. Cleveland faces the problems faced by most American cities: poverty, unemployment, and strained race relations. In 1966 the city was torn by riots. After the riots several citizens took the initiative and acted to structure new programs for the city. Paul Briggs, the new superintendent of schools, began a school modernization program which placed special emphasis on job training through expanded vocational education programs. A group of Cleveland businessmen formed the Businessmen's Interracial Committee and the Inner City Action Committee to provide increased institutionalized contacts with the black community. These groups also emphasized jobs and job training.

In a study of the employment situation in Cleveland, the committees identified these critical problems: There were few jobs for unskilled black workers, and there were few workers for many semiskilled jobs. The skills of the local work force did not correlate with those needed for the available jobs.

The prosperity of the Cleveland SMSA,[1] in which only 2.5 percent of the workers were unemployed, contrasted with the conditions in the five ghetto districts: Hough, Kinsman, Glenville, Near West and Central, where 15.5 percent of the blacks were unemployed. For out-of-school youth between the ages of 16 and 26, unemployment exceeded 58 percent. Over 40 percent of the black workers were classified as underemployed, and less than 2 percent were employed in professional, technical, or managerial occupations. Twelve thousand families earned less than $2,000 per year, and one-fourth of all families—black and white—lived in rat-infested dwellings. To expand economically, the city needed trained workers. To survive socially, it needed to develop opportunities for the blacks.

The General Electric Company. Robert Corning, vice president of General Electric and general manager of the Lamp Division, was one of the Cleveland businessmen who realized that a stable environment was necessary for effective and efficient operation of his business. The General Electric Company was about the sixth largest business in Cleveland, employing some 9,700 salaried and hourly workers. Like other large employers, its financial stake in Cleveland was high, represented by investment in buildings and equipment for some twelve factories. Eleven of these plants were part of the Lamp Division, one of GE's oldest and most important divisions.

The Lamp Division employed some highly skilled engineers, many unskilled operatives, and a few semiskilled workers, who were usually promoted from the ranks. In some plants the more recently recruited workers had not been sufficiently skilled or motivated, the turnover rate was high, and management feared that the company's production efficiency would be affected. As a result, GE began to participate in training programs with AIM-JOBS (the local Concentrated Employment Program) and with the Opportunities Industrialization Center. Neither program had provided a complete solution to the unique psychological needs of the hard-core unemployed, however, and the company decided to seek further manpower training assistance. Specifically, Robert Corning and other Cleveland business executives wanted to create an on-the-job training program that would build positive attitudes and behavior patterns, teach some skills, increase motivation, reduce turnover, and insure a continuing supply of competent workers.

---

[1] The SMSA (Standard Metropolitan Statistical Area) is a term used by the census bureau to define the boundaries of large metropolitan areas.

The Woodland Plant. General Electric owned a building on Woodland Avenue in the central ghetto. It had been constructed in 1929 as a one-stop service center for many GE products. Later many smaller, geographically decentralized service centers were opened, and during the 1950's the company began to phase out its operations in the Woodland building. By 1967, the plant was used only occasionally as a warehouse.

GE had contemplated selling the Woodland facility, which had a tax value slightly in excess of $1 million. However, Charles J. Miller, regional vice president of General Electric, suggested that the company should consider the possibility of putting the building to some socially constructive use. Therefore, Robert Corning and his assistant, Marc D'Arcangelo, began to consider alternatives for the Woodland building.

Corning learned that the Businessmen's Interracial Committee had completed a series of studies of education and employment. The chairman of this committee, Ralph Besse, informed Corning that the Woodland building could house a program that both the Businessmen's Interracial Committee and Paul Briggs, the Superintendent of Schools, had been discussing. This was the shop program, which had been designed to combine both business and school disciplines in a new approach to job training. The idea was that business would provide skills training in actual production shops, and the school system would provide educational support programs specifically related to vocational needs. The entire program would be conducted in a factory setting rather than in a school environment. In a later meeting between Corning and Briggs, Briggs also suggested that the program could concentrate on the high school dropout, and thereby alleviate a city social problem while providing business with trained workers. Corning and Briggs subsequently decided to work out a specific plan.

CONCEPTUALIZATION

In Cleveland, as well as in other American cities, high school dropouts and hard-core unemployed had continued to defy the efforts of both business and the schools to stop the unemployment-welfare cycle. Corning and Briggs hoped that, by combining the experience of businessmen and educators, they might develop a plan which would eliminate the faults of previous training programs. These earlier programs had failed to train and motivate the worker because they did not treat the total individual. Training programs

148

sponsored by business taught specific skills in a work-oriented environment without providing individualized instruction or academic and social training, and tended to treat the trainee solely as a skilled operative. Training programs sponsored by school or training agencies taught attitudes and work procedures in classrooms, but classroom training often proved insufficient once the student was confronted with an actual job. Furthermore, existing training programs usually ignored the many and diverse reasons for motivational problems, as they tended to group all trainees into one homogeneous mass called "dropout" or "unemployed."

Briggs and Corning wanted to design a program which would focus on the individual worker and the individual job. They wanted to train workers on an individualized basis in an environment that simulated the world of work. They also felt that skills training should be supported by academic and social courses which were directly related to the needs of a particular job.

With these objectives in mind, Corning and Briggs decided to create a factory school at the Woodland plant for youths up through the early 20's who were not enrolled in public schools. Within this plant there would be a number of production shops, sponsored by companies in Cleveland, in which the trainees would work. These shops would function as small, independent factories. They would have their own equipment, product line, supervisory personnel, and income statement. The sponsoring company would manage the shop and provide both the raw materials and a sales outlet for the production of the shop. After the completion of training, individual workers would be employed by the training company.

The work training in the program would emphasize job readiness. The production shops, functioning as microcosms of larger factories, could accurately simulate both the technical and the human requirements of real jobs. The worker would produce real products and would learn skills directly related to his permanent job. Trainees would also benefit from individual supervision, since supervisors in real factories seldom have the time to assist individual workers.

The emphasis on job readiness and motivation extended to the social and academic training as well. Although this part of the training would be conducted under the auspices of the school system, an effort would be made to avoid a classroom atmosphere so that the trainee would not be reminded of previous failure. Instruction would be given by coaches in offices rather than by teachers in classrooms, and the program would be directed by a general manager rather than by a principal. This instruction would be offered on an individual or small-group basis, and would be tailored to the needs of the individual.

All academic and social training was designed to complement skills training. Two types of education would be provided:

> *Worker-oriented*—Arithmetic and reading courses would be designed around a particular job and taught with the materials of that job. For example, a trainee might learn reading from an auto mechanics manual, rather than from the literary classics. He would also learn basic things about how the working world functions, such as how time clocks work and how to calculate gross and net income.

> *Person-oriented*—Supportive courses were designed to aid those parts of the trainee's personal life which would affect his working life. Black history and culture courses would attempt to increase racial pride; health instruction would improve his attendance record, and counseling services would deal with personal problems, which might affect his ability or desire to work.

Trainees could acquire academic training on their own initiative or on the recommendation of their foremen. The coaches and the materials for instruction would be available at all times.

The program was designed to take an average of six months, but the duration of training and the specific content of the curriculum would be tailored to the needs of each worker. Each trainee would be promised employment upon graduation, and all training would be directed toward this employment.

Corning and Briggs realized that the employment of workers by many companies within the Woodland Center might create certain undesirable conditions. Wage differentials would be created, and employment by individual companies would also restrict transfers between shops. Briggs and Corning wanted to permit the trainees to explore various jobs to find the ones that best suited them. Consequently, it was decided that the Cleveland Public Schools would form a nonprofit holding company called "Woodland Enterprises" to employ all workers in the center. This holding company would permit a uniform rate structure and unrestricted transfer, and it would also enable the center to train dropouts who were under age. After training, however, the workers would still receive permanent employment with the companies that trained them.

To further motivate the workers, Briggs proposed to make the Woodland plant a community center by building bowling alleys, game rooms, and meeting rooms. If Woodland could become a community center, the trainees might take increased pride in their training program, and other community members would be encouraged to enroll.

150

Diversifying the Program. Dropouts have differing needs, and some enter programs in which they do not fit, and fail again. It seemed desirable to have several different programs located at Woodland Center, so that the dropouts could see alternative possibilities and transfer into the program that best satisfied their needs. Consequently, Briggs proposed that the School System's Work-Study Program also be placed in Woodland.

Like the Shop Program, the Work-Study Program provides both vocational and academic training for high school dropouts. Unlike the Shop Program, however, Work-Study terminates in a high school diploma. Its academic component is more intensive, lasting for several years, and its students have seemed to be highly motivated. Combining the Work-Study and the Shop Programs could have a beneficial effect for both. Shop program trainees would come in contact with Work-Study trainees, who were working to obtain a high school diploma, and possibly a better job, and some might be tempted to transfer to the Work-Study Program. The less able Work-Study trainees might transfer to the Shop Program. In addition, the shops in the Woodland Center would provide some clerical employment for the Work-Study students. Thus the center would present models of two types of dropouts—those being trained for a job, and those being trained for a job and a diploma.

Reactions to the Proposed Program. The Program had considerable appeal for the executives at General Electric, who believed that by working with the school system they might be able to reduce the number of dropouts and perhaps break the spiral leading to unemployment and welfare. Participation in the program would also permit General Electric to upgrade the potential of its own work force. The executives felt that their Woodland plant would be a perfect location for such a program.

If it participated, General Electric would be required to rent space, place a production unit in the shop, train managers, and develop its trainees for jobs in the corporate plants. Although it seemed likely that the shop would lose money, accurate cost estimates were difficult to determine. The net loss for the shop would depend upon the rate of learning and the overall efficiency of the trainees. According to the Lamp Division's most pessimistic projections, the annual loss of training two groups of 40 workers for six months each would approximate $50,000–$70,000. In commenting upon these projections, however, Marc D'Arcangelo noted that the company would not be surprised if this training program unleashed great productivity from the unskilled trainees.

Other business firms also received the program enthusiastically.

For them, the Woodland Center provided an opportunity to train skilled workers while helping to solve one of Cleveland's pressing urban problems. Although no specific commitments were made, several of the major businesses in Cleveland seemed inclined to participate.

The program also had considerable appeal for the school system. It would provide a solution to the system's most urgent problem, the high school dropout; enable the schools to expand the vocational education curriculum; and create an innovative partnership between the schools and local industry.

If the program were started, Paul Briggs felt that the federal government might pay for the expenses relating to teachers and rehabilitation, excluding those remodeling projects covered by special foundation grants. It would also pay for audiovisual and other equipment covered by the Elementary and Secondary School Education Act of 1966. As stipulated by law, the federal government would pay 50 percent of the building maintenance. These costs might amount to $3 million, calculated on the basis of 1,000–1,500 trainees at $2,000–$3,000 per trainee. The school system would have to hire the top administrators, pay for maintenance, other start-up costs, and some of the expenses related to the academic courses.

Based on the enthusiasm for the program, General Electric decided to donate their plant on Woodland Avenue to the school system for a job training program. They also agreed to sponsor a training shop in the plant. On January 10, 1968, in a speech before an urban problems session of the National Industrial Conference Board, Paul Briggs announced the program. He stated:

> This week the Cleveland Public Schools finalized an agreement with the General Electric Company that promises to make history in American Education. We will take over a former General Electric plant of over 200,000 square feet near the heart of the ghetto. The schools will use it to have a new kind of training for unemployed out-of-school youth. Here under one roof will be located components of education and on-the-site employment. Students will receive salaries from the first day of enrollment, as they will be [working] in actual production . . . units . . . operated by a number of Cleveland industrial firms.

This program will be a bridge between unemployment and conventional employment.

Nine days after the announcement, on January 19, 1968, Briggs and D'Arcangelo went to Washington to discuss the concept with the Department of Labor. Representatives of the department were quite excited about the program, and asked when it would be operational. They were told six months. They replied that they would like to see the program started earlier. Briggs and D'Arcangelo left Washington feeling optimistic about obtaining funds for the program.

The school system began the planning process. In February planning and development grants totaling $70,000 were received from three foundations. In March initial staffing was begun. Al Cunningham, a director at the Rodman Job Corps Center in Bedford, Massachusetts, was hired to be the center's general manager.

At the same time, Briggs began to contact local business firms. In the early months of 1968, definite commitments were made by General Electric, Western Electric, and Ohio Bell. Other companies also began to express an interest.

National Alliance of Businessmen: MA-3—JOBS. On January 24, 1968, while the Woodland Center was being planned, President Johnson announced the creation of the National Alliance of Businessmen. The alliance, directed by Henry Ford II and composed of business leaders throughout the country, made a commitment to hire and train the hard-core unemployed in a program called "Job Opportunities in the Business Sector" (JOBS). To encourage participation and to make the program financially attractive to business, President Johnson asked Congress to authorize MA-3 (Manpower Administration) funds to be used to reimburse companies hiring the hard-core unemployed.

Congress approved the appropriation, but demanded that other urban programs be either curtailed or modified to meet the regulations of the MA-3. The Department of Labor was reluctant to curtail the Woodland Project, feeling that it was exceptionally innovative and progressive. The Woodland Program was more advanced and sophisticated than the MA-3, which was designed to motivate businesses to start simple training programs. The Woodland Project provided a more complete solution to the problems of training the hard-core unemployed. Modification of the project to satisfy MA-3 requirements would have restricted its operation.

However, while the Department of Labor wanted to maintain the Woodland Project intact, it was conscious of the problems and responsibilities incurred in administering a new federal training act. It had to use the first set of projects to help to establish national guidelines and standards for the entire program. The funding of a slightly divergent program like the Woodland Project might make the establishment of these standards and guidelines difficult. Therefore, while the department agreed to be flexible, it asked the school system to tailor the project to the regulations of the MA-3.

To create a framework for business sponsorship, the department asked the school system to find a third party to sponsor the program. The Greater Cleveland Growth Association (the Cleveland Chamber of Commerce) agreed to act in this capacity. Originally, the principals in Cleveland had believed that the Growth Association could serve as a "permissive contractor." On further interpretation of the MA-3, the association was forced to assume the full responsibilities of a contractor. To further institutionalize business involvement, the workers were to have specific jobs before entering the program. This meant that Woodland Enterprises could no longer serve as the employer. Hence, transfers would be limited and workers would be paid according to the prevailing wage rate of other employers. The guidelines of MA-3 also forced the school system to rearrange the schedule of the program and shorten both the training period and the academic component.

The New Program. Briggs decided to apply for a consortium program in the Woodland Center. (In a consortium program, a group of companies creates a combined training program in one location, and each company commits itself to a certain number of jobs.) Funding, training, and reimbursement would be administered by the Greater Cleveland Growth Association. A program was designed which would last 14 weeks: The first two weeks would consist of basic orientation, the next four of elementary education and skills training, and the last eight of general skills and on-the-job training. The Woodland Center would be used solely for the six-week orientation.

This program was not nearly as comprehensive as the Shop Program. However, William Adams, president of the Growth Association, and Paul Briggs tried to make some changes which would improve it. They contacted AIM-JOBS, an organization of local businessmen funded by the Department of Labor as part of the Concentrated Employment Program. AIM had extra training funds that it agreed to allocate to supplement the MA-3 program. It would sponsor a two-week orientation program away from the center. At the end of the two weeks, AIM would evaluate each student and then make recommendations for the full MA-3 program. After training, AIM-JOBS would provide counselors to ease the transition to the full-time job.

To further strengthen the MA-3, Corning and Adams felt that an in-service training program for supervisors from business was needed to ease the transition to the job itself. This training would sensitize the supervisors to the unique problems of the hard-core unemployed. It would help them develop human relations expertise and the ability to motivate their trainees. The training plan would include material on the psychology, sociology, and culture of the Negro; an orientation to the inner city; and some sensitivity training in interpersonal skills. The addition of the in-service training program was critical because it would help to make the line-supervisor a participant in the training process.

Briggs and Adams also wanted to increase the flexibility in the MA-3. More flexibility could be achieved if the Growth Association applied to serve as the employer as well as the contractor. Under this plan, the GCGA would hire all 1,000+ workers. After the training period they would "sublet" the workers to particular companies for the remainder of the year. Since all the trainees would be employed by the same company—the GCGA—the flexibility inherent in the Shop Program could be restored. A uniform wage structure with achievement-based incentives and an unrestricted transfer policy could be maintained. Finally, if the Growth Association served as the employer, the individual companies would be freed from bureaucratic entanglements with the government. This would permit small companies to participate in the center.

THE FUNDING PROCESS

The First Application. By mid-May plans were being developed for two programs: the original Shop Program and the modified MA-3. While some companies were exploring the possibility of developing and funding "shops" for the Woodland Center, the Growth Association and the school system were preparing an MA-3 application for the Department of Labor. This application, which was submitted on May 5, 1968, called for the creation of a 16-week training program. During the first two weeks, AIM-JOBS would provide an orientation fully subsidized by the government. Then the trainees would select their company, enter the Woodland Center, and begin a six-week introduction to work. Individual companies would assist in the design of this section, which would be followed by eight weeks of on-the-job training, either in the Woodland plant or in the field. The companies would agree to ultimately employ 1,020 workers. Because the center projected a dropout rate of one-third, 1,530 workers were to be recruited and trained.

The program was estimated to cost $3,436,164 or $3,369 per successful trainee, exclusive of the costs of the AIM-JOBS program. The Growth Association requested that the federal government pay

$3,185,159 or some 93 percent of the total budget. Fifty-five percent of the costs were employee wages (trainees were to be paid $1.60 or $1.75 per hour). Twenty percent of the costs were for instruction. Operation and maintenance accounted for 15 percent and overhead for 10 percent.

The Department of Labor received the application favorably but felt that certain modifications were necessary. The use of the Growth Association as the employer was not consistent with the purpose of the NAB–MA-3 program, since this program had been created to stimulate business firms to hire and train the hard-core unemployed. The goal was to provide a direct institutionalized relationship between the trainees and their employing companies. The use of the Growth Association as the employer, while possibly beneficial to the Woodland Program, was at variance with the rules of the MA-3. The department did not accept the idea of "subletting" workers, and decided that only a company offering a permanent job could serve as employer. Therefore the Growth Association was asked to submit a new application in which it would be the contractor and the individual companies would be the employers.

The Second MA-3 Application. On June 3, 1968, a new MA-3 application was made to the federal government. The Growth Association was still listed as the contractor and the school system as the subcontractor, but now individual firms were to serve as employers. The total cost was largely unchanged, but major sections were re-allocated to the individual companies. This new proposal placed certain restrictions upon the program. With the individual companies employing the workers, transfers would be eliminated, vocational training restricted, and wage differentials created. Proposed health services that could have been provided by the Growth Association in the Woodland facility now would have to be provided separately in each firm's home office. Supervisory training would be eliminated.

This second application was not accepted because the one-third dropout rate proposed by the Growth Association violated the MA-3 regulations. Only those workers receiving final employment would be eligible for reimbursement.

The Third MA-3 Application. The Growth Association and the school system were informed that a contract for 1,000 workers, each with definite jobs, budgeted at $2 million, or $2,000 per worker, would be accepted. On July 25, 1968, such a program was submitted to the Department of Labor. The next day the contract was signed.

156

With the $2 million from the Department of Labor, the MA-3 program was funded. The Shop Program, however, was not. A decision on the final status of the two programs had to be made.

Paul Briggs held meetings with Robert Corning and Marc D'Arcangelo of GE and with Bill Adams of the Growth Association to discuss the merits of the two programs. The two programs are compared in Table 1.

Paul Briggs wanted to retain both programs. The MA-3 was funded and could start operations on a large scale immediately. The Shop Program was not funded. Its implementation would depend upon the willingness of individual companies to support a shop without federal reimbursement.

The Woodland Center in Three Parts. On June 28, 1968, Paul Briggs, Robert Corning, William Adams, and Jack Tankersly [2] announced that the center, which was slated to open in September, would provide the following:

> A three-dimensional approach, putting together under one roof, a factory-school that gets at:
>> Basic and remedial education
>> Training in job skills
> in order to:
>> Develop a new source of manpower for local business and industry
>> Provide jobs immediately for the unemployed
>> Reclaim the high school dropout and reduce the dropout rates by making available more relevant training opportunities

Three groups were to be trained in three distinct programs.

1. JOBS--MA-3

The school system and the Growth Association agreed to accept

---

[2] Mr. Tankersley, President of The East Ohio Gas Company, was NAB chairman for Greater Cleveland.

TABLE 1:

	Shop Program	MA-3 Modified
Lenth of training	6 months	16 weeks
Length of employment	6 months +	1 year minimum
Union restrictions	None	Subject to rules of individual companies
Opportunity for change	Transfer to or from work-study programs; re-enter school; switch job or company	Cannot transfer between jobs in the center
Academic program	Black history and sociology, math, English, etc.	Basic education and counseling
Motivation	Shop concept: real production shop, degree of worker control, incentives, interaction with surrounding shops; after a 6-month period, with community	Incentive system based on learning
Training	Workers remain in training until ready; academic and vocational supervision tailored to individual needs. Personal as well as skills training	Workers removed from center at established intervals; 2-week AIM-JOBS orientation
Government requirements	None	All responsibility to GCGA
Funding	Uncertain sources of funds	Assured federal funds
Facilities	Loaned by industrial companies	Little funding for facilities because of high risk to company if worker leaves and it is not reimbursed

the $2 million of MA-3 funds in order to train 1,000 hard-core unemployed workers. The program would include five phases:

1. Recruitment and selection by AIM-JOBS.
2. Personnel processing and employment by participating businesses.
3. Enrollment in the Woodland Job Center for orientation, counseling, basic education, job skill training, and supportive services.
4. On-the-job training by employer at the center or at the employer's place of business.
5. Full-time employment follow-up.

Within a month after the announcement, companies in Cleveland had pledged all 1,000 JOBS commitments.

2. Job Training for New Workers—The Shop Program

Those companies that desired to adhere to the original shop concept could participate in the center through the Program of Job Training for New Workers. Designed for the 16- to 22-year-old dropout needing training for immediate job placement, this program would operate in three concurrent phases.

1. *Immediate Employment*—The trainee would be placed upon entry in a job in a shop operated by one of the participating companies.
2. *Skill Training*—The trainee would be given specialized skill development for immediate job placement and for job advancement.
3. *Basic and Remedial Education*—Communication, computation, consumer economics, work-study attitudes and habits, the free enterprise system, and citizenship education would be included in this phase.

General Electric and Western Electric made definite commitments to the Job Training for New Workers Program, which were nonreimbursable. Ohio Bell and General Motors also seemed likely to participate in the program.

3. Work-Study

The existing Work-Study Program of the school system would also be included in the center. Designed for the 18- to 21-year-old dropout wishing to return to school part time, the program provides a six-week pre-employment orientation to the world of work followed by a cooperative course of study composed of enrollment in high school courses and part-time employment leading to high school graduation and full-time employment. An average of 300 Work-Study students would be in training at the Woodland Center at all times.

The following starting schedule was devised by the school system:

July 1–28	GCGA contracts for job commitments
	Planning and development of staff of jobs program
August	Facility renovation
July-August	Attempt to find participants for the shop program
September 1	Work-study program moved to center
September	First MA-3 and shop trainees enrolled
November-December	Full capacity reached

FURTHER ALTERATIONS IN THE WOODLAND PROGRAM

The Woodland Center was an especially complex and ambitious undertaking, and before the center could be opened, inevitable problems arose which caused further delay and alteration. The principal difficulties centered around funding problems, center/company relations, and recruiting. Some of these problems merely slowed progress, while others offered opportunities for innovative changes.

Funding problems delayed the opening of the center. The school system did not have the funds to begin a major rehabilitation of the Woodland building. This program was partially solved on November 22, when Governor Rhodes appropriated $2½ million for rehabilitation and program development in the Woodland Project. However, the MA-3 funding restricted monies for capital equipment. Under the conditions of the MA-3 reimbursement (see Figure 1) the total cost of the contract for each worker would be repaid to the company in equal daily installments for one year, as long as the worker remained employed. If the trainee should quit before the end of the year, the company would forfeit the remainder of its reimbursement. Companies were unwilling therefore to allocate large sums of money for capital equipment early in the year, since a high turnover rate would mean considerable financial loss.

The business community presented additional problems for the Woodland Project. Despite aggressive education efforts by the

160

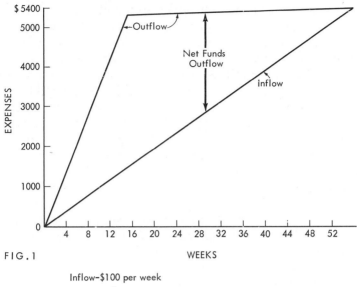

FIG.1

Inflow—$100 per week

Outflow—Cost of first six weeks of MA -3 training=$2,600
Cost of next eight weeks of MA -3 training=$2,600

Growth Association and the NAB, it proved difficult to develop close relations between the center and the companies. The smaller companies had not participated in the design of the MA-3. Many were wary of dealing with the federal government, and some did not fully understand the nature of the job commitments when they agreed to participate in the excitement of early July. Contact was further restricted by the off-site nature of the project. Many companies were training only a few workers, and they preferred to use equipment in their own plant rather than move it to another location.

Recruiting problems also delayed the opening. AIM-JOBS was to provide trainees for the Woodland Project, but the relationship between the two parties was somewhat ambiguous. AIM was funded and evaluated by the Department of Labor on its ability to place workers in jobs. During 1968 it was required to make 4,000 placements, but it was not clear if the 1,000 Woodland trainees were to be included in this quota. AIM therefore decided to give preference to its original commitments. Thus, although 30 to 90 workers were to enter training every two weeks, during the first three two-week periods, AIM-JOBS recruited groups of only 14, 13, and 4 workers for the program. By the end of four months, only 169 workers had begun training.

Although AIM had freedom in allocating its placements, the Woodland Center could accept only those recruits certified by AIM.

As the number of trainees fell below expectations, the Woodland Center was forced to maintain a high counselor-trainee ratio, and funds were wasted. To secure additional trainees, the center received permission from the Department of Labor to use the Ohio Bureau of Employment Services (OBES) to recruit workers for the program. Although trainees recruited by OBES would not be eligible for the two-week AIM-JOBS orientation, the center was willing to forgo this training if a continuing supply of workers could be provided. In November 1968 a recruiter was hired, and the OBES office was opened in the center to provide direct recruiting. The center and the bureau started an intensive campaign to recruit boys who had just dropped out of high school. The preliminary results of the campaign were excellent.

With insufficient commitments from the companies and a limited number of workers, the center could not begin full-scale training operations; without capital equipment, the "real production shop" could not be simulated. The shop was the innovative core of the Woodland Program, as it was to provide special skills training and motivation. Without capital equipment there could be no shops, and the workers would have to be processed to their employing companies as quickly as possible.

Implementation of the MA-3. After the center opened, additional changes were made in the program. The failure of MA-3 funding to provide the equipment for training made it impossible for the center to simulate the environment of industry. Complications in dealing with several federal agencies, many businesses, and many state and city government agencies caused further adjustments. Also, the peculiarities of each new group of trainees increased the need for improvisation. Consequently, the program was shortened and more directly oriented to the needs of the individual companies.

In practice the MA-3 program began to differ markedly from the Shop Program. The lack of capital equipment meant that the trainees had to begin skills training in an actual corporate environment fairly soon. The failure of companies to take an active role in the planning of their training programs, and a combination of few trainees plus extensive training tasks per company prohibited the creation of production shops and structured academic programs in the MA-3. As a result, the MA-3 was no longer a shop program with different funding because the emphasis was changed from that of a permanent production shop to that of a short and flexible training program.

However, although the MA-3 was made shorter and more flexible, the close interaction between the trainee and his employing company was maintained. Skills training in both the MA-3 and Shop Program was oriented to the needs of specific companies; the academic curriculum was also designed around particular company requirements and subject matter related to employment. (For example, one course contained a week-long unit called "How to be Able to Calculate Your Gross and Net Income.") Participating companies were urged to use their own employees as trainers, and counselors who had never been in a factory before were sent to visit each participating company so they might better understand specialized jobs.

The following example illustrates how the MA-3 was modified in practice: The Hough Handyman Corporation Training Program trained 27 hard-core unemployed, who were also militant blacks. The staff of the center assembled loose building materials from throughout the Woodland plant. With these materials the workers built, plastered, destroyed, and rebuilt various objects so that they could learn the skills of construction and repair. Then the staff created three different academic reading courses until they found one that motivated the trainees. Through this type of improvisation, the program was able to adapt a unique group of black workers to a unique training task.

One successful MA-3, sponsored by East Ohio Gas, trained 15 gas-line helpers in a six- to eight-week course. Most on-the-job training occurred in the field, although the East Ohio supervisors used the Woodland plant for some preliminary skills instruction. The academic courses and counseling provided at the center were developed with the help of the company and were directly related to the needs of the job. All 15 trainees were still employed by Ohio Gas three months after training.

In a program that involved a consortium of Cleveland banks, 13 workers were trained in general banking procedures. First, the staff of the center and bank personnel met to design a training program around the banks' job qualifications, which included good technical skills, attractive personal appearance, and reliable attendance. The banks provided personnel to teach the trainees about banking procedures, and the center developed a course to teach reading. Topics such as Operations of Banks and How to Manage Money were included as the basic subject matter. The center also developed a course on personal appearance with the assistance of a local black charm school consultant. This consultant instructed the trainees on such topics as how to pick up something while wearing a mini-skirt. Finally, since these trainees were women and attendance was important, a short course on birth control was developed.

Results of the MA-3. Although the neatly tailored MA-3 of early June was no longer intact, in its first four months of operation the Woodland Center could be termed "a qualified success." Through

December 31, 1968, 109 workers had completed training and another 50 remained in the center. By January 16, 1969 the record of the 71 men who had completed training had been tabulated. Of the 71, 31 had not remained on their original job. However, 23 of the 31 had found other employment, and one had enrolled in a community college. Only 7 were unemployed.

There were several reasons for the unemployed percentage in this group of trainees. Many of the initial recruits had been "program hoppers," men who enter every new training program and then quit once on the job. Second, one of the companies involved in the MA-3 program lost a government contract and was forced to lay off all nine of its trainees shortly after they started work. Since it appeared that the company might rehire them, six of these workers obtained other employment on a temporary basis, two entered other training programs at Woodland, and one chose to enroll in college.

THE SHOP PROGRAM

The Shop Program began more slowly than the MA-3. For the committed companies, General Electric and Western Electric, the creation of a shop required allocating funds, installing equipment, hiring personnel, and developing a training program. Since these companies were entering the center without reimbursement, they were very careful in their planning. In addition, the creation of Woodland Enterprises, a nonprofit holding company that would serve as the employer, took several months.

Western Electric. Late in October, Western Electric became the first company to open a shop in the Woodland Center. The program was started because Western Electric felt that the new hard-core workers would not be accepted by groups in the plant. They would not receive assistance from their fellow workers, and the on-line supervisors would not have the opportunity to give them the necessary guidance. Western Electric therefore created a modification of the sheltered workshop at the Woodland plant and assigned one line supervisor to conduct the training.

The workers in the shop were to assemble line changers for telephones. After testing and an initial orientation, the workers went into the shop to begin assembling the changers under the supervision of the Western Electric trainer. They then received skills training for six hours per day and academic training for two hours. While in the shop, the workers received the minimum salary of $1.60 per hour, but were eligible to receive hourly incentives of $.30 to $.40.

The first group of trainees spent from three to four and a half weeks in the shop. Although the Shop Program was originally planned to last six months, it was felt that the center's primary goal should be to get the workers onto the job as quickly as possible. The experience of the Western Electric shops indicated that training would have to vary with the abilities of the workers and the complexity of the tasks.

By January 1969, 12 workers had been trained in the Western Electric shop, and all of these are still employed by the company. Meetings are currently being held at Western Electric to determine skill requirements for 1969.

General Electric. At the time of this writing (January 1969), the General Electric shop was scheduled to open at the end of February 1969. Unlike the Western Electric shop, which offers training in one labor-intensive skill, the General Electric shop will be an expensive and complex permanent production and training center. The shop will train workers in a variety of jobs, including assembly of light bulbs, connectors, and thermal units and the cutting and packaging of tungsten. These jobs will provide the workers with a broad training experience in skills and attitudes.

General Electric first allocated $50,000, hired a foreman and part-time experienced production man, and began an extensive renovation of the 80' x 80' area in which the shop is located. $22,000 of the $50,000 was allotted for the renovation. During the last months of 1968, the two men worked to transform the empty warehouse area into a production shop.

The shop is intended to train 100 workers per year, with some 15 to 20 in the shop at one time. Training time will average over two months, but a trainee will remain in the shop as long as it takes to make him job ready. However, once job-ready, trainees will be encouraged to leave and accept employment in a General Electric or other factory.

The General Electric program is an ambitious undertaking. With a potential of 15-20 trainees in five occupation categories, each requiring some capital investment, the shop is designed to function like a small factory. However, the high projected turnover and the academic training make the shop more complex than a normal factory. General Electric is willing to plan the program carefully because the company feels that it is an innovation that can provide a prototype for other training programs. Mr. D'Arcangelo expressed the company's feelings as follows:

> The MA-3 is a good program, but it trains skills. We see attitudes and behavior as a basic problem for the younger worker from the inner city. We have two manpower needs—motivating unskilled

workers and identifying workers who can be upgraded to skilled positions. Through the shop, we hope to concentrate on the attitudes of the trainees and motivate them to be productive workers. While the workers are undergoing the intensive shop training, we hope to be able to work with them individually and determine which workers have the potential to be upgraded.

The MA-3 will eventually run out. Paul Briggs still has the building, and he still has the concept, so the shop alternative is still open. We will have our shop operating, and Western Electric opened this week. Other companies will follow. Soon there will be new kinds of money available from the federal government and the states for innovative subvocational training. If our programs are successful, they can still provide the prototypes for the future.

Discussion

BY   RICHARD B. FREEMAN *

There are many ways to prepare individuals for the world of work. Vocational training in secondary schools, apprenticeship programs, post-secondary study in special institutes (as in cooking or barber schools), college education, graduate or professional school training, and formal or informal on-the-job training programs are just some of the possible routes to employment. In recent years the U.S. has relied extensively on formal school preparation, usually resulting in a high school diploma, to teach the general skills and to certify persons for the further training required for employment.

Individuals who find this system of schooling uncongenial are at a disadvantage in the labor market. There are few direct paths to good jobs for the dropout: The usual education or training ladders are closed to them. Other phenomena, such as minimum wage laws, are also likely to create unemployment among low-skilled workers. As a consequence, unemployment has been concentrated among the less educated.

Tight labor market conditions and public concern over the plight

---

* Richard B. Freeman is an assistant professor of economics at Harvard University and the University of Chicago.

of disadvantaged workers have combined in the 1966–69 period to create new programs for the hard-core unemployed. New mechanisms for training have been developed to provide dropouts with the opportunity to learn general and specific job skills. The General Electric Woodland Job Center is a case in point. At this center, dropouts ranging in age from 16 to 22 are offered a spectrum of academic and job-training opportunities. The creation of *additional options* in preparing for work and of alternative methods for learning academic skills is certainly desirable for the labor market.

Whether current programs like the Job Center are successful, on the other hand, is less clear. Administrative difficulties, inherent probably in all innovative acts, hamper the programs. The lack of scientific testing, moreover, creates problems in interpreting the record of only 7 unemployed of 71 graduates. Would the job trainees have obtained work elsewhere in a tight labor market? Are they "displacing" other potential workers? What about the trainees who do not remain on their original job? Is "success" due solely to the tight labor market?

To answer these questions and to evaluate the efficacy of programs requires an analysis of similarly placed non-Job Center workers. Until that is done, it will not be possible to determine the value of programs of this kind. As innovations in the labor and education markets, such programs for the disadvantaged are probably a priori "good things." Innovations must, however, meet the market test to become true successes in a competitive economy.

7

The Workers' Defense League

BY *EDWARD C. PINKUS* *

INTRODUCTION

During the 1950's and the 1960's, civil rights groups have strongly criticized the construction industry because of the small number of nonwhite building trades craftsmen. Statistics on minority participation in apprenticeship programs lend weight to the criticism. In January of 1967 there were 122,000 registered (and an unknown number of unregistered) building trades apprentices in the United States.[1] They were distributed in the following basic trades:[2]

Bricklayers	9,000
Carpenters	23,000
Electricians	25,000
Ironworkers	7,000
Painters	6,000
Pipe Trades	25,000
Sheet metal workers	12,000

---

* Edward C. Pinkus is a labor lawyer and a member of the bar in California and the District of Columbia. He is presently pursuing a graduate degree in labor law at the Harvard Law School. The author is grateful to Ernest Green, Charles Bremmer, and other members of the Workers' Defense League staff, for their help in the preparation of this study, and to Virginia M. Sullivan for editing the manuscript.

1 See Appendix A.

2 F. Ray Marshall and Vernon M. Briggs, Jr., *Equal Apprenticeship Opportunities: the Nature of the Issue and the New York Experience,* No. 10 in a series of Policy Papers on Human Resources and Industrial Relations published jointly by the Institute of Industrial Relations (University of Michigan at Ann Arbor and Wayne State University at Detroit) and the National Manpower Policy Task Force. © 1968.

According to the 1960 census, only 2.52 percent of the total number of apprentices in the building trades were nonwhite; there were only 79 nonwhite apprentice electricians, and only 62 nonwhite apprentices in the plumbing and pipe-fitting trades. In 1960 there were no Negro apprentices in five New York City construction unions—plumbers, steam fitters, sheet metal workers, ironworkers, and mosaic and terrazzo workers.

Criteria for admission into an apprenticeship program include education, work experience, residence, citizenship, police clearance, military service, physical ability, written tests, and oral interviews.[3] An apprenticeship program typically consists of on-the-job training accompanied by classroom instruction, and is usually of four or more years duration. While progressing through a program, an apprentice earns an increasing percentage of the journeyman's wage. (See Appendix D.)

A variety of factors—poor education, inadequate information, discrimination—have contributed to the limited participation of Negroes in the building trades. Proposed remedies for this problem have ranged from emphasizing objective testing procedures in selecting apprentices to the complete abolition of apprenticeship training.

One organization, the Workers' Defense League, has had considerable success in placing nonwhites into building trades apprenticeship programs. The Workers' Defense League (WDL) is a private nonprofit organization which, in conjunction with the A. Philip Randolph Fund, has developed a program of preapprenticeship recruitment and training for placing minority group members in building trades apprenticeship programs. Since 1967 the program has been financed in large part by federal funds.

WDL began its efforts to recruit and train youths for entry into building trades apprenticeship programs with the publication, in 1963, of a guide to apprenticeship openings in New York City. The guide listed the requirements, filing fees, and application procedures for some 3,000 openings—information not generally available until then. In late 1963 WDL opened an office in the Bedford-Stuyvesant section of Brooklyn and by mid-1964 had begun to actively disseminate apprenticeship information, as well as recruit potential applicants. Civil rights demonstrations at construction sites punctuated WDL's transition from publicity to recruitment and training.

The Workers' Defense League's preapprenticeship training program is currently supported by a variety of agencies including the U.S. Department of Labor and the Ford Foundation. In addition to

---

[3] See Appendices B & C.

its headquarters and two field offices in New York City, WDL now has operations in Buffalo; Cleveland; Newark; Boston; Rochester, Nashville; Lexington, Kentucky; and Mount Vernon, New York.

THE WDL PROGRAM

Since 1964 WDL's primary strategy for increasing nonwhite participation in the building trades has been *preapprenticeship,* that is, recruiting and training youths to pass existing apprenticeship examinations and not attacking the tests, or otherwise seeking to lower apprenticeship admission standards. While working within the framework of existing programs and institutions, WDL does not hesitate to challenge discriminatory procedures and to question the relevancy of some apprenticeship admissions criteria.

WDL follows a program which has been worked out by experimentation over a period of years. This program consists of six parts:

1. Recruiting of qualified nonwhite youths.
2. Testing and evaluation of recruits' abilities.
3. Counseling.
4. Preparation of documents and apprenticeship applications.
5. Tutoring.
6. Follow-up and supportive services.

The typical WDL recruit goes through the following procedure. He fills out a simple WDL application form. He is given the Otis Quick Scoring Test to indicate aptitude and intelligence. He receives counseling regarding the various building trades and the requirements for admission to their apprenticeship programs.

When he has chosen a program and has been accepted by WDL, WDL assists the recruit with the application procedures. This includes help in assembling such necessary documentation as birth certificate and high school diploma, and help in filling out the often complicated apprenticeship application form. Arrangements are made for a medical examination when required. Loans are available for admission fees and tools, and tutoring is provided to help him pass the written examination. If he needs a job during the tutoring period, WDL helps him find one.

When the recruit has finished training, WDL gives a mock oral interview to prepare him for the interview he will eventually face before an admissions committee probably composed entirely of whites. WDL then assembles its recruits for the actual examination and makes certain that all go to the correct location, on time, and with the necessary credentials and supplies. A long time—sometimes several months—may elapse between examination and acceptance; WDL assists in finding interim employment. Once the recruit passes the test and is accepted into an apprenticeship class, WDL attempts to maintain personal contact in order to ensure that he does not drop out of his apprenticeship program.

This study is divided into two main parts. The first contains a more detailed description of the WDL program, mainly as it was developed in New York City. The second part concerns problems and evaluation of the program. A great deal of information regarding background and the New York City program has been drawn from the Marshall and Briggs manuscript,[4] which is the pioneer and most comprehensive study of WDL to date. Some data have also been taken from *Black Builders*, R. B. Goldmann.[5] Information regarding WDL's activities in Buffalo and Nashville was gathered during this writer's interviews with WDL staff members in those cities, and this study focuses on those two cities in addition to New York.

Recruitment. When WDL opened its Bedford-Stuyvesant field office in 1964, a group of Brooklyn ministers promised to supply a list of 600 prospective minority applicants for building trades apprenticeship programs. The list, supposedly compiled during civil rights demonstrations at construction sites, was never forthcoming. WDL then compiled its own roster of qualified nonwhite youth with the help of youth employment organizations, churches, civil rights groups, schools, and fraternal organizations. WDL gathered 700 names; 300 showed up for WDL testing and screening. Many of the 300 turned out to be ineligible for apprenticeship programs, and WDL was forced to turn away the unqualified recruits.

Since then, WDL has tried to minimize the discomfort of turning away recruits by developing selective sources of qualified recruits. These include:

1. *High Schools*—Since a high school diploma is required by many apprenticeship programs, WDL works with high school guidance counselors and talks to student assemblies in order to promote interest in the building trades.
2. *Parents*—Parents influence the career decisions of their children, but are likely to share the American bias against manual labor. WDL tries to influence parental attitudes by speaking at PTA meetings.

---

[4] Marshall & Briggs, *op. cit.*
[5] Ford Foundation Assessment Paper, 1968.

3. *Local YMCA's*—The YMCA's are a source of young Negroes in transit from rural areas to cities.
4. *Local bars and pool rooms*—These are not always a good source of qualified youth, but in some cases are middle-class social centers where WDL finds good recruits.
5. *Organizations in contact with minority youth*—These include churches, civil rights groups, and such government programs as the Job Corps, the Neighborhood Youth Corps, and the Concentrated Employment Program.
6. *The underemployed*—Many young Negro high school graduates are working as stock clerks, gas station attendants, and culinary employees.

The relative degree of success in recruiting from each of these various sources differs from city to city. In Bedford-Stuyvesant, where the WDL program has become well known, word of mouth has become a prime source. In Cleveland, high schools and recent high school graduates are the best sources; whereas in Rochester the high schools have not proved to be a fruitful source. WDL's recruiting experience in Buffalo and Nashville suggests some of the underlying factors which affect the suitability of particular sources.

WDL's sources of recruits in Buffalo have been varied and have included poolrooms, word of mouth, and "through the streets." Distribution of written promotional material has recently been started. Some recruitment has been done directly at high schools. But in June, when virtually all high schools graduate, only a few apprenticeship programs including the plumbers and steam fitters are open for applications. Electricians, for example, recruit for apprentices in January, February, and March, and youngsters graduating in June often aren't willing to look ahead so far. One Buffalo high school in June of 1968 had three graduates with bricklaying training, but none could get into the bricklayers' apprentice program at that time of the year.

Recruitment efforts in Buffalo have concentrated mainly on high school graduates with some work experience. Table 1 indicates the education and work experience of the 53 applicants whom WDL recruited in Buffalo in October 1968. Forty-one of the 53 had prior work or military experience. Of the 30 recruits for trades other than roofing, 24 were high school graduates and one of the 24 had completed one year of college.

There are several reasons for the recruiters' emphasis on work experience which, though particularly strong in Buffalo, also exists in other cities. Men with work experience perform better in oral

TABLE 1: WORKERS' DEFENSE LEAGUE
BUFFALO: WORK EXPERIENCE AND EDUCATION OF OCTOBER, 1968, RECRUITS *

Trade	No. of Applicants	Education	Prior Experience
Ironworker	22	16 high school graduates or equivalent.	18 with prior work or military experience, ranging from 3 months as waiter to 3 yrs. as drill operator, and including railroad switchman, die cutter, tool-maker apprentice, gear assembler (automotive), chemist's helper, and grinder.
Roofer	20	11 completed 11th grade; 4 completed 10th; 2 completed 9th; and 3 completed 8th.	15 with prior work or military experience, ranging from 4 months as restaurant worker to 3 years as crane operator, and including steel or common laborer (3), paintmaker, assembly worker press operator and clerk (2).
Electrician	1	One year of college	Laborer, steelworker and 3 months as electrician's helper.
Welder	1	High school graduate.	Grinder (4 months); conveyor (2 months).
Tool & die Worker	1	Completed 11th grade.	None.
Draftsman	1	High school graduate.	5 years as a clothes presser.
Carpenter	2	Both high school graduates.	One with 2½ years as laborer; one with 3 years Army and 3 years Air Force.
Plumber	2	One high school grad; one completed 9th grade.	One (the high school grad.) none; one with 2 yrs. as meat cutter apprentice.
Immediate employment without WDL training	1	High school graduate.	5 years air force.
Machine Shop	2	One high school graduate; one completed 11th grade.	One (the high school grad.) with 2½ years as machine operator; one with none.
Total:	53		

Source: Information obtained from the Workers' Defense League.

interviews. Many unions give substantial weight to work and military experience in making a final rank list of apprenticeship applicants. A man with work experience is likely to appreciate the value of a good job and to have a higher aspiration level, which lessens the likelihood of his dropping out of an apprenticeship program once he has been admitted.

Buffalo WDL has made some effort to recruit from the Buffalo Puerto Rican community, but with almost no success. The Buffalo carpenters and cement finishers, for example, require only a 10th grade education. Many Puerto Ricans meet the minimum qualifications but are unaware of the possible opportunities in the building trades. Since there may be a languague barrier, WDL started, in December of 1968, to distribute recruiting literature in Spanish.

Recruitment in Nashville has followed the same basic pattern as in New York and Buffalo but with some variations. Nashville has one black radio station and WDL started using it for weekly spot announcements, featuring a different craft each week, even before any apprenticeship program was open for new applicants. When programs are open, spots for the particular program are broadcast daily. Newspapers are also used but only for regular news stories; want ads draw too many whites, probably because whites have been more successful in the past than nonwhites in finding jobs through want ads. The main emphasis of the radio spots is money—the potential earnings in the building trades. Once a potential recruit has been attracted by that initial lure, other advantages of the crafts are emphasized. The early ads and radio spots did not mention that high school graduation is a requirement in all but three of the Nashville building trades. As a result, many non-high school graduates were attracted, most of whom had to be turned down.

Other recruitment sources in Nashville have been churches (all ministers read special letters to their congregations), community centers, spring dances, and college students helping with recruitment. High schools have been a prime target. WDL set up an outdoor table in the neighborhood of one high school, with loudspeakers playing rock and roll music. The virtues of apprenticeship training were then extolled to the gathered crowd. (It is perhaps appropriate to note that WDL's senior field representative in Nashville was formerly an automobile salesman.) High school guidance counselors are urged to recommend building trades apprenticeships.

Testing and Screening. WDL personally interviews each recruit and gives him the thirty-minute Otis Quick Scoring Test of Mental Ability. At least through 1965, the interview and test were used to help select those recruits who were most highly qualified and most likely to succeed in the apprenticeship examinations. Since 1965, as the tutorial program has improved and experience has been gained, WDL has been able to accept some recruits with less excellent qualifications and to adjust tutoring to individual differences and needs.

WDL's tutor in Nashville thinks that the Otis test is adequate to ascertain learning ability and general aptitude, the purpose for which it is designed, but that it does not show in what specific areas a given individual needs special help. The tutor is trying to design a test for this purpose. No minimum Otis score is a prerequisite to entry into the Nashville WDL program. (Cities with more applicants than Nashville can be more selective, but do not rely upon a minimum Otis score as an automatic cutoff point.) Nashville accepts some trainees with quite low Otis scores, who may need 8 or 12 rather than 4 weeks to prepare for an apprenticeship test. Some low Otis-scorers have qualified for TVA training programs, but most other successful WDL trainees have had higher scores.

Counseling. Many recruits know little about specific building trades and apprenticeship programs. This lack of knowledge is acute among ghetto youths whose fathers, relatives, and friends are unlikely to include building trades craftsmen. WDL once asked 40 recruits what kind of work they thought operating engineers perform; the most common response was "they run subway trains." The aim of WDL's counseling is to inform each potential applicant about the specific nature of each trade, and about the employment opportunities in each; the recruit must then choose the program which best suits his needs, abilities, and aspirations. In practice, the selection of a trade is often determined by the programs open for new apprentices at the particular time.

Many potential applicants who are clearly not destined for the building trades come into the WDL offices. They may lack some essential qualification, or have misunderstood the services offered by WDL. Such persons are referred to other agencies and sources of employment whenever possible.

Preparation of Documents and Apprenticeship Applications. Most apprenticeship programs require applicants to have such documents as a birth certificate, high school diploma, medical certificate, and driver's license. WDL assists applicants in obtaining the necessary documents. The application for admission into an apprenticeship program is often a lengthy and complex document, which must be carefully prepared and filed at a particular time and place. The 1966 application for the sheet metal workers apprenticeship program, for example, was nine pages long. WDL must supervise and assist applicants in the preparation and filing of the applications in order to ensure their completeness and accuracy.

Tutoring. Tutorial sessions run for a maximum of six weeks, with about nine hours of tutoring a week. Tutoring is strictly unidirectional—aimed at the apprenticeship test. No attempt is made at more general education. WDL does not try to correct educational deficiencies but only to prepare applicants to pass a single apprenticeship examination.

Apprenticeship tests may be administered by the union-management joint apprenticeship committee itself, or by a state employment service, or a private independent testing agency engaged by the committee. WDL tutors gather as much information as possible about the particular test to be given. Library research, consultation with test experts and interviews with applicants who have taken tests are among the sources of information. In some instances, a tutor can accurately predict the exact test to be given, but it is dangerous to limit tutoring to an exact test because the test may be changed. Then applicants may be unprepared or psychologically unable to handle the different questions.

Through its experience with many tests, WDL has learned that most apprenticeship examinations cover five areas: mathematical computations, mathematical problem solving, spatial relationships, mechanical reasoning, and verbal reasoning. In each area the tutors deal only with those kinds of problems that may be on the examinations. If an applicant asks a question about some other aspect of the area the tutor will not answer the question, but will tell the applicant not to worry because it won't be on the test.

Special emphasis is placed upon quick answers because the time for examinations is limited, and rapid work is necessary to complete them. WDL students drill by constant repetition, using sample questions prepared by the tutors, and they learn to do problems almost by rote. They are also instructed in the art of test taking—when to guess and when not to guess, whether wrong guesses will be penalized; when to go for speed and when to go for accuracy.

Academic tutoring alone is not sufficient to attain the goals of WDL's tutorial program. WDL considers discipline and socializing equally critical ingredients of success. The tutoring program therefore encompasses the further objectives of shaping attitudes, instilling self-confidence in recruits, increasing their aspiration levels, and training them to accept the discipline of the workplace and deal with the kinds of problems that will arise on the job. The tutors are selected for their ability to relate to WDL's recruits. They are young Negro males who believe in the importance of WDL's work and who

176

are knowledgeable about apprenticeship examinations and testing procedures. They are willing to work evenings and weekends when necessary to provide special tutoring or counseling; preferably they have had some experience with the labor movement; and most are college graduates with some prior experience in education.

In Nashville, WDL's senior field representative has expanded the tutoring program to non-high school graduates who are preparing to take the Nashville Board of Education's General Education Development examination (GED) for a high school equivalency diploma. The field representative, his secretary, his mother and 14 other volunteers (10 of whom are white) donate two hours of their time to this activity each Saturday. Most of the 26 tutees in the current class were originally prospective WDL trainees, but the GED program is not limited to WDL rejects. It is a community program offered to all non-high school graduates. Black power advocates have criticized the use of white tutors, but GED has not been able to find enough black volunteer tutors. There are no reportable results yet. Three students took the GED test before the course was completed and against the advice of the tutors; all three failed. The rest of the group has not yet been tested. There have been attendance problems—it takes many Saturdays to cover the math, English, social studies and science necessary for the GED. Whites in their 40's and late 30's, many of whom are teachers by profession, have been effective GED tutors. The GED program is a spontaneous offshoot of WDL's activities but is a completely independent program and receives no WDL funds.

Supportive Services and Follow-Up. WDL's activities do not cease once an applicant has successfully completed a written apprenticeship examination. After an applicant has been accepted into an apprenticeship program, there may be a delay of up to several months before he actually starts work and training and begins to draw his apprenticeship wages. WDL helps him find interim employment, preferably of a kind which pays less than the starting apprenticeship wage.

WDL continues to follow the progress of its applicants after they have started their apprenticeship programs. Some men stop in or phone WDL periodically on their own initiative. The WDL staff phones others, sends out follow-up cards, and arranges periodic meetings. WDL also asks its successful applicants to aid in recruiting new applicants.

A variety of supportive services have been developed as needed. WDL has arranged for free medical examinations through the Medical Committee for Human Rights. Applicants in need are granted loans for application and initiation fees (which can run into hundreds of dollars) and for tools. WDL is able to finance notary fees, photostatic copies of transcripts and records, and transportation costs for needy applicants. It also prepares discrimination complaints to be lodged with appeals boards within the building trades and with public antidiscrimination agencies.

In brief, WDL assists its applicants in every way necessary at each step of the way from recruitment to attainment of full journeyman's status. Because of ignorance and misunderstandings, verbal communication is often the only effective means of reaching recruits. Phone calls and face-to-face contact are the most extensively used means of communication. On one occasion WDL learned that ghetto youths do not know what registered mail is and will not accept or call for a registered letter. On another occasion WDL advised 27 recruits by letter to bring photographs of themselves to a meeting. Twelve of the 27 failed to comply with the request. (Luckily, the WDL staffer had the foresight to bring a Polaroid camera.) In addition to the tasks of recruitment, screening, tutoring, counseling, placement and follow-up, it is a major function of the WDL staff to keep each recruit effectively informed of his status and of the exact nature of every step to be taken at each stage of the program.

PROBLEMS AND EVALUATION

Evaluation Criteria. There is no clear and universally-accepted criterion for evaluating the success of WDL and similar programs. It is possible to judge WDL in various terms (success in meeting its own declared objectives, relation to the labor market, cost-benefit efficiency, and social utility) and reach different conclusions, depending upon the criterion selected.

Possible criteria range from the purely subjective to the highly objective. The application of objective criteria is especially dependent upon reliable data, and any program like WDL should strive to maintain accurate, comprehensive, and current data for evaluation purposes. There are two monthly reports for each WDL office—one for WDL's own administrative headquarters and one for the Department of Labor. The forms for the Department of Labor's Monthly Activity Reports on Outreach Programs are ambiguous. (See Appendix E for the statistical abstract of the report of the Brooklyn office for the month of October 1968.) Several of the report categories are meaningless, and it is impossible to reconcile the figures given in subcategories with the broader totals. WDL staff members say that they have received different explanations and instructions from different people in the Department of Labor. WDL's own internal reports are more clear and consistent, but could stand improvement.

The most basic criterion is the number of WDL applicants who have been accepted into apprenticeship programs and have commenced work as indentured apprentices. As of October 1968, the oldest WDL office—Bedford-Stuyvesant—had recruited 2,056 potential trainees, of whom 816 have undergone one or more sessions of tutoring and 272 have become indentured apprentices. Performance in the newer offices is more modest: Buffalo placed a total of 68 indentured apprentices during the period May 1967 to October 1968, and Nashville placed a total of 20 during the period May to November 1968. The total number of WDL recruits placed as indentured apprentices outside of the Bedford-Stuyvesant office was 290 as of September 1968; WDL projects that the total will rise to 575 by mid-1969. These figures represent a significant increase in minority participation in apprenticeship programs, though, as will be seen in subsequent sections of this paper, dropout rates require some discounting.

The cost of WDL's program may be indicated by the following figures for the Bedford-Stuyvesant office from its inception in 1964 to mid-September 1968.[6]

Source of Funds	Funds Spent
Total Taconic Foundation funding	$115,000
Brooklyn share of Ford Foundation 1967 grant	26,400
Brooklyn share of Department of Labor 1967 grant:	44,000
Total Funds Spent	$185,400
Number of persons recruited, trained, and placed over this period:	365
Average cost per trainee placed:	$ 508

Some adjustments are necessary. WDL provides some benefits, such as job development and referral service, to recruits who do not qualify for its program. On the other hand, post-indenture dropouts may be viewed as increasing the per capita cost figure of the remaining apprentices, although the dropouts, too, have had the benefit of tutoring and other services.

---

[6] Source: Goldmann, *Black Builders, op. cit.*

The cost and number of WDL recruits who are placed as indentured apprentices are helpful tools of analysis but are by no means self-sufficient evaluative concepts. The number of indentured apprentices alone does not indicate the rate of progress in overcoming the cumulative effects of past inequalities and in planning for future needs. Nor are cost figures meaningful unless compared with other programs and possible alternative uses for funds.

Recruitment and Selection Standards. Judging from the quality of WDL's recruits, WDL is not presently a program for "hard core" youth, however that term may be defined. Even for those apprenticeship programs which do not require a high school diploma, WDL prefers high school graduates because of the greater likelihood of their success. At the same time, an effort is made to reach non-high school graduates, at least in cities where the WDL program has become well established.

A 1968 survey of 48 WDL applicants in New York City tends to confirm the view that WDL's recruiting is oriented more toward the middle class than the hard core. The survey was designed to ascertain family background, education, and views on race relations. Forty of those surveyed were undergoing tutoring for the sheet metal apprenticeship examination, and eight for the bricklayers'.

The applicants were found to be between the ages of 17 and 22. Most had lived with both parents or were still living with parents or relatives. The father was the provider for more than half of the families, and the majority of the fathers were laborers, craftsmen, or service workers. The survey commented that the individual homes of the applicants did not evidence the type of family disorganization syndrome characteristic of the neighborhoods in which the families were located.

Two-thirds of the 40 sheet metal applicants surveyed were high school graduates, and only three had not finished 11th grade. Four bricklayer applicants had finished 10th or 11th grade, and the other four had completed 9th grade.

A majority of the 48 did not believe that racial discrimination was a barrier to their employment opportunities. Almost one-quarter subscribed to the view that large numbers of Negroes are unemployed because they don't want to work. Some 85 percent expressed no preference between whites and nonwhites as fellow employees. The survey commented that the 48 WDL applicants "are not only not particularly bitter or angry as are many ghetto youth, but many of them seem rather naive given the realities of life for Negoes in the United States. . . ."

There are practical justifications for WDL's selectivity. First, high school diploma requirements which prevail in many apprenticeship programs require the exclusion of a vast segment of ghetto and minority youth.

Second, the white youths against whom WDL applicants must compete in apprenticeship programs are not hard core. The educational background of the 65 apprentices in the Spring 1965 sheet metal workers apprenticeship program in New York was as follows:

Type of Diploma	Number of Recipients *
Academic	21
General	21
Commercial	7
Vocational	4
No diploma	4
High school equivalency	2
Mechanical	1
Technical	4
Other	1

* Source: Marshall and Briggs, based upon a survey conducted by WDL.

Of the ten who scored highest on the apprenticeship examination, eight had academic diplomas.

Third, it may be that once a program is well established in a particular city WDL could expand its tutoring techniques to accommodate a broader segment of ghetto youth. But such expansion would require more funds, additional tutors, and possibly the extensive redevelopment of tutoring techniques. It might also encounter considerable resistance from the building trades unions, which might view any substantial lowering of the quality of WDL recruits as a threat to the standards of the apprenticeship programs.

Fourth, even setting selection standards at a level of educational parity with white apprentices might not suffice to meet WDL's goals. Because of his inferior schools, the skills and testing ability of a black high school graduate may be comparable to those of a white who has only completed 10th grade. In order for WDL applicants to compete effectively, they often must have one or two years more education than their white competitors. Black applicants are at a further disadvantage in those trades where the white apprentices are predominantly the sons or nephews of journeymen; such whites have an acculturation, which is an advantage on mechanical aptitude tests and in oral interviews.

Whether or not one agrees that the various practical considerations justify WDL's selectivity, "creaming" has been an effective and efficient selection method for promoting WDL's specific goals as currently defined. It should, however, be recognized that even within WDL's select group there are different categories or recruits who may derive different benefits from the program. For example, Buffalo's recruiting intake includes both graduates who have had no work experience and for whom apprenticeship programs are initial entries into the labor market, and high school graduates who have been working for several years for whom apprenticeship programs are an opportunity to upgrade their position in the labor market. The benefits are also different for recruits who succeed in becoming indentured apprentices, remain so for only a short time and then move on, or return, to other occupations.

WDL's stated position regarding selection criteria is ambivalent. While there is no denial of selectivity, recruitment and selection standards have never been clearly defined in terms of education, work experience, and family backgrounds, and some WDL staffers claim that there has been some lowering of standards, particularly in New York, as the program and techniques have been perfected.

The scope of recruitment and the standards of selection can be changed by circumstance as well as by design. The senior field representative in Buffalo finds the major recruitment problem to be that WDL is running out of high school graduates with work experience. One New York staff member observes on the basis of his experience that there has been a decline in the quality of recruits in Harlem, and he has the impression that the same is true in Brooklyn. Expansion of the WDL program has increased the number of referral sources and made it more difficult to focus on high quality recruits. Moreover, as the staffer put it, "there's a lot of competition for black heads."

In Nashville the competition for qualified Negro youths is heightened by the presence of two black universities. Many blacks aspire to college, and WDL feels that it is competing directly for potential college students. WDL recruitment is made more difficult by a general Negro disdain for the building trades. Blacks in Nashville generally come into contact only with non-union black building tradesmen who work longer hours for lower wages than union journeymen. The senior field representative recalls that his own attitude in high school was that anyone who took shop was a "dummy." He does not feel that WDL has been getting the quality he would like to see in recruits.

The WDL tutor in Nashville finds that many high school graduates seem to be defective in basic skills, although many went to very good high schools. The better students often go to college, as do many mediocre ones. (The entrance requirements at Tennessee Agricultural and Industrial State—the black counterpart of the University of Tennessee—are very low.) WDL is left with students who were slow in school, though some are quite bright. The tutor feels the recruitment program should aim for better students who can do well in the building trades. So far, in Nashville WDL has been reaching neither the very best nor the very worst students.

With recruitment and selection, as with other aspects of the program, the results differ from city to city, and from neighborhood to neighborhood within cities. Selection standards will continue to vary by locality as long as WDL continues its flexible and pragmatic approach of allowing accommodations between its own standards and goals on the one hand and external labor market conditions on the other.

Tutoring and "Test-Busting." Many of WDL's tutoring techniques for "test-busting" were developed in the course of four successive examinations for the New York Sheet Metal Workers Local 28 apprenticeship program. The first was in February, 1965, when Local 28 held an open examination to select an apprenticeship class of 65. Of 340 applicants, 50 were Negroes and Puerto Ricans, with 28 of the Negroes recruited by WDL. WDL gave its recruits no tutoring other than a small amount of work in vocabulary and algebra. Twenty-two percent of the whites who took the test placed in the top 65. The highest scoring WDL recruit placed 68th; the next highest scoring Negro placed 97th. Three of the whites who scored in the top 65 declined positions, and the WDL recruit who scored 68th became the first Negro ever admitted to the Local 28 apprenticeship program.

In November, 1965, another exam was held by Local 28 for another class of 65 apprentices. This time more advance notice was given. The 25 WDL applicants were given 2 months of tutoring, $2\frac{1}{2}$ hours a day, 5 days a week. The tutoring was aimed at the particular kind of test, with no effort being made to provide general education. Fourteen of the 25 WDL applicants (56 percent) placed in the top 65. Fifty-one of the 135 white applicants (38 percent) placed in the top 65. The intensive tutoring had increased the percentage of WDL recruits who qualified from zero in the first test to 56 percent in the second.

A third apprenticeship exam was given in November 1966. Thirty-two of 147 applicants were Negroes recruited and tutored by WDL.

Twenty-four of the 32 Negroes (75 percent) placed in the top 65, compared to only 21 percent of the whites. Negroes achieved 9 of the top ten scores; one Negro turned in a perfect test paper. The officials of the Local 28 apprenticeship program refused to accept the spectacular success of WDL's applicants, declaring that they suspected "some nefarious means." Twenty-one of the 24 successful Negro applicants were finally admitted to the program under a court order.

The fourth exam was in November 1967. Thirty-four out of 400 applicants were WDL tutees. Eighteen of the 34 (53 percent) were admitted to the apprenticeship program. Taking the four exams together, WDL's tutoring techniques had succeeded in placing a total of 57 Negroes in Local 28's apprenticeship program, approximately 20 percent of all persons admitted.

Despite the improved tutoring techniques, WDL's test-busting program is in some ways vulnerable to changes in the tests. Until mid-1968, apprenticeship committees in New York used either one standard test (General Aptitude Test Battery) or various other tests selected and administered by New York University. Particularly in the case of the GATB test, WDL tutors have had great success in anticipating the nature of the questions and effectively tutoring for them, even in the two problem areas. Recently some apprenticeship committees in New York have changed to tests selected and administered by a different testing service in the New York Metropolitan area.

WDL has had markedly less success with tests of the new service than with prior tests, partly because of the increased difficulty of the math problem solving and verbal reasoning sections (the two areas most difficult for WDL trainees and least suitable for WDL's "drill" methods of instruction), and partly because constant shifting of tests by the new service interferes with accurate anticipation by WDL tutors. WDL's lack of success with the new tests is illustrated by the results of three recent examinations. Sixty-two WDL trainees took the April 1968 sheet metal test; 11 passed. Twenty-three WDL trainees took the July 1968, steam fitters' test; 4 passed. Forty-three WDL trainees took the October 1968, sheet metal test; 9 passed. WDL planned to challenge the steam fitters' test at the December 1968 hearings of the New York State Human Rights Commission, but the sheet metal workers' union is negotiating with WDL, because the craft needs new men and doesn't want the apprenticeship class held up by litigation.

WDL's experience with three rounds of testing for the sheet metal workers' apprenticeship program in Nashville affords another example of roadblocks to successful test-busting. The Nashville sheet metal union announced an apprenticeship test to be given in early October 1968 for a class of ten apprentices. WDL had only four weeks to tutor its applicants, most of whom were high school graduates, out of school for quite some time. WDL's Nashville tutor knows which of the available tests is used by each apprenticeship program. At one time the sheet metal apprenticeship committee relied solely on the GATB test, but before WDL began operating in Nashville, the committee had added a special math and spatial relations test to be given with the GATB test. WDL's tutor assumed that the special test would contain more complex math than GATB, and tutored accordingly. Seven WDL applicants took the GATB, given several days before the special math test, and all seven passed. These seven, and five whites, then took the special math test. Four of the five whites passed. All seven of the WDL applicants failed. The special test did not deal with geometry and other complex math, but rather was the same kind of test as GATB—addition, subtraction, multiplication, and division—but using fractions, decimals and mixed numbers rather than whole numbers. The tutor had erred; his tutees were unprepared to handle simple math with decimals and fractions, and were at a psychological disadvantage as well.

As a check, WDL made up its own test containing the same kinds of math questions as had appeared on the special test. When the WDL applicants who had failed the special math test also failed the WDL Sample test, WDL backed off from lodging any strong complaints of discrimination. An additional reason for forbearing from high-pressure protest was the announcement of a second test.

The sheet metal apprenticeship class was to consist of ten apprentices, for which there were now six openings, since only four people had passed the special math test. The apprenticeship committee announced that the program would be held open for 30 days and a new test given. The applicants who had taken the first test were ineligible for the second under union rules which barred them for six months from further tests. Furthermore, no one who had failed the first round of testing could be accepted into the apprenticeship program because the tests were required for acceptance. WDL was very much disappointed at having to recruit new people for the second round, only 2½ weeks away. A total of five people took the second tests in early November 1968. Two WDL trainees, and two whites passed. Two openings still remained in the apprentice class. The committee then announced a still further extension and a third round of testing. WDL decided not to recruit for round three because of the difficulty of recruiting qualified people in the month of December when employment in Nashville is at a peak.

Several conclusions are suggested by WDL's testing experiences.

WDL's test-busting techniques, which have achieved some spectacular successes, are substantially dependent upon accurate analysis of prior examinations and prediction of the nature of questions on future tests. Unannounced changes in tests or testing practices and procedure can undermine the results of long hours of tutoring. Even where test changes are without discriminatory intent, WDL's staff feels that the better-educated whites have a distinct advantage over WDL recruits with respect to taking and adapting to tests. Testing does not occur in a vacuum, and the success of WDL's program is dependent not just upon refined tutoring methods, but constant adjustment of those methods to changing tests and competition.

Dropouts from WDL. One goal of WDL and similar organizations is to prevent young Negroes from dropping out of programs in which they have enrolled. There is a definitional problem involved in judging WDL's success in meeting this goal.

Recruits are lost in the early stages of the WDL program for many reasons: some lack a birth certificate or medical certificate; some do not possess the qualifications required by the apprenticeship program which interests them or which is available at the time; some lie during the initial interview in the hope that their qualifications will not be checked; many simply change their mind or just never show up again. WDL does not, however, consider youths who leave prior to indenture a problem calling for any remedies at the present time, and accordingly does not include such youths in its definition of dropouts. Its definition of *dropout* is instead limited to the indentured apprentice who leaves his apprenticeship program. This definition of dropout as exclusively postindenture obscures some important points regarding the preindenture stages of the WDL program.

Many WDL recruits leave the program at various stages prior to indenture and for a variety of reasons. The single most serious cause of preindenture dropout is probably the many delays between the steps which precede the start of an apprenticeship program. The Cleveland carpenters, for example, accept apprenticeship applications in October; the written examination is given in November; the oral interview is in December; acceptances are announced in January; the apprenticeship program finally starts in February. Particularly critical is the delay between acceptance into an apprenticeship program and the actual start of work and training, which is often as long as several months.

The delay problem is further aggravated by some unions' policy of accepting applicants without regard to the availability of work. For example, 17 WDL applicants took the Nashville ironworker ap-

186

prenticeship examination on June 1, 1968. All 17 passed. Only one has been referred to a job, and that is some 80 miles from Nashville. The root of the problem is that the ironworkers, like other Nashville unions, set periodic test dates and accept apprentices even if there is no job demand.

Similarly the Buffalo WDL interviewed between 75 and 100 recruits to select 22 applicants for the ironworkers' apprenticeship examination in 1967. Fourteen of the 22 took the examination, and all 14 passed. Only one has actually been placed on a job as an indentured apprentice. For the 1967 Buffalo steam fitters' examination, WDL selected 28 recruits. Nine failed to obtain the necessary medical certificate. Of the remaining 19, 15 took the examination, and 4 were finally accepted into the apprenticeship program. An unusual amount of persistence is required to overcome the discouragement caused by so many delays.

Many applicants are lost during the tutoring sessions. Absenteeism is a common problem, which often requires individual attention from the tutors. In Harlem, WDL recently sent letters to the parents of applicants (many did not know that their sons were in the WDL program) in an effort to improve attendance. On one occasion in Nashville an applicant missed several classes in a row. The tutor knew that the man could be found in a particular bar at the same time every day. The tutor made a visit at the appropriate time, had a few drinks with the applicant, and talked the matter over; the applicant resumed attendance the next day.

Turning to the area of postindenture dropouts, WDL claims that in New York City the rate has been held steadily at about 6 percent, which is viewed as a low rate.[5] In Nashville, however, 20 WDL applicants have become indentured apprentices, 8 have dropped out voluntarily and one dismissed. All 9 of the dropouts were roofers. Neither an examination nor a high school diploma is required to become a roofer in Nashville, and WDL is acting merely as a referral conduit and not providing any preapprenticeship tutoring. The particular kind of roofing from which there have been dropouts is hard, dirty work. WDL's Nashville staff is not particularly worried by the roofer dropouts.

The postindenture dropout rate in Buffalo is 41 percent, considerably higher than that of New York, and the reasons for the high rate are more complex than in Nashville. As of December 1968, 28 of

---

[5] WDL's follow-up procedures—phone calls, visits, letters and periodic meetings —are not stringent enough to determine the current status of every WDL apprentice. The actual rate may therefore be higher than 6 percent.

WDL's cumulative total of 68 indentured apprentices had dropped out of building trades apprenticeship programs in Buffalo. The cement finishers, roofers, and plumbers were particularly hard hit, with dropout rates of 100 percent, 50 percent and 53 percent respectively. Roofing and cement finishing are relatively difficult and unattractive trades, but the high dropout rate among plumbers is more difficult to understand. The senior field representative in Buffalo thinks one significant cause of dropouts is the long period which often elapses between acceptance into an apprenticeship program and actual commencement of work. The Buffalo plumbers and carpenters tend to accept into their apprenticeship program more men than the number for whom there is work available. Such practices aggravate the problem of the time gap between acceptance and work.

WDL in Buffalo started recruiting for carpenter apprentices in December 1967. The apprenticeship examination was given in April 1968, and three WDL candidates passed. No jobs were then available. One of the three joined the military, one went to college, and the third left Buffalo. When work finally became available for carpenter apprentices in October or November of 1968, the man who had left Buffalo was contacted and brought back because the joint apprenticeship committee was very anxious to have at least one black apprentice. One apprentice plumber dropped out because he was not called to work. The plumber's problem was probably due to general unavailability of work at the time rather than to discrimination. The ironworkers gave a test in August 1967. Eighty applicants took it; 14 were WDL. All 14 WDL applicants passed and were placed on an eligible list. Only one, a thirty-year-old man with military experience, was accepted into the class of 25 apprentices. (A second was later accepted.) The remaining 12 stayed on the eligible list until it expired.

No Buffalo apprentice has been known to quit solely because of discontent with the pay, although one sheet metal apprentice was unhappy when he was placed in shop work where the rate is lower than in field work—a pay differential of which WDL had not been aware. Two WDL applicants who ranked at the top of the class for the bricklayers' apprentice program dropped out. WDL could not confirm their reasons, although one returned to his previous job at a factory which had been on strike during the bricklayers' recruitment period.

Some applicants accepted into Buffalo apprenticeship programs drop out to go to college. An apprentice ironworker starts his apprenticeship program at $4.00 an hour; the ironworkers' program is therefore attractive to youths waiting to start college or saving to go to college. (There have, however, been no dropouts from the iron-workers' program.)

A WDL staff member in New York suggests that part of the cause of the high dropout rate in Buffalo may be the disparity between the low starting wages of most apprentices and the high journeyman's rate sometimes emphasized by WDL recruitment publicity. In addition, there are well-paying industrial jobs available in Buffalo. A youngster may try an apprenticeship program paying a starting rate of $2.50 an hour and decide to switch to an industrial job paying $3.50 rather than serve the time necessary to progress to a higher rate in the apprenticeship program.

In December 1968 the staff of the Buffalo WDL office prepared a special report on dropouts in Buffalo. Table 2 shows the results. Eight of the 28 dropouts were men accepted into apprenticeship programs but not assigned to any work as of the time of dropping out. Seven dropped out because they did not like the work or found it too difficult or insecure. Two who dropped out enrolled in college. Some had assorted other reasons for quitting and some gave no reason, many switched to other occupations. Several trades had no dropouts and one had a 100 percent dropout rate.

Several important conclusions are consistent with the Buffalo dropout survey. Work in the building trades as a whole may be much less desirable in Buffalo than in New York City. Buffalo has far, far fewer of the large office and apartment construction projects that provide steady, long-term employment for so many apprentices and journeymen in New York City. Buffalo contractors therefore probably provide less stable employment than New York contractors. The apprenticeship programs of some of the building trades may be administered much less efficiently than others. In Buffalo, as in many cities, the building trades may to some extent be serving as a training ground for other industries, and some WDL dropouts would therefore be more employable in general as a result of their experience in the building trades.

The high dropout rate in Buffalo may also be due in some part to lack of diligence on the part of WDL in screening, in counseling, and particularly in follow-up procedures; or, the techniques developed in New York may need change or improvement to succeed in Buffalo. Furthermore, it is possible that WDL should not recruit for some of the building trades in some cities. In any event, it is clear that the dropout problem at least in Buffalo calls for continuing WDL attention.

Leadership and Administration. A large part of WDL's success is due to effective leadership and administration, but some leadership

TABLE 2: WORKERS' DEFENSE LEAGUE (BUFFALO): DROPOUTS AS OF DECEMBER, 1968 *

Trade	# of Indentured Apprentices	# of Dropouts [1]	Reasons for Dropping Out
Sheetmetal workers	9	4	No union assignment (1); didn't like type of work (2); quit and left Buffalo (1). (One now working at Bethlehem Steel; one driving a truck; and one working in a flour mill.)
Steamfitters	7	None	
Ironworkers	2	None	
Electricians	2	None	
Asbestos workers	2	None	
Plumbers	10	5	No union assignment (3); withdrew before being dismissed from apprenticeship program (1); school (1).
Roofers	17	9	No union assignment (4); didn't attend union school (2); didn't like work (2); injured (1). (One now working at Bethlehem Steel; one applied to Steamfitters; two going to college.)
Cement masons	8	8	Didn't like work (1); work too hard (1); left Buffalo (1); medical reasons (1); in jail in Canada (1); did not want to risk job insecurity (1); no reason (2). (One now working at Bethlehem Steel; one a department store junior salesman.)
Carpenters	3	None	
Bricklayers	8	2	One went back to old job; one never showed up at apprentice school.

Totals:	68	28	In addition to the above, 3 out of 5 WDL-placed industrial apprentices dropped out: one employee of Bethlehem Steel returned to a hospital job; one survey assistant entered Project JUSTICE. The two are still industrial apprentices working at General Motors and Bethlehem, respectively.

Source: Information obtained from the WDL.
[1] Leaving for military service not included in dropouts.

problems now appear to be emerging. Key leaders are spread thinly and, because of WDL's success, are increasingly in demand to consult and assist with other programs. The increasing size and geographic dispersal of the staff dissipates the personal influence exercised by key leaders. Such problems are not unique to WDL and can be controlled by a reasonable degree of leadership continuity combined with skillful selection of new staff. Institutionalization is a challenge to any program pioneered by a few strong and devoted leaders, but many other programs have survived the vicissitudes of expansion and leadership turnover.

The WDL staff has remained lean. The basic personnel of each field office consists of a senior field representative, a junior field representative, a tutor, and a secretary. Field representatives carry out recruiting, selecting, interviewing and counseling activities. They also deal with joint apprenticeship committees to learn the time, place and admissions procedures of the apprenticeship programs in the various trades. Tutors are responsible for the classroom preparation of applicants for the written apprenticeship examinations. All staff members participate in the follow-up and supportive services.

In addition to the eight field offices, WDL recently opened a national administrative headquarters in Brooklyn. The central administrative staff has about ten members including the Director, assistant director, Executive Secretary, tutor coordinator and their secretaries.

To date, there appear to have been no serious administrative conflicts between field staff and central administrators. But one administrator expresses concern for problems which may arise as increasing staff size diminishes informality and the influence of personal leadership. There has been some administrative resistance to the amount of time spent by Nashville staff members on the General Educational Development (GED) program.

Virtually all of WDL's staff members are Negroes. Marshall and Briggs concluded in their study that the staff should be so composed because of the credibility gap between the black community and the apprenticeship establishment, the need to instill in applicants racial pride and a will to succeed, and the necessity to visit the ghetto to talk with recruits and their parents. As WDL progresses, the credibility gap presumably narrows; however, the other factors may remain constant. WDL might benefit from adding to each office's staff a building trades union official or member, at least on a part-time or consulting basis, to act as a liaison between WDL and the unions. A white staff member might best serve this function.

Obtaining good tutors is a substantial problem. WDL's national tutor coordinator states that a good WDL tutor must combine two critical qualities: knowledge of, and a feeling for mathematics and, more important, an ability to relate to ghetto youths. This combination is difficult to find.

Many WDL applicants have been out of school for several years, and are no longer (if they ever were) at home in the classroom. For them, the examination looms large at the end of the road and causes many to freeze at the outset. The tutor must offer such recruits continual reassurance and incentive to maintain their classroom attendance and attention. White female schoolteachers have served well in Nashville's GED program, but WDL does not believe they would be effective in the WDL program, where there is more time pressure because of shorter notice before exams and where discipline is a much greater problem.

Relationships with Unions. As civil rights criticism of discrimination in the building trades intensified during the 1950's and 1960's, union and apprenticeship officials often became defensive. They felt that the building trades were being unfairly singled out for a problem that is common to many other social institutions. They resented government action which appeared to them to be a "numbers game" of quotas and preferential treatment under the mantle of "affirmative action,'" and they feared that craft standards would be undermined by flooding the market with underqualified, and only partly trained, apprentices.

Against this background, WDL made two related decisions which seem to have been important in the success of its program. One decision was not to challenge the apprenticeship system, seek lowering of apprenticeship entry requirements, nor to interfere with other apprenticeship admissions procedures in order to increase minority participation. The other was to seek actively to establish sound working relationships with union officials.

Many trade unionists initially suspected the Workers' Defense League of having Communist affiliations, but they soon learned that it was a pragmatic organization seeking neither to produce a civil rights confrontation nor to embarrass the building trades unions. By limiting its activities to placing minority group members into existing programs without altering their structure, WDL has been able gradually to win the confidence of many union leaders. It has regularly sought and received advice from AFL–CIO civil rights staffs at both the national and local levels. Most major craft unions in New York City, though not legally required to do so, now give WDL sufficient advance notice to assure adequate opportunity for the filing of minority applications. In 1967 the chairman of the New York City and State Building Trades councils declared that WDL applicants have proven to be "good apprentices," and urged local unions to cooperate with WDL's program. The AFL–CIO's 1967 constitutional convention endorsed WDL, and in February 1968 the AFL–CIO Building and Construction Trades Department pledged support of WDL's program.

WDL's relationships with building trades unions are probably sounder than those of any other preapprenticeship organization. However, there are still problems. Endorsements at the national and state levels do not guarantee enlightened cooperation at the local level. Many craft locals are powerful and quite autonomous. Some have been distinctly less cooperative than others. WDL's program can be readily thwarted, at least temporarily, by a variety of discriminatory techniques and even by plain indifference. WDL's efforts to build sound relationships, however, have contributed considerably to the lessening of such hostility.

WDL's experience in Nashville suggests that special arrangements may be useful in southern cities. When WDL's Nashville office opened, its staff included a representative of the local building trades council, known as a "tradesman specialist."

Relationships with Employers. Apprenticeship programs are commonly administered by joint union-management apprenticeship committees. Employers have equal representation with unions on the committees. In keeping with the general weakness and disorganization of construction contractors in their relations with craft unions, employer representatives on the joint apprenticeship committees tend to be passive. In some situations, the union representatives have absolute control and can effectively prevent employer access to apprenticeship data. WDL feels that, in general, employers in the construction industry have not been fully aware of their powers and duties in the area of apprenticeship training.

On-the-Job Reactions. Apprenticeship programs teach skills through on-the-job training and related classroom instruction. Classroom instruction may be a full-time course which precedes the start of job-site work or an evening program concurrent with full-time work. In some programs, employers pay the apprentices' wages while they attend classes during the working day.

At the job site, apprentices have their first substantial contact with the journeymen of their craft. The journeymen teach the practical skills and applied techniques which the apprentice is to learn in his years of on-the-job training. A concerted refusal on the part of journeymen to teach apprentices could effectively hinder an apprenticeship program. Short of such extreme reaction, the attitude and cooperation of the journeymen greatly affects the quality and tone of apprenticeship training.

Considering the building trades' historic patterns of racial discrimination and strong resistance to change, one might have anticipated a variety of problems at the job site as WDL's successful recruits began their work. Job site integration, however, has been the most minor problem in the WDL program. Subject to some qualifications noted below, WDL's recruits have generally made a smooth transition into apprentice status.

During their WDL training recruits are taught that a certain degree of hazing of apprentices is customary in many of the building trades. Ironworkers, for example, traditionally call apprentices "punks." An apprentice who knows this in advance is much less likely to feel that he has been insulted by a racial slur. WDL emphasizes the goal of becoming qualified journeymen, not that of overcoming the accumulated prejudices of union craftsmen. It attempts to turn out tough, practically oriented apprentices who will be able to withstand racial and other pressures in the course of their apprenticeships.

The contractors who employ apprentices have varied in their attitudes—from neutrality to enthusiasm. One contractor called all his employees together and announced that he would fire anyone showing racial bias. Another held individual conversations with every one of his employees. More typical, however, is the contractor who remains passive, absorbing minority apprentices without any special preparation. Contractors' discussions of racial problems generally tend to be with foremen rather than with rank and file journeymen, even though it is the journeymen who must teach the apprentices the skills of the trade.

While contractors differ in their approaches to on-the-job integration of minority workers, any contractor who is bidding for government jobs subject to the Civil Rights Act is likely to view WDL as an asset, indeed a boon, in helping to satisfy affirmative action requirements. Such a contractor may or may not make an effort to smooth the on-the-job transition; his main concern is simply to have enough Negroes on the job no matter what the nature of their relationship with their fellow workers.

Union officials understand the need for compliance with the Civil Rights Act, and the business agents and apprenticeship committees have generally been cooperative in solving job-site problems. Even in unions whose officials have resisted WDL's apprenticeship efforts, job sites have generally been immune from any official interference with minority apprentices, although some joint apprenticeship committees tend to delay processing complaints of minority apprentices.

Those job site problems which do arise are generally the product of individual relationships between apprentice and rank and file journeymen. Some physical altercations have occurred, but they are infrequent, and not always a product of racial tension.

A problem which is more serious and also more frequent is the failure or refusal of journeymen to offer proper teaching and training to minority apprentices on the job. Although similar complaints are heard from white apprentices, in some instances the journeymen's attitudes seem discriminatory. The problem varies in intensity from trade to trade. In New York City, there have been a number of complaints by WDL sheet metal apprentices that the journeymen monopolize the work of setting up machines, and that they limit the apprentices to pushing the button to operate them. One sheet metal apprentice in his fourth term told WDL he would be willing to take a cut in pay to go back and learn some of the skills and techniques he had missed. Another, earning $3.00 an hour in the second year of the sheet metal program, resigned to work at $1.90 an hour in the electricians' apprenticeship program, where he felt he would learn more. Only in the sheetmetal trade in New York does the problem reach significant dimensions. There have been no such complaints from the carpenters or plumbers, and most WDL trainees in ironworking have progressed so rapidly in their training that they are earning over scale.

While WDL's trainees have, in general, worked into sound relationships with journeymen on the job, it does not follow that they feel wholly accepted and part of their crafts. Many WDL apprentices approach their first job site assignment with trepidation, particularly when they are among the first Negro apprentices. For their part, many journeymen view minority workers as a threat to their job security and are not as enlightened as their union leaders about the compelling necessity for affirmative action. A few WDL apprentices have complained about, or expressed unhappiness at, not really being accepted in their crafts. WDL's view is that if lack of acceptance doesn't interfere with training and work, attitudes and acceptance by journeymen do not affect the practical goals of the WDL program.

In dealing with the specific incidents which, from time to time, do arise, WDL first talks with the apprentice and then with the union. It never deals directly with the contractor. WDL reports that virtually all job-site problems, except teaching difficulties in the sheet metal program, have been easily resolved.

Relationships with the Government. Various kinds of legislation, regulations, and rulings have helped to provide a favorable climate for WDL's programs: state fair employment practices laws, federal and state apprenticeship regulations, NLRB rulings, executive orders, antidiscrimination clauses in government contracts, and the Civil Rights Act of 1964. Judicial remedies have aided WDL at several critical junctures and have greatly assisted in increasing the objectivity of admissions standards and fairness in the administering admissions procedures.

There are several federal administrative agencies concerned with apprenticeship: the Secretary of Labor's Advisory Committee on Equal Opportunity in Apprenticeship and Training; the Labor Department's Bureau of Apprenticeship Training; and the Manpower Administration's Apprenticeship Information Centers. In theory, both the Bureau of Apprenticeship Training and the Apprenticeship Information Centers are to be sources of apprenticeship information. The Apprenticeship Information Centers are supposed to supply recruits for apprenticeship and preapprenticeship programs. In actuality, WDL has supplied far more information than it has received, and the Apprenticeship Information Centers have supplied no recruits. The most important federal activity is funding: The day-to-day administration of WDL's apprenticeship program is now entirely financed by federal funds.

Transferability. There are two aspects of transferability. The first is the extent to which the WDL program as developed in New York City can be transferred and successfully applied in other cities. The second is the extent to which WDL's techniques are applicable to other programs designed to increase minority group employment opportunities.

At the time of their writing, Marshall and Briggs felt it was too early to evaluate the geographic transferability of WDL. The recent evidence from Buffalo and Nashville suggests that the program is in some measure transferable. WDL's prime goal—preparing and training minority youths for placement in apprenticeship programs—is being achieved in these cities by means of the program and techniques developed in New York.

A major qualification to this observation arises from the post-indenture dropout problem which exists in Nashville and is serious in Buffalo. It is too early to tell whether the dropout problem can be remedied by more diligent use of the recruitment, selection, counseling, and follow-up techniques developed in New York. It may be that labor markets in some areas are more suitable than others to WDL's program, and it may be that, in a given city, some specific trades are less amenable than others. It does not follow from the basic transferability of WDL's program that it would be possible to implement it successfully in every apprenticeship program of every city. Pressure from the federal government and civil rights groups, the existence of a large minority population, and a large volume of construction work may all be essential to the success of transfer attempts.

Marshall and Briggs also concluded that a prime ingredient of the success of WDL and similar programs is the dedication and devotion of staff members to a carefully circumscribed goal. This writer agrees that, particularly in the early stages of a new program, staff members must be prepared to work long hours and to experiment with a variety of measures and techniques. Unfortunately, society has a limited supply of dedicated, brilliant pioneers capable of making the break throughs necessary to the success of new programs. Long-term survival depends upon the establishment of routines that do not depend on brilliant leaders to succeed. The major lesson for other minority opportunity programs provided by WDL may be that staff members must be capable of relating effectively to those whom they seek to help.

Model Cities and Future Prospects. Apprenticeship is not the only route to journeyman status in the building trades, and in fact, only a rather small proportion of journeymen have entered their trades through the apprenticeship system. The 1963 *Manpower Report of the President* projected that from 1960 to 1970 the three crafts which meet the highest proportion of their manpower needs through apprenticeship programs—electricians, bricklayers and sheet metal workers—would meet only 36 percent, 22 percent and 21 percent, respectively, of their needs. This suggests that there may be other routes toward increased Negro participation in the building trades.

WDL is currently extending its activities beyond preapprenticeship training. In Buffalo, it is administering a program, Project JUSTICE, designed to upgrade to union journeymen blacks such as non-union craftsmen who already have some experience in the building trades. In Boston, WDL is participating in a pioneer agreement whereby a certain number of minority group craftsmen will work on Model Cities projects without going through the formal apprenticeship system.

In 1967 the Buffalo building trades took 200 apprentices, of whom 50 were WDL trainees. The field representative, however, fears that WDL's 25 percent share of new apprentices cannot be maintained long enough for blacks to become a significant force in the Buffalo building trades unions. Moreover, Buffalo's apprenticeship programs as a whole are not keeping up with the growth of the construction industry. The size of apprenticeship classes is too small in relation to the 15,000 journeymen in the Buffalo building trades; even with a steady 25 percent share of apprenticeships for blacks, it would take many years to correct the imbalance of past discrimination unless apprenticeship programs were dramatically expanded. As WDL now stands, it may be just performing a service for Buffalo unions which feel they must have some blacks and can best obtain them through WDL.

In Nashville, the senior field representative estimates that the building trades are 50 percent non-union. Those contractors who have both union and non-union crews use the non-union crews wherever they can to make a higher profit. There are several black contractors—all non-union. Non-union employees earn less and have less assurance of learning a trade. Nashville's 50 percent non-union factor helps account for its relatively small number of apprenticeship opportunities. For example, in December 1967, Cleveland had openings for 120 apprentice plumbers, while Nashville had openings for perhaps 10 or 20.

Nashville is part of the Model Cities program, which unions may see as a route to increased unionism in the building trades. The Nashville Model Cities Citizens Committee wants black contractors to have some of the work, and indeed Model Cities construction workers are supposed to come from target neighborhoods. However, there are not enough qualified craftsmen in Nashville's target areas, and the black contractors are not equipped to train any substantial number of new ones. Meanwhile, there is increasing pressure on the unions to raise their black membership.

Model Cities therefore has the potential of opening routes into the building trades unions for blacks who presently work for non-union contractors. If the unions become involved in Model Cities, there will be training programs, and WDL's future in Nashville may well be linked to such programs.

There are, of course, many cities other than Nashville in the Model Cities program, and the next big step for WDL may be to concentrate on providing minority representation in Model Cities projects.

APPENDIX A:* APPRENTICES IN SELECTED CONSTRUCTION TRADES REGISTERED WITH STATE APPRENTICESHIP AGENCIES OR BUREAU OF APPRENTICESHIP AND TRAINING FOR THE CALENDAR YEAR 1965

Trade	Active at Beginning of Period	Apprentice Actions for Period			Active at End of Period
		New Registrations	Completions	Cancellations	
Brick, stone, & tile	8,389	3,181	1,342	1,042	9,186
Carpenters	24,345	10,068	3,272	6,935	24,206
Cement masons	1,701	602	297	340	1,666
Electricians	20,585	7,181	3,327	2,330	22,109
Glaziers	1,002	379	222	146	1,013
Lathers	1,992	369	268	432	1,661
Painters	6,586	2,735	969	2,022	6,330
Plasterers	1,431	391	181	306	1,335
Plumbers, pipefitters	21,837	6,222	3,050	2,312	22,697
Roofers	2,226	1,277	272	824	2,407
Sheet metal workers	10,285	3,452	1,477	1,514	10,746
Structural ironworkers	5,223	2,379	870	829	5,903
Not classified above	4,623	2,664	620	994	5,673
Total	110,225	40,900	16,167	20,026	114,932

* Source: Marshall & Briggs. [All appendices have been taken from Marshall and Briggs.]

199

APPENDIX B: MINIMUM QUALIFICATIONS FOR SELECTED APPRENTICESHIP PROGRAMS IN NEW YORK CITY*

Local Craft Unions	Grade Completed	Residence Requirement	U.S. Citizenship or Declaration of Intention	Age (yrs.) Minimum	Age (yrs.) Maximum	Age (yrs.) Veterans' Maximum	Police Clearance Required	Test Scores Minimum Passing	Test Scores Out of Maximum Points
Bricklayers Local 34	12th	3 yrs.	Yes	17	21	25	—	—	—
Carpenters—District Council	12th	—	Yes	17	25	—	be willing to sign a statement indicating any police record	—	—
Electrician Local 3	12th	5 yrs.	Yes	18	21	—	—	65	100
Ironworker Local 40	10th	—	Yes	18	28	—	—	pass aptitude test	—
Ironworker Local 580	12th	—	Yes	18	25	—	must not have drug addiction record	71	100
Metal Lathers Local 46	12th	3 yrs.	No	18	25	—	—	—	—
Painters—District Council 9	12th	—	No	18	25	—	—	letter of reference	
Plasterers Local 60	9th	1 yr.	No	18	21	26	—	—	—
Cement Masons Local 780	8th	—	No	18	21	25	—	—	—
Plumbers Local 1	12th†	3 yrs.	Yes	17	21	25	—	—	—
Plumbers Local 2	12th†	3 yrs.	Yes	18	21	25	be willing to sign statement attesting to lack of criminal record	—	—
Roofers Local 8	12th	3 yrs.	U.S. citizenship only	18	30	—	—	70	100
Sheetmetal Workers Local 28	11th	—	No	18	23	25	—	—	—
Steamfitters Local 638	12th	3 yrs.	Yes	18	24	28	Yes	55	100

* Grades must average at least 70 percent.

† Source: New York State Commission for Human Rights, Analysis of Apprenticeship Selection Standards (March 1968).

APPENDIX C: SELECTION STANDARDS: SUMMARY OF MAXIMUM POINTS ASSIGNED FOR APPRENTICE QUALIFICATION IN NEW YORK CITY*

	General Education	Technical Education	High School Grades	Work Experience	Seniority	Military Service	Written Tests	Oral	Other	Total Points
Bricklayers Local 34	15	—	—	—	10	—	50	25	—	100
Carpenters—District Council	10	10	—	—	—	—	55	25	—	100
Electricians Local 3	—	—	—	—	—	—	—	—	—	—
Ironworker Local 40	5	—	—	—	—	—	40	25	30†	100
Ironworker Local 580	—	—	20	—	—	10	45	25	—	100
Metal Lathers Local 46	10	—	30	—	—	—	35	25	—	100
Painters—District Council 9	10	—	—	—	—	—	25	10	—	55
Plasterers Local 60	15	20	—	20	10	10	—	25	—	100
Cement Masons Local 780	50	20	—	—	10	5	—	25	—	100
Plumbers Local 1	—	10‡	80	10‡	—	—	—	10	—	100
Plumbers Local 2	—	—	45	—	—	—	45	10	—	100
Roofers Local 8	—	—	30	—	—	5	40	25	—	100
Sheetmetal Workers Local 28	—	—	—	—	—	—	750	150	—	900
Steamfitters Local 638	—	—	—	—	—	—	90	10	—	100

* Source: New York State Commission for Human Rights, *Analysis of Apprenticeship Selection Standards* (March 1968).

† Based on competitive Physical Agility Test.

‡ Maximum points given for technical education or work experience.

APPENDIX D: APPRENTICE AND JOURNEYMAN WAGES IN NEW YORK CITY, 1967-8

| | Wage Rates | |
Trade	Apprentice (beginning rate)	Journeyman
Bricklayer	$2.90 hr.	6.00 hr.
Carpenter (construction)	3.00 hr.	$5.80 hr.
Electrician	1.90 hr.	6.23 hr.
Electric motor repairman	60% of Journeyman	N.A.*
Folding box adjustor	1.95 hr.	N.A.
Glazier	2.70 hr.	5.40 hr.
Ironworker	4.35 hr.	6.55 hr.
Marble setter	80.00 wk.	5.05 hr.
Plasterers	66.25 wk.	N.A.
Plumber	1.90 hr.	8.00 hr.
Roofer	2.50 hr.	5.61 hr.
Sheet metal worker	2.25 hr.	6.20 hr.
Steamfitter	2.25 hr.	5.50 hr.
Stone derrickman and riggers	3.00 hr.	N.A.
Stone setter (mason)	2.88 hr.	5.96 hr.
Structural steel & bridge painter	3.50 hr.	5.50 hr.
Wire, wood, and metal lathers	3.15 hr.	6.00 hr.

Source: Joint Apprenticeship Program of the Workers' Defense League—A. Philip Randolph Educational Fund.
* [Not available.]

MONTHLY ACTIVITY REPORT ON OUTREACH PROGRAMS

CONTRACTOR'S NAME	Joint Apprenticeship Program of the Workers' Defense League, A. Philip Randolph Educational Fund	CITY	Brooklyn, N. Y.

Report for Month	October, 1968	Contract No.	34-7-0025-000
Starting Date	Jan. 1, 1967	Completion Date	Jan., 1969

Number of Trainees in Contract 250

	Monthly Total	Cumulative Total to Current Date
1. Potential Trainees Recruited	200	2056
Referrals by Apprenticeship Information Center	0	0
2. Referred for Appraisal (List by Name for current month—Page 2)	0	0
3. Status of Applicants in Supportive Services:		
a. Undergoing Tutoring	60	816
b. Full Applications on file with Joint Apprenticeship Training Committee	100	480
c. Awaiting JATC Exams	100	390
d. Passed Exams and Waiting JATC Action	0	299
e. Indentured (List by name for current month—Page 3)	11	272
f. Documents obtained:	150	2322
(1) Birth Certificate		
(2) High School Diploma		
(3) High School Equivalency		
4. Applicants dropped from Supportive Services		
a. Voluntary	0	117
b. Dismissed	0	0
5. Indentured apprentices dropped (see page 4)		
a. Voluntary	2	4
b. Dismissed	0	0
6. Applicants not indentured by JATC	0	0

Discussion

QUINN MILLS °

The Workers' Defense League—A. Philip Randolph Fund currently conducts outreach, counseling, and tutoring programs in eight cities with the purpose of apprenticing minority group youth to the building and construction trades. This program has become the prototype for similar efforts conducted by various groups including the Urban League, local Building and Construction Trades Councils, and the Opportunities Industrialization Center in over 52 cities. The proportion of blacks entering apprenticeship programs had climbed from about 3.5 percent only a few years ago to 7.5 percent by late 1968.[1] The WDL-type program has become the major method of formal recruitment of black youth for building trades apprenticeship.

The strategy of the WDL to date has been to accept the standards and selection procedures determined by the joint apprenticeship councils of the various trades, and to recruit and prepare minority group youth to meet and pass entrance requirements. Only in cases of overtly discriminatory standards or methods of selection has WDL challenged the joint committees. WDL tactics inevitably involve selecting better qualified youth, reflecting the preference of apprenticeship committees for well-educated and highly instructed youth. As described by Mr. Pinkus, the program involves six steps: recruiting, testing, counseling, preparing of apprenticeship applications, tutoring for entrance exams, and follow up.

The program has developed some degree of rapport with employers and unions in the building and construction industries,

---

° D. Q. Mills is an assistant professor of Industrial Relations at the Massachusetts Institute of Technology.

[1] Racial integration in the building trades follows the pattern of most American industries. Roughly the same proportion of construction workmen are blacks as the proportion of the population generally. However, blacks are concentrated in lower-skilled employment, particularly in the laborers classification. The proportion of blacks in the skilled mechanical trades (e.g., plumbers and electricians) is definitely low, as is the case among skilled trades in other major industries such as automobiles, steel, electric utilities, etc.

204

based, apparently, on the latter's respect for the thoroughness of the WDL effort and for the competence of its recruits. Program directors exert considerable effort to become familiar with the peculiar characteristics of employment and labor relations in construction. Familiarity with the industry allows well-considered initiatives and develops cooperation with labor and contractors. Thus, in several cases joint apprenticeship committees have begun to notify the WDL of apprenticeship openings privately and well in advance of general publicity.

There are currently several problems affecting the operation of WDL programs, none of which appears likely, however, to imperil their existence or effectiveness. First, there has been a rather high rate of WDL dropouts from apprenticeship programs in certain crafts and cities. Second, the recruitment of qualified applicants has become more difficult. Third, conditions (especially with respect to the nature and volume of work) have not been as favorable to placing and retaining apprentices in some cities as in others. The transferability of the WDL approach to weakly unionized areas, to depressed building markets, etc. is likely to be difficult. Fourth, as a greater number of programs are created, obtaining qualified staff becomes increasingly difficult. Orientation of people from other industries to construction practices has proven difficult.

A group of more basic issues may also be raised regarding programs which prepare minority group youth for apprenticeship. First, integration of the building trades will be necessarily slow if it is accomplished only through indenturing apprentices. For most building trades in most of the country (excluding primarily the mechanical trades and all crafts in the large Eastern cities) informal means, rather than apprenticeship, are the major source of manpower. National policy regarding integration of the trades should concern itself with informal routes of entry as well as with apprenticeship.

Second, the WDL approach has thus far avoided serious efforts to enlarge apprenticeship classes, to alter selection criteria, to modify techniques and periods of training, etc. Issues regarding size and content of apprenticeship are, of course, of wider significance than race specifically. It has been a strength of the WDL approach that it concentrates on its primary objective, apprenticeship opportunities for blacks. However, if informal or nonapprenticeship entry routes to the trades are to be exploited or created for blacks, the difficult issues of insuring training and compensation standards, continuity of employment for trainees, etc., must be faced. Clearly the quality and content of training are critical to the trainee's ability to earn the wage, find jobs, and remain in the industry, and be accepted by other craftsmen. Further, WDL has been able to largely ignore the industrial relations problems respecting workers' rights and privileges, which would occur in a non-union context.

Finally, programs of preparing for apprenticeship are subject to the basic perils of all manpower programs. First, if economic conditions worsen significantly there will be few jobs available for entry to the trades. Second, program staff tend to conceive of the program process itself (recruitment, tutoring, etc.) as the objective of the program, concentrating on processing people through a series of procedures rather than on adapting procedures to the placement of applicants in apprenticeship programs. Consequently, administrators must keep clearly in mind the objectives of the program (in this case, to apprentice nonwhite youths to the building trades), and retain flexibility in the elements of the program. WDL appears to have had remarkable success thus far in avoiding this bureaucratic snare.

8

Project 100,000

BY *HAROLD WOOL* AND *ELI S. FLYER* *

INTRODUCTION

The military services, by any quantitative measure, rank as the nation's largest single employer and trainer of manpower. During the past decade, the number of men on active duty has ranged between 2.5 and 3.5 million. To maintain these strengths, the armed services have recruited between 500,000 and 1.0 million new entrants per year, both through voluntary programs and the draft. Since most new entrants enter service shortly after leaving school, with little or no relevant occupational training or work experience, the Department of Defense has also been compelled to operate the nation's largest vocational training establishment. Although this occupational training is designed to meet specific military needs, most of it has some potential transferability to civilian jobs: Only 14 percent of enlisted positions are in strictly military-type skills, such as infantry, armor, or artillery.

The sheer magnitude of the military personnel operation and its high national priority for men and resources have stimulated—and made possible—numerous innovations over the years in the selection, training, and management of personnel. The armed services have pioneered in the use of psy-

---

* The authors wish to express their appreciation to Mr. Irving Greenberg and Mr. Frank McKernan, project directors for Project 100,000 and Project Transition, respectively, who provided essential information and helpful comments on this paper.

chological tests; they have introduced many innovations in training methods, ranging from audiovisual aids, training simulators, and related devices to the use of instructional TV and programmed learning. The military have also pioneered in applying operations research techniques to solving complex problems of personnel assignment, distribution, and management. Thus, as in other fields of technology, the armed services have often served as a vast national proving ground for testing new methods and approaches to the management of personnel.

The present paper describes two of these most recent program innovations, assigned the code names of "Project 100,000" and "Project Transition," respectively. These projects are not focused on exploiting any single new technique or gadget, but they do provide for the application and further exploitation of recent advances in the art of personnel selection and training. Nor are they designed for uniquely military objectives; although, as we shall see, they are compatible with, and do offer a potential for, significant "payoff" in meeting military manpower program objectives. Rather, they have had in common the primary objective of utilizing the military manpower system, with its established capability for the training of manpower, to advance a high priority national manpower objective: increasing the skills and employability of disadvantaged youth.

The first of these programs, Project 100,000, provides for the acceptance into service, as volunteers or draftees, of large numbers of young men who would not previously have qualified, primarily because of failure to receive certain minimum scores on the written qualification tests; it also provides for their training and utilization in a wide spectrum of military skills. A related effort, Project Transition, is designed to assist these and other servicemen nearing the end of their tours of duty to prepare for future civilian work careers through programs of counseling, training, education, and job placement.

In this paper we shall review in turn: (1) the policy considerations leading to the initiation of each of these programs, (2) a description of the programs and of their results to date, and (3) some possible implications for employment policy both in the military and civilian sectors of the economy.

SOME POLICY PERSPECTIVES: THE ROLE OF MENTAL APTITUDE STANDARDS

In order to qualify for military service, young men must meet certain minimum mental, physical, and moral standards of fitness based on examinations conducted for all the services at Armed Forces Examining and Entrance Stations in major cities throughout the country. The basic physical and moral standards have not been materially modified since the end of World War II, but the administration of these standards has been changed over the years, mainly for the purpose of greater uniformity and reliability. The mental standards have, however, fluctuated considerably over this period. A description of these mental standards provides an essential backdrop for considering the recent program initiatives under Project 100,000.

Since the closing years of World War II, all military services have established certain minimum passing scores on a psychological test or tests as necessary conditions for enlistment or induction into service. Reliance on these psychological tests has stemmed from the operational need for an objective and rapid method of mass screening to predict trainability and potential usefulness in military service.

The standard screening test used since 1950 has been the Armed Forces Qualification Test (AFQT). This test includes one hundred questions equally divided among four subtest areas: vocabulary, arithmetic, spatial relations, and mechanical ability (i.e., ability to interrelate tools and equipment). Scores are normally expressed as percentile scores. A percentile score of 10 represents the score which would be attained or exceeded by 90 percent of the "standard" population, as established originally by World War II testing experience. For qualitatively allocating new entrants, certain broad mental groups have been established, based on the scores on this or an equivalent test as indicated below:

Mental Group	Percentile Score
I	93-100
II	65-92
III	31-64
IV	10-30
V	9 and below

Mental Group III corresponds to a range of about one standard deviation of the population mean and may be construed as the "average" group in terms of mental ability. Mental Groups I and II correspond to the "above average" groups; Mental Groups IV and V, to those "below average."

In addition to the AFQT, the military services have made increased use of aptitude test batteries in the initial selection and classification of personnel. These test batteries are designed to predict the success of individuals in various occupational areas, such as mechanical, technical, clerical, or combat. Individuals applying for enlistment under certain options providing for assignment to a particular school or occupational area must receive minimum qualifying scores in the corresponding aptitude area. In addition, in the past decade the aptitude tests have been used as a supplementary screening device for applicants or draft registrants receiving marginal passing scores on the AFQT, i.e., Mental Group IV's.

The extent of historical fluctuation in entry standards based on these or predecessor tests is suggested by the following summary:

- During the closing years of World War II, initial selection standards had been reduced to a level which permitted large numbers of functionally illiterate individuals to qualify for service. Special training units, providing up to 12 weeks of initial literacy training, were established for those classified as illiterates or slow learners. Estimates based on Selective Service data indicate that by the close of the war less than 5 percent of all men aged 19–25 years had been disqualified solely because of failure to meet mental requirements.

- In the years immediately following the end of World War II, qualification standards were raised by all the services, as they adapted to the needs of a much smaller regular force.

- Under the Selective Service Act of 1948, the Congress prescribed for the first time a statutory mental standard for induction, equivalent to a percentile score of 13 on the AFQT. Enlistment standards however continued to be set unilaterally by each service and were generally higher than the draft standard.

- In June 1951, in the face of a shrinking manpower pool during the Korean War, this standard was lowered to a percentile score of 10. This standard applied only to draftees; however, under Department of Defense policy the same minimum score was set for enlistees, as well, as part of a "qualitative distribution" policy to assure a proportionate qualitative allocation of new enlisted entrants into all services.

- With a reduction in requirements for new personnel and a growing manpower pool of draft availables following the end of the Korean War, the Department of Defense requested and obtained authority from Congress in 1958 to modify the standard of qualification for service, except in periods of declared war or national emergency. Under this authority, the mental test standard for draftees was raised by requiring those scoring in Mental Group IV on the AFQT to pass certain supplemental aptitude test batteries. Concurrently, enlistment standards were raised in all services to at least the 21st percentile on the AFQT, with supplementary aptitude tests or educational requirements imposed by most services for those in the marginal Group IV category.

The raising of mental test standards in the late 1950's and early 1960's was justified by military officials on two main grounds: (1) increasing requirements for higher aptitude personnel capable of training and assignment in the more technical specialties and (2) evidence that, irrespective of occupational specialty, individuals with low test scores, i.e., Mental Group IV's, accounted for a disproportionate share of disciplinary problems. Under conditions of a growing total pool of draft-available men, an increase in mental test standards had therefore seemed both feasible and desirable from a military personnel management standpoint.

These relatively high qualification standards for service were however subject to criticism for several reasons. The increase in mental test standards following 1958 was inevitably accompanied by a sharp increase in the percentage of draft-age men rejected for service. Department of Defense estimates indicate that the overall rejection rates, i.e., the percentage of all draft-age men in the population who would have been disqualified for military service for all causes—mental, physical, or moral—rose from about 24 percent during the Korean War period to 32 percent in August 1958–60 and to an estimated peak of 35 percent in 1964. The major factor in this increase was clearly the raising of mental standards. Between the early 1950's and 1964, the estimated proportion of all youth disqualified solely because of mental test failure had nearly doubled: from less than 8 percent in 1950–53 to about 15 percent in 1964. An even higher proportion of youth, moreover—probably about 20 percent—failed to qualify under the more selective enlistment standards then in effect.

Two other aspects of the rejection rate statistics have also commanded attention in this context. Draftee rejection rates, as measured by results of preinduction examinations, were found to vary widely among the various states, and also by race. Geographically, the draftee rejection rates for all causes, in the period August

1958–December 1965, ranged from 35.6 percent in the West North Central states to 57.9 percent in the East South Central region. This variation was due entirely to sharp regional differences in failure rates on the mental tests, which ranged from 9.2 percent to 37.0 percent. Further, Negro rejection rates for all causes were nearly twice as high as those of white youths. Negro draftee rejection rates due to mental test failure alone averaged 57.5 percent, as compared with only 14.0 percent for white youths. In the Southern states fully 70 percent of the Negro draft examinees failed the mental tests.

It was evident that the existing draft standards, and even higher enlistment standards, had effectively barred a substantial proportion of our nation's youth from military service. Included among these rejectees were many young men who had attempted to volunteer and had been denied the opportunity to serve. Inevitably, the effect of these policies was to narrow the source of volunteers for service and to concentrate the military service obligation upon a more limited population group. For these reasons, the premises underlying existing military selection procedures were subjected to critical review as part of a broader Department of Defense study of the draft and of related military manpower policies conducted in 1964–65.

When viewed in simplistic terms, the available research evidence appeared to support existing judgments that those with low scores on the psychological tests were poor "risks" for military service. Available statistics based on such criteria as training attrition, unsuitability discharge rates, and rates of promotion indicated that— quite consistently—Group IV personnel performed more poorly than those in higher mental categories.

However, this experience alone did not provide a basis for determining an appropriate cutoff score or a passing standard on the tests. It was equally clear from the existing evidence that a large majority of the Group IV personnel had completed training and had performed satisfactorily in a wide range of military skills.

The contention that low test scores were necessarily predictive of high disciplinary problems was also found to be questionable as a result of more recent research. For example, a longitudinal study of over 73,000 airmen originally enlisted by the Air Force in 1956 found that the unsuitability discharge rate of 5.6 percent for Group IV airmen who were high school graduates was less than half the corresponding rate of 12.4 percent for non–high school graduates in Mental Group I. Not surprisingly, the attitudinal and emotional factors associated with successful adjustment to a high school environment were much more directly relevant to successful adjustment to military life than mental attainment as such.

Also important in influencing revision of military qualification standards was the increased recognition of the unique role of the armed services as a training institution. Beginning with the enactment of the Manpower Development and Training Act in 1962, the federal government had undertaken a direct and substantial commitment for the training or retraining of workers as a major aspect of its national manpower policy. Succeeding measures, including laws establishing the Job Corps and the Youth Conservation Corps, placed prime emphasis on the development of needed skills for underprivileged youth in order to help them compete more effectively in the civilian job market. It appeared to top officials that the armed services, as the nation's largest employer of youth and largest single training institution, could contribute to such efforts, and that this could be done as a by-product of their primary mission of training men for occupational duties in military service, with little or no incremental cost.

PROJECT 100,000

Description of the Program. Based on all these considerations, a carefully phased reduction in mental qualification standards was initiated in November 1965 shortly after the Vietnam force buildup was begun. The initial reduction in standards, applicable only to draftees and Army enlistees, consisted of deleting certain of the supplementary aptitude test requirements for individuals having percentile scores of 16–30 on the AFQT. Even this limited reduction in standards resulted, in the following 11 months, in enlistment or induction of more than 30,000 entrants who would not have previously qualified for service.

In August 1966 this policy was broadly expanded and given national prominence in an address by Secretary McNamara in which he announced his intention of accepting for service up to 100,000 men per year who would not have been acceptable under then-existing standards. Although stressing the capability of the military services to train and utilize these men effectively under job-oriented rather than academic-oriented training methods, he linked this new effort directly to the war against poverty: "The poor of America have not had the opportunity to earn their fair share of this nation's abundance, but they can be given an opportunity to serve in their nation's defense and they can be given an opportunity to return to civilian life with skills and aptitudes which for them and their families will reverse the downward spiral of human decay."

Specifically, Secretary McNamara directed that in the initial year of the program—a 12-month period beginning in October 1966—the armed services accept some 40,000 men who failed to meet either current aptitude test or medical standards but who could be expected—when exposed to military training or to a brief period of remedial medical attention—to fully qualify and perform military duties. In the following year and in subsequent years, the goal would be to accept 100,000 such men per year.

To implement this policy, the following revisions in acceptance standards were placed in effect:

(1) Mental standards for induction and enlistment were lowered in October and December 1966 to qualify individuals with scores as low as the 10th percentile on the AFQT who were (a) high school graduates or (b) non-high school graduates receiving a passing score on certain supplementary aptitude tests; that is, passing one out of seven aptitude areas if scoring between 16 and 30 on the AFQT, or two out of seven aptitude areas if scoring between 10 and 15 on the AFQT.

(2) Medical standards for enlistment were also lowered in 1967 to accept volunteers with any one of 15 specific defects correctable in six weeks or less. Typical remedial defects listed were: overweight, underweight, hernia, pilonidal cyst, and deviated nasal septum.

To assure achievement of the Project 100,000 manpower procurement goals, detailed quotas for "new standards" accessions were allocated to each military service, based on the total number of entrants to be procured by each service either through enlistment or induction, and on other relevant factors such as each service's occupational requirements and training capabilities. Since the Army was scheduled to enroll nearly two-thirds of all new enlisted accessions into service in fiscal year 1967, it was allocated the largest quota. Under this procedure, any service normally not requiring draftees, which could not procure its quota of such new standards entrants through enlistment, would be allocated a corresponding number of such entrants through the draft. (The latter procedure has not, however, proved necessary.)

Three other key policies were established from the outset in management of the program. These were:

1. The minimum standards of performance established by each military service would not be reduced.
2. Extra time and effort would be spent, when required, to help new standards entrants achieve satisfactory performance.
3. The results of the program would be monitored in detail to assure that its goals were being attained.

Overall responsibility for supervising the program was assigned to the Assistant Secretary of Defense for Manpower and Reserve Affairs in consultation with the top manpower officials of each of the military departments.

As a matter of policy, care was taken to avoid singling out the new standards men or treating them as a special group. They were to be trained in all of the 18 basic training centers operated by the military services, and assigned to advanced training on the basis of their aptitude test scores and classification interviews. However, special training units—already in existence at a number of centers—were established at each recruit training center to assist individuals who needed special help, whether new standards or old standards men. These units provided special assistance on specific aspects of the basic training curriculum. In addition, in the past year, literacy training units were set up to upgrade the reading ability of entrants found to have less than a fifth grade level of reading. At the same time, a more long-range effort was initiated to modify technical training courses and methods, so that these men, if otherwise qualified, would have a wider range of occupational training opportunities in the services.

Program Results. Detailed statistics covering experience in the first two years of Project 100,000 are presented in the Appendix at the end of this discussion. They include data on the number and characteristics of the new standards entrants, their occupational assignments, and their performance to date. Where applicable, comparisons are presented for control groups consisting of representative samples of old standards entrants in each service who entered during the same time period. Key findings are summarized below:

1. *Progress in meeting accession goals*—The goal for the first two years of the project, October 1966–September 1968, was to accept 140,000 new standards entrants. The number actually enrolled totaled 140,667 (Table 1), about 9 percent of all new enlisted entrants into service during this period. Of this total about one-half were enlistees (volunteers); the remainder were draftees. The proportion of volunteers rose significantly during this two-year period—from 34 percent in the first 12 months to 58 percent in the second year of the project. About 94 percent of the new standards entrants were accepted under the revised mental standards and only 8,800, or 6 percent, under the medically remedial program.

Of the total accessions into the program, about 97,000 (slightly more than two-thirds) went into the Army; the remainder entered the three other services.

2. *Characteristics of new standards entrants*—The following is a

statistical profile of the new standards entrants accepted under the reduced mental standards, compared with the control group. (More detailed statistics appear in Tables 2 and 2a.):

	New Standards Entrants	Control Group
Race: Percent nonwhite	39.6%	9.1%
Educational Attainment		
Percent high school graduates	43.3%	79.2%
Median school grade	10.6 years	11.9 years
Median reading level (grade)	6.1 years	10.9 years
Employment and Earnings (Prior to Entry into Service)		
Percent not employed	38%	n.a.*
Percent employed earning less than $60 per week	18%	n.a.
Region of Residence (Preservice)		
Percent from Southern states	47%	30%

* Not available.

It will be evident that based on available criteria, the new standards entrants as a group exhibit characteristics normally associated with the poverty syndrome. They include a disproportionate number of nonwhites; their formal educational attainment is only one year below that of the control group, but actual reading ability is 4.8 years lower; over half the new standards entrants were either without jobs or were employed at very low wage levels (under $60 per week); a disproportionate number came from the Southern states. (The differential characteristics of the Negro accessions, as shown in Table 2, will be discussed in more detail below.) It should be noted, however, that relatively low scores on military aptitude tests are by no means limited to youth from any single socio-economic class. Thus, the new standards draftees as a group were older than the volunteers, included a much smaller percentage of unemployed, and reported substantially higher preservice earnings than did the enlistees.

3. *Performance in Basic Trianing*—All enlisted personnel entering service must successfully complete basic training to be retained in service. This training includes initial indoctrination into military life, familiarity with certain basic hand weapons, and other skills and

knowledge required of all military personnel. Nearly 96 percent of all new standards entrants successfully completed basic training; this was only slightly lower than the completion rate of 98 percent for other entrants. Moreover, only about half of those failing to complete basic training satisfactorily were separated from service for such reasons as unsuitability, inaptitude, or behavioral problems; the remainder received medical discharges because of pre-existing conditions.

This low attrition rate is due in part to the fact that basic training imposes limited mental demands upon trainees; success is measured primarily by practical performance tests in relatively simple training routines (and by absence of serious behavioral problems) rather than by written tests. However, the procedures instituted at the training centers to assist individuals experiencing difficulty with particular phases of the training clearly contributed to the very high completion rate. About 13 percent of new standards trainees were recycled or assigned to remedial training units for brief periods, as compared with only 4 percent of personnel with higher AFQT scores.

Those who are recycled are reassigned to a training company in an earlier phase of the training cycle so that the trainee has an opportunity to repeat a portion of the curriculum. Recycling usually adds one or two weeks to the total training time.

The training cadre may decide that the man needs more attention than he can normally receive in a regular training company. Each Basic Training Center has a remedial training unit (usually called "Special Training Company") that provides concentrated attention to trainees who need physical conditioning, have motivational or adjustment problems, or are slow learners. A trainee may stay in a Special Training Company a day or a month; the average is 11 days. He then returns to a regular training company.

One of the additional innovations introduced into the recruit training programs after some initial experience was remedial reading training for those new standards men found, upon testing, to be seriously deficient in their reading ability. Small remedial reading training programs were initiated at recruit training centers by the Navy and Air Force in 1967; the Army started a similar program on a larger scale in April 1968. During the first two years of the program, about 6 percent of the new standards men received such training; present plans provide for a doubling of this overall proportion in 1969. Under current procedures, the Army assigns to the program men who test below a fifth grade reading level on a standard reading achievement test. This training precedes basic military training and is designed to upgrade men to a fifth grade reading level in periods up to six weeks. Instruction is conducted either by enlisted personnel, such as college graduate draftees with degrees in education, or by civilian instructors. Special training materials—adult in approach and oriented to the service environment—have been developed for this purpose. Army reports indicate that out of a total of 7,681 who entered this program between April and December 31, 1968, 5,761 (75 percent) were able to reach a fifth grade reading level, usually in a three-week period. An additional 1,001, or 13 percent, failed to reach this level; 225 were dropped for nonacademic reasons, and 694 were still enrolled at the end of the year.

4. *Performance in skill training*—Upon completion of basic training, new entrants are assigned for training in specific military occupational specialties. This training may be provided either in formal programs at service schools or training centers, or through on-the-job methods after direct assignment to an operating unit. The Army and Marine Corps normally assign all new entrants to either advanced combat training or to entry-level specialist training following completion of basic combat training. The Air Force and Navy assign varying proportions of their recruit trainees to formal specialist courses. As a result of relatively high aptitude standard qualifications for entry into these courses, only about half of the Air Force new standards entrants and 5 percent of the Navy entrants were assigned to formal skill training courses.

Many of these courses, other than those in the ground combat skills or in certain semiskilled occupational areas, make significant mental demands upon the trainee. In view of earlier research findings, relatively high failure rates from such courses could be anticipated for new standards entrants assigned to the more technical courses. As shown below, the overall attrition rate in skill training courses has, in fact, been significantly higher for new standards men than for other trainees.

More detailed statistics by occupational area for the Army and Air Force (Table 3) indicate that new standards entrants experienced relatively low failures in combat training or other nontechnical courses, such as service and supply-handling occupations. Relatively high failure rates (15 percent or higher) were experienced by those new standards men given to courses in the technical, mechanical, and administrative skills. The overall record is however considered quite satisfactory. For the Department of Defense as a whole, about nine out of ten new standards men successfully completed their occupational training. Those who did not were generally assigned to less demanding occupational areas. It is expected that a program to simplify training courses as well as more refined screening criteria, will further reduce this rate.

ATTRITION RATES FROM TRAINING COURSES

	PERCENT DROPPED FROM TRAINING	
	New Standards Entrants	Other Trainees Attending Same Courses
Army	8.8%	4.1%
Navy	16.8	6.7
Air Force	13.5	4.0
Marine Corps	3.4	n.a.*

* Not available.

5. *Occupational assignments*—Upon completing their formal training, enlisted entrants are assigned to duty in a particular occupational specialty. The distribution of new standards entrants by broad occupational area is shown in Table 4; a more detailed distribution, showing the 15 occupational groups to which such personnel were most frequently assigned is shown in Table 5. At the outset of the program, concern was expressed that these entrants would be heavily concentrated in the infantry and in related combat specialties, where their opportunities for acquiring skills transferable to civilian life would be quite limited. About 38 percent of these personnel were, in fact, assigned to such specialties, as compared with 30 percent of those in the control group.

The relatively large concentration in the ground combat occupations resulted from two factors: the large buildup requirement for combat specialists during this period in the Army and Marine Corps, and the role played by aptitude testing in classification, which restricted the opportunities of new standards men for assignment to the more technical specialties. A majority of the new standards men were, however, assigned to a wide variety of other specialties with greater potential usefulness in civilian work careers. These include service occupations, mechanical repair skills, clerical occupations, and even certain technical occupations, such as radio operators and medical specialists.

6. *Post-training performance*—The data bank maintained on Project 100,000 entrants includes a number of items relevant to an assessment of their performance of military duties following completion of training. Among the available indicators are: (1) attrition rates from service after specified periods for such reasons as bad conduct, unsuitability, etc.; (2) advancement rates; (3) incidence

of disciplinary problems; and (4) efficiency ratings. The results of these in-service follow-ups are summarized below:

a. *Attrition rates*–At the end of 1½ years of active service, about nine out of ten new standards entrants were still on active duty. Attrition rates were lower in the Army than in the other services, partly because of differences in discharge practices among the services (Table 6). Data for directly comparable control groups showed that these attritional rates were higher than for old standards entrants (8.8 percent to 4.8 percent). The loss rate for new standards men, however, is considered to be at an acceptable level. As shown in Table 7, less than half of all new standards men who separated during this period had been discharged because of poor performance or unsatisfactory behavior; the remaining separations were due to disability, death, or other causes.

b. *Advancement rates*–Data on the pay-grade distribution of new standards entrants after 19–21 months of service are presented in Table 8. Comparison with control groups indicates a somewhat slower rate of grade advancement for the new standards men. The differences to date are relatively small in the Army, Air Force, and Marine Corps; they are much more pronounced in the Navy, which relies to a greater extent upon formal testing as a condition for grade advancement.

c. *Disciplinary problems*–Available data indicate that the incidence of disciplinary problems among the new standards men has been relatively low. After 19–21 months of service, less than 4 percent of all new standards men had received a court martial conviction, while 17 percent had received nonjudicial punishments for lesser offenses. Control group data are not yet available.

d. *Supervisory efficiency ratings*–Ratings are routinely recorded for enlisted personnel at one-year intervals. Results of such ratings for new standards men entering service during 1967, as well as for control groups are shown in Table 9. While new standards men generally received lower supervisory ratings, the disparity was not great. About 90 percent of the new standards men in each service received ratings which classed them as good performers or better. These ratings were received, however, while performing the simpler jobs in each military service.

The Role of the Negro in Project 100,000. In recent years, Negroes have constituted about 10 percent of the strength of the armed services and a similar proportion of all enlisted entrants into service. These proportions are roughly comparable with the proportion of Negro youth in the population of military service age (about 11–12 percent). Yet, as noted above, Negroes comprised 38 percent of all new standards entrants during the first two years of Project 100,000. This apparent disparity is a direct consequence of the fact that—as in other tests involving educational skills—Negro youth, as a group, have scored much lower on the AFQT than white youth. The extent of this disparity is shown in the following table.

ESTIMATED DISTRIBUTION OF MALE YOUTHS, 19–21, BY AFQT MENTAL GROUP (1960) *

PERCENT DISTRIBUTION

AFQT Mental Group	Percentile Score	TOTAL, ALL GRADES			HIGH SCHOOL GRADUATES ONLY†		
		Total	White	Negro	Total	White	Negro
Group I	100-93	8.7	9.8	.4	6.8	7.5	.4
II	92-65	26.1	29.0	3.9	29.4	32.1	5.1
III	64-31	36.8	38.6	23.7	45.6	46.6	36.8
IV	30-10	20.5	17.7	41.2	16.9	13.2	50.0
V	9 or below	7.9	4.9	30.8	1.3	.6	7.7

* Source: Rernard D. Karpinos, "The Mental Qualification of American Youth for Military Service and Its Relationship to Educational Attainment," Proceedings of the Annual Meeting of the American Statistical Association, Social Statistics Section (1966), pp. 92–111.
† Excludes men with one or more years of post–high school education.

In the estimates above the results of military examination for youth of both races have been standardized by race and educational level according to the distributions of all male youths, aged 19–21, in the 1960 census. The *relative* frequency of Negro youth in the Group IV category is about 2½ times as great as that of white youth, and nearly six times as great as for white youth in the lowest (Group V) category. The contrast is even greater when limited to high school graduates. The reduction in mental test qualifying scores within the Group IV range under Project 100,000, thus inevitably resulted in a relatively large proportion of Negroes among the new standards entrants.

These comparisons explain some of the other differential characteristics of the Negro new standards entrants shown in Table 2. Among the new standards men, 73.4 percent of the Negroes were in the lowest AFQT score group (Percentile Scores 10–15) as compared with 62.0 percent of the white entrants. A large proportion of the Negroes included in the new standards group (60.2 percent) had completed twelve or more grades of school, whereas only 32.4 percent of the white new standards men were high school graduates. Yet, despite having more education, the reading achievement level of the Negro new standards men (6.1 years) was about the same as that of the white men (6.2 years).

The lower mental test scores of the Negro new standards entrants also help to explain the differential pattern of occupational assignment of Negro and white entrants. Among Negro new standards men, 43.1 percent were assigned to infantry and combat specialties, whereas only 34.2 percent of the white entrants were assigned to this occupational area. (Table 4.) Correspondingly fewer of the Negroes were assigned to skills such as communications, equipment repair, and the crafts occupations. It should be noted, however, that the proportion of Negroes assigned to medical and dental specialties and clerical duties was slightly higher than for white men. Some of these differences result from variations in the proportion of Negroes among new standards entrants in the four services—each of which has a distinctive occupational structure. Generally, they reflect the higher aptitude test qualifications established in all services for assignment to the more technical skills—and the handicaps of many Negro youths in meeting these formal test standards.

Finally, one of the more significant comparisons resulting from the available statistical materials is the difference in the "survival" rates in military service between black and white new standards men (Table 6). Among all new standards entrants into service during the first fifteen months of the program, 93.8 percent of the Non-Caucasians (nearly all Negro) were still in active service, as contrasted with 89.2 percent of the white entrants. Stated differently, the failure rate of the Negroes was about half that of the white group. These differentials hold true for each service and for each entry period. More intensive evaluation has indicated that this differential holds separately both for high school graduates and non–high school graduates, so that the observed relationship cannot be explained by the larger proportion of high school graduates among Negroes in Project 100,000.

More detailed analysis of these differences and of other performance measures is planned. But if ability to complete an initial tour of duty is an acceptable criterion, these initial findings suggest that low-aptitude Negroes are more often successful than low-aptitude Caucasians. One possible explanation is that the present AFQT and aptitude tests may, in fact, be culturally biased to a measurable degree, and that these tests need revision or supplementation by other types of selection criteria. Intensive research on this and related aspects of the mental testing procedures has been initiated by the Department of Defense.

A Preliminary Appraisal. Experience under Project 100,000, to date, has a number of important implications, both for military manpower programs and for related efforts in the civilian sector of the economy. From the standpoint of the military manpower manager, the experience summarized above provides substantial support for the conclusion recently affirmed by Secretary of Defense Clifford that "Project 100,000 has been a spectacular success." The most tangible evidence of this success is the fact that over 90 percent of these men, previously considered not qualified for service, were in fact performing effectively after one year of service. The performance data reviewed above do indicate that, as might be expected, some marginal costs have been entailed in this result. For example, training attrition rates for these entrants have been somewhat higher—primarily in the more demanding occupational fields—and a modest proportion of these men have required more time and attention in completing their initial training programs. These incremental costs are however substantially less than had been originally anticipated.

On balance, the experience to date clearly supports Secretary McNamara's original premise that previous minimum mental standards were unduly restrictive and had deprived many young men with high motivation and performance potential of an opportunity for entering military service. The fact that one-half of the new entrants under Project 100,000 were volunteers suggests that a continuation of the current lower standards could make a significant contribution toward reducing reliance upon the draft in the event of a future reduction of military manpower requirements.

This experience has not only demonstrated the feasibility of lowering the passing scores under existing testing procedures but has also highlighted the need for developing improved selection criteria particularly adapted to measuring performance potential of youth from educationally disadvantaged backgrounds. A substantial research effort toward this objective has been initiated; under it a number of alternative selection instruments less dependent upon pencil and paper testing and cognitive factors are now being evaluated by the Department of Defense personnel research laboratories.

An important factor contributing to the success thus far achieved

223

by Project 100,000 was the early recognition by top management of the Department of Defense that the reduction in entry standards would inevitably have consequences for—and require certain adjustments in—the entire system for training and utilizing personnel in the armed forces. One of the first policy decisions for Project 100,000 was to avoid any form of separate identification of the new standards entrants, except for statistical purposes. They were assigned to the same basic training units as all other personnel, and measured under identical performance criteria. Besides avoiding any stigma associated with their low test scores, this procedure provided the opportunity for low-aptitude men who needed help in training to be assisted by better-qualified buddies in the same unit. At the same time, procedures for remedial and literacy training were established to assist those individuals requiring special assistance—not all of whom, incidentally, were in the new standards category. There is general agreement among top officials that this approach—as distinct from a policy of initial segregation of these new entrants in special units—has been an important ingredient in the success of the program.

Progress has also been made in adapting occupational training courses, both in content and method. This was accomplished initially by providing research funds to the services to evaluate and modify a number of representative courses considered particularly adaptable for new standards men. Innovations and experience derived from these pilot projects are now being extended to a number of other courses. Since there are many hundreds of separate training courses conducted by each of the military services, this program is a continuing effort, and there is much scope for continued improvement in this area.

While considered emphasis has been placed on adaptations in the training system, the military classification system—the process of selecting men for assignment to various training programs and occupational specialties—was not materially altered during the initial phases of Project 100,000. Under existing procedures, the services still relied primarily on aptitude tests in their occupational allocations of new personnel, using computerized systems to optimize these assignments. Aptitude test standards for entry into many technical and support-type occupations are higher than those for combat assignments. One result of this was a relatively large allocation of new standards men to combat specialties. This result has been considered undesirable for two reasons: first, the possible impact upon the combat units of having too many lower aptitude men at one time; second, the obviously more limited opportunities in combat units for acquiring training transferable to civilian work careers. In

view of these considerations, the military services have been reviewing their assignment procedures, and gradually reducing the proportion of new standards men being assigned to combat occupations.
The ongoing research to develop improved selection methods has
obvious potential for application to the classification system as well.

One other application of aptitude testing in the military personnel
system has an important bearing upon the effectiveness of Project
100,000. Aptitude tests are not used in the Army merely for initial
selection and classification of personnel; they also play an important
role in determining eligibility to re-enlist. Under existing Army regulations, enlisted personnel in the Group IV category are generally
considered ineligible for re-enlistment unless they pass certain supplementary aptitude or skill knowledge tests. These rules were established about ten years ago to preclude the entry into the career force
of enlisted men with limited potential for advancement into the noncommissioned ranks. Aptitude tests were used for this purpose because of limited confidence in the reliability of supervisory ratings.
If present practices are continued, their effect will be to limit significantly the opportunity of many new standards men to remain in
military service on a career basis, even if they have performed at a
fully satisfactory level in their assigned duties. A clear challenge here
is to find suitable alternative measures of career potential, based
upon more reliable performance measures than the results of written
tests geared mainly to predicting success in formal training courses.

Thus far we have discussed some of the more immediate military
manpower management implications of Project 100,000. One of the
major objectives of this effort, as originally outlined by Secretary
McNamara, was to provide undereducated youth drawn from poverty backgrounds with an opportunity to acquire skills and work
experience which would aid them materially in future civilian work
careers. Since the program has been in effect for a little more than
two years, most of the participants are still in active service; therefore, no data on the postservice experience of these men is yet available. A program for systematic follow-up research is being developed, however, designed to provide comprehensive information on
the postservice economic, vocational, and social adjustment of new
standards separatees, as compared with appropriate control groups
without military service experience.

There are several ways in which exposure to military service and
training may be expected to assist men in their postservice work
careers. The military system imposes certain basic personal and
social disciplines which are equally important for successful adjustment in civilian work environments. An honorable discharge therefore represents a potentially useful certificate for entry into civilian

jobs, particularly for young men lacking other certificates such as a high school diploma. In addition, a majority of those in Project 100,000, as we have seen, have received training in vocational skills which have counterparts in civilian life. A 1964 Census Bureau survey of veterans under age 35 indicated that about one-third had made some direct use of their military training in their current civilian jobs.

It is evident, however, that Project 100,000 entrants assigned to combat specialties have not, in the course of their regular military training, received an occupational skill that is directly transferable to civilian employment. Others have been trained in specialties having restricted openings in civilian life or which may require considerable additional training to meet civilian job standards. Still others may have occupational preferences very different from the particular specialty they have been assigned to while in service.

These were important considerations in the initiation of a second program—Project Transition—which will be described below.

THE TRANSITION PROGRAM

In his Manpower Report to the Congress in April 1967, President Johnson noted the extensive training contributions of the armed services, and the potential for expanding these contributions under Project 100,000. He recognized that "there are, of course, some military specialists whose training does not lend directly to civilian employment." To help the latter, he directed the Secretary of Defense: "to make available, to the maximum extent possible, in-service training and educational opportunities which will increase their chances for employment in civilian life."

To implement this policy, manpower planners in the Department of Defense were faced with a formidable, and in many ways, unprecedented task. In the following fiscal year, the armed services were scheduled to return some 900,000 servicemen to civilian life, including the first wave of draftees inducted after the Vietnam force buildup in 1965. These men would be separated from service at several hundred military installations throughout the country—many shortly after returning from duty in Vietnam, other overseas areas, or from naval shipboard duty. In a highly prospering economy, it could be assumed that a large proportion of these returning servicemen would make a satisfactory and rapid adjustment to civilian careers. Some would undoubtedly resume their education, aided by the GI Bill of Rights; some would return to jobs held before entering service; still others had clear vocational objectives and with their prior civilian training and skills acquired in service could be expected to move toward these objectives with no special assistance.

By the same token, many other servicemen needed, and would probably welcome, special assistance to help prepare them for future civilian careers. A pilot survey conducted at a large military base in mid-1967 confirmed this premise: 65 percent of the servicemen interviewed who were approaching the end of their tour of duty and were not planning to re-enlist indicated that they were willing to participate, in off-duty time, in training courses of their choice to help prepare for future civilian jobs.

Based on these initial assessments, the objectives of the program were more specifically defined by the Secretary of Defense as designed to meet "the four basic needs of the man leaving the service: counseling, skill enhancement, education, and job placement." Initial estimates indicated that of the 900,000 servicemen who would leave service each year in the immediate future, some 350,000 would probably need counseling, and, of these, about 150,000 would need skill training or additional education; while many others would seek placement assistance for already acquired skills. The following policy guidelines were established for the program which was identified as "Project Transition":

1. The program would be available to enlisted personnel having from one to six months of service remaining.
2. Top priority in assistance would be given to the following target groups: combat-disabled personnel, combat personnel with no civilian-related skill, other servicemen with no previous civilian occupation or civilian skill, and those ineligible for re-enlistment.
3. The program would be a voluntary one. It would be conducted on off-duty time, except to the extent that the unit commander authorized training during duty hours.
4. Counseling of potential separatees would be an essential element of the program. For individuals eligible to re-enlist, the choice of continuation in service, as well as of civilian training and job opportunities, would be presented.
5. The strengthening of basic educational skills would be emphasized in the case of individuals with less than a high school education.
6. Skill training courses would be offered only when they reflected actual job requirements; training would be job-oriented.
7. In addition to use of any available capacity for civilian-oriented occupational training on the military base itself,

maximum training support and participation would be sought from both the private and public sectors of the economy.

8. Job placement assistance would be offered in collaboration with the United States Employment Service and private industry.

9. Provision would be made for systematic follow-up and evaluation procedures.

In June 1967 pilot Project Transition programs were established at five military bases—one from each military service—as well as at the Walter Reed Army Hospital. The program became operational in January 1968, and by the end of the year was functioning at 254 military bases mainly in the continental United States. The program is directed by a small staff in the Office of the Assistant Secretary of Defense for Manpower and Reserve Affairs. However, administration of the program is highly decentralized: The key link in the effort is the Project Transition officer, who is responsible for managing the program at each of the participating military bases.

The first step for an enrollee is completing a questionnaire regarding his skills, education, and work experience; his plans concerning re-enlistment or separation from service; and his career and training preferences. This is followed by a counseling interview in which the counselor advises as to relevant training and job opportunities and helps enrollees select the courses most useful to them from a list of those available at the particular installation.

Skill training offered is largely at the entry level; course lengths vary from 50 to 400 hours, depending upon type and complexity. The sponsorship and conduct of the training courses involve a unique combination of resources of the military services; federal, state, and local agencies, and the private sector (including both major corporations and small local businesses).

The military services provide Transition enrollees access to regular technical training courses offered at the installation, on a space available basis; in addition, opportunities are provided at the base for on-the-job training in both trade and technical skills such as computer data processing activities.

Public agency training participation has taken several forms: The Labor Department allocated $877,000 in fiscal year 1968 and over $1 million in fiscal year 1969 under the Manpower and Development Training Act for training courses conducted at or near military bases. In addition, courses are supported by federal agencies, such as the Post Office, as well as by state and local agencies, to assist men to qualify for jobs in these agencies, with particular emphasis on the law enforcement field.

Private business participation in the training programs has included conducted formal training courses at or near military bases by many major national corporations in such skills as auto mechanics, service station management, electronics, hotel-motel management, appliance repair, and sales management. In addition, small businessmen in communities adjacent to military bases have been invited to sponsor on-the-job training programs often involving only one or a few persons. All of these courses are designed to meet specific job needs of the sponsoring firm, thus assuring a direct linkage between training and placement.

Objectives of educational programs offered under Project Transition range from helping some to complete a high school or even eighth grade equivalency to providing opportunities for others not previously oriented to college, to qualify for admission into college programs. Resources used include local civilian schools, courses offered at military bases through the United States Armed Forces Institute, extension courses, General Education Development tests, and the use of self-study programmed instructional materials.

The following summary statistics indicate the status of the program at the end of November 1968—11 months after its formal initiation:

- 347,000 prospective separatees (26 percent of those eligible) had received Transition questionnaires.
- 279,000 had been counseled, that is, 81 percent of those questionnaired.
- 154,000 of those counseled who did not plan to re-enlist expressed a desire for training.
- 51,000 of the latter group had actually entered training or education programs; of these, 35,000 had completed training; 14,000 were in training, and 2,000 had dropped out for various reasons.

Statistics are not yet available on the placement record of Project Transition graduates or on the extent to which this training has contributed to their post service employment and vocational advancement. Nor are detailed statistics yet available on the characteristics of those trained—with one exception: Reports indicate that 19 percent of those who have entered Transition training through November 1968 were nonwhite, a somewhat higher proportion than their ratio in the eligible population.

Strengths and Weaknesses of Project Transition. Until more detailed results become available, no full appraisal of this new program can be attempted. Based on discussions with staff responsible for administering the program, we may identify certain of its strengths and limitations. Following are some of the more promising features of the present program.

- As noted above, it represents a unique combination of military and civilian government agencies, and private resources, engaged in a cooperative effort on a voluntary and largely decentralized basis. The Department of Defense has served as a catalyst in bringing together a wide range of services from both the public and private sector; it has not attempted to duplicate services provided by the latter.
- Certain obvious benefits have accrued to both civilian government agencies and business firms that have sponsored job-oriented training programs under this arrangement: In a tight labor market it has provided them early access to a highly desirable pool of civilian labor force entrants–men who have already successfully completed periods of military service and training, who are disciplined and motivated, and who are available for job training on a part-time basis while still on the military payroll.
- It has broadened both the occupational and geographical horizons of many of these men; has reduced their risks of transitional postservice unemployment; and has provided them, in a direct way, with an expression of the public interest and concern for their future welfare.
- Finally, it offers the potential of important benefits to the armed services in their voluntary recruitment programs: Young men may be much more receptive to enlisting (either for a single tour or a full career) if they receive tangible assurance that military service combined with Project Transition training will provide productive careers during and after military service.

There are however a number of recognized problems—some of them inherent in the present design of the program.

- The program may not be reaching large numbers of servicemen within the primary target group for assistance. Under current Army regulations, servicemen returning from one-year tours of duty in Vietnam with five months or less remaining in their tour of duty, are eligible for immediate discharge upon returning to the United States. There is no provision for voluntary extension of such tours of duty for the sole purpose of receiving Transition training. Thus, many combat veterans who might most benefit from this assistance can be helped only to a limited extent, primarily through the programs's counseling features. There are obvious problems, too, in establishing satisfactory programs for naval personnel afloat and others in isolated duty locations. Moreover, there is some danger that—as with civilian manpower training programs—training agencies, when faced with limited quotas and a large pool of potential applicants, will tend to "cream" the most promising prospects (based on aptitude and educational criteria) rather than those most needing help.

- Since the program is decentralized, its success depends to a considerable extent upon the support and initiative of local military commanders. Many bases have done outstanding and imaginative jobs in advancing Project Transition; others have lagged. Extensive use is being made of the information media and also base visits to promote this effort, which the Secretary of Defense has given his strong support.

- Initial counseling of separatees is recognized to be one of the critical links in the success of the program. The nationwide shortage of qualified counseling personnel affects Transition and also civilian manpower programs. To alleviate this shortage, military and civilian personnel are being trained to perform basic counseling services at a subprofessional level. In addition, a pilot program is being planned to develop more effective counseling strategies.

- Finally, the ultimate payoff from the program will depend upon the effectiveness of placement of Transition graduates. The emphasis upon job-linked training programs provides some built-in assurance of a good placement ratio. The entire program, however, will be crucially tested in the event that a large scale exodus of men from the services following the termination or scaling down of the Vietnam War were to coincide with a slackening in the present high level of labor demand.

TABLE 1: NEW STANDARDS ENTRANTS* BY PROGRAM, ENTRY SOURCE, AND SERVICE
October 1966—September 1968

	Total	New Mental Standards	Medically Remedial
Entry source			
Enlistees	70,079	61,257	8,822
Inductees	70,588	70,588	—
Total	140,667	131,845	8,822
Service			
Army	96,985	94,785	2,200
Navy	16,579	13,334	3,245
Air Force	13,735	11,261	2,474
Marine Corps	13,368	12,465	903
Total	140,667	131,845	8,822

* In subsequent tables, "new standards entrants refers" only to those accepted under the revised mental standards, and excludes the medically remedial group.

TABLE 2: SELECTED CHARACTERISTICS OF NEW STANDARDS ENTRANTS BY RACE AND OF CONTROL GROUP
October 1966—September 1968

	NEW STANDARDS ENTRANTS				Control Group*
		NON-CAUCASIAN			
Characteristic	Caucasian	Negro	Other	Total	Group*
Race (percent distribution)	60.4%	38.1%	1.5%	100.0%	†
AFQT Percentile Scores					
31 and over	—	—	—	—	83.2‡
21-30	6.8	2.9	3.8	5.3	
16-20	31.2	23.7	25.1	28.1	16.8‡
10-15	62.0	73.4	71.1	66.6	
Total	100.0	100.0	100.0	100.0	100.0‡
School Grades Completed (percent distribution)					
13-16	2.0	4.2	7.2	3.0	23.2
12	30.4	56.0	46.9	40.3	56.0
9-11	45.0	35.4	36.2	41.3	18.0
8	15.0	3.2	7.2	10.4	2.0
7 or less	7.6	1.2	2.5	5.0	0.8
Total	100.0	100.0	100.0	100.0	100.0
Median Reading and School Grade Levels					
Reading level	6.2	6.1	6.1	6.1	10.9
School grade level	10.1	11.3	11.0	10.6	11.9

* Entrants selected by each service as representative of accessions during October 1966—September 1968, under previous mental standards. See text for detailed description.
† Caucasian—90.9%, Negro—8.8%, Other—0.3%.
‡ Based on total accessions during period, exclusive of new standards entrants.

TABLE 2a: HOME GEOGRAPHIC AREA OF NEW STANDARDS ENTRANTS BY RACE AND OF CONTROL GROUP
October 1966—March 1968

Geographic Area*	NEW STANDARDS ENTRANTS				Control Group†
		NON-CAUCASIAN			
	Caucasian	Negro	Other	Total	
Total United States	100.0%	100.0%	100.0%	100.0%	100.0%
Northeast	20.6	14.2	2.6	17.9	20.9
New England	5.1	1.3	0.5	3.6	5.0
Middle Atlantic	15.5	12.9	2.1	14.3	15.9
North Central	26.6	16.9	6.9	22.6	33.9
East North Central	19.5	14.4	2.0	17.3	23.5
West North Central	7.1	2.5	4.9	5.3	10.4
South	36.2	64.2	13.2	46.6	27.7
South Atlantic	16.0	32.7	2.9	22.2	12.5
East South Central	9.2	14.3	1.3	11.0	6.4
West South Central	11.0	17.2	9.0	13.4	8.8
West	16.6	4.7	77.3	12.9	17.5
Mountain	4.3	0.7	22.4	3.2	4.3
Pacific	12.3	4.0	54.9	9.7	13.2

* The states within each geographic area are:
  New England: Conn., Maine, Mass., N.H., R.I., Vt.
  Middle Atlantic: N.J., N.Y., Pa.
  East North Central: Ill., Ind., Mich., Ohio, Wisc.
  West North Central: Iowa, Kan., Minn., Mo., Neb., N.D., S.D.
  South Atlantic: Del., Fla., Ga., Md., N.C., S.C., Va., D.C., W.Va., Puerto Rico
  East South Central: Ala., Ky., Miss., Tenn.
  West South Central: Ark., La., Okla., Tex.
  Mountain: Ariz., Colo., Idaho, Mont., Nev., N.M., Utah, Wyo.
  Pacific: Alaska, Calif., Hawaii, Oregon, Wash.
† Entrants selected by each service as representative of accessions during October 1966—March 1968 under previous mental standards.

TABLE 3: PERFORMANCE OF NEW STANDARDS ENTRANTS IN ENTRY-LEVEL OCCUPATIONAL TRAINING BY OCCUPATIONAL AREA
Army and Air Force

Department of Defense Occupational Area *	PERCENT DROPPED FROM TRAINING	
	Army†	Air Force‡
Infantry, gun crews, and allied specialists	2.4%	—
Electronic equipment repairmen	25.5	—
Communications and intelligence specialists	18.7	—
Medical and dental specialists	17.7	19.2%
Administrative specialists and clerks	17.8	14.6
Electrical/mechanical equipment repairmen	16.9	20.3
Craftsmen	8.8	9.2
Service and supply handlers	5.2	10.4
Total	8.8%	13.5%
Other entrants attending same courses	4.1%§	4.0%§

* New standards entrants attended 145 different types of skill courses in Army; 60 in Air Force. For purposes of presentation, these courses are grouped by DoD occupational area. Excludes areas with fewer than 100 trainees.

† Based upon experience for the period August 1967 to June 1968.

‡ Based upon experience for the period April 1967 to July 1968.

§ Percent dropped from training is based on current or past experience for each service.

TABLE 4: ASSIGNMENT BY OCCUPATIONAL AREA
(all services)

DEPARTMENT OF DEFENSE OCCUPATIONAL AREA	NEW STANDARDS ENTRANTS				Control Group
		NON-CAUCASIAN			
Title	Caucasian	Negro	Other	Total	Control Group
Infantry, gun crews, and allied specialists	34.2%	43.1%	39.4%	37.7%	30.5%
Electronic equipment repairmen	1.9	1.6	1.3	1.8	6.2
Communications and intelligence specialists	4.7	3.1	3.3	4.1	7.3
Medical and dental specialists	1.2	1.4	0.9	1.2	3.7
Other technical and allied specialists	0.3	0.4	—	0.3	2.4
Administrative specialists and clerks	9.8	10.9	10.4	10.3	13.5
Electrical/mechanical equipment repairmen	17.3	12.6	16.1	15.5	20.0
Craftsmen	10.0	7.2	10.9	8.9	5.2
Service and supply handlers	20.6	19.7	17.7	20.2	11.2
Total	100.0%	100.0%	100.0%	100.0%	100.0%

TABLE 5: ASSIGNMENT OF NEW STANDARDS ENTRANTS BY OCCUPATIONAL GROUP

(fifteen most common assignments)

DEPARTMENT OF DEFENSE OCCUPATIONAL GROUP Title	Percent Assigned to Each Occupation
Infantry	20.7%
Artillery, gunnery, rockets	8.8
Food service	7.3
Supply and logistics (clerical)	5.9
Wire communications (installation and maintenance)	5.2
Motor transport	4.8
Material receipt, storage, and issue	3.8
Combat engineering	3.7
Automotive repair	3.6
Administration (clerical)	3.2
Construction	2.6
Radio and radio code	2.5
Aircraft repair	2.4
Military police	2.4
Marine operating crafts	2.2
Subtotal—15 most common assignments	79.1%
All other assignments	20.9%
Total assignments	100.0%

TABLE 6: ATTRITION RATES FROM SERVICE, BY ENTRY GROUP, AS OF 30 SEPTEMBER 1968

DATE OF SERVICE ENTRY (MONTHS OF SERVICE IN PARENTHESES)

Service	Oct-Dec 66* (22-24)	Jan-Mar 67 (19-21)	Apr-Jun 67 (16-18)	Jul-Sep 67 (13-15)	Oct-Dec 67 (10-12)	Total Oct 66-Dec 67 (10-24)
Army						
New Standards						
Caucasian	12.7%	10.4%	8.2%	7.1%	5.0%	7.8%
Non-Caucasian	7.2	6.2	5.5	4.0	2.4	4.4
Total	10.3	8.7	7.1	5.9	3.9	6.4
Control Group†	5.8	5.1	3.9	2.7	2.6	4.2
Navy						
New Standards						
Caucasian		20.4	19.1	14.7	11.4	15.7
Non-Caucasian		12.5	6.4	9.1	5.3	7.9
Total		18.4	16.4	13.5	9.9	13.9
Control Group†		6.7	5.4	4.3	3.2	4.8
Air Force						
New Standards						
Caucasian		16.9	28.2	17.5	13.2	18.0
Non-Caucasian		9.9	14.5	9.8	4.9	8.8
Total		13.9	22.3	14.7	9.0	14.0
Control Group†		8.2	6.7	5.2	3.4	5.9
Marine Corps						
New Standards						
Caucasian		26.1	26.5	17.0	15.2	19.8
Non-Caucasian		23.2	18.5	14.7	13.6	16.1
Total		24.9	23.1	15.8	14.5	18.1
Control Group†		10.7	11.0	11.6	9.8	10.7
Dept. of Defense						
New Standards						
Caucasian	12.7	13.6	12.2	10.4	7.6	10.7
Non-Caucasian	7.2	8.2	7.6	6.4	4.1	6.2
Total	10.3	11.6	10.5	8.7	6.0	8.8
Control Group†	5.8%	5.9%	5.0%	4.3%	3.4%	4.8%

* Only the Department of Army had new standards accessions during this period.
† Control Group data based upon analysis of data files furnished by each service for men with the same length of service, except for the Army, which provided attrition data in a special report.

TABLE 7: ATTRITION FROM SERVICE OF NEW STANDARDS MEN BY CAUSE—DOD AS OF 30 SEPTEMBER 1968

DATE OF SERVICE ENTRY (MONTHS OF SERVICE IN PARENTHESES)

Attrition Category *	Oct-Dec 66 (22-24)	Jan-Mar 67 (19-21)	Apr-Jun 67 (16-18)	Jul-Sep 67 (13-15)	Oct-Dec 67 (10-12)	Total Oct 66-Dec 67 (10-24)
Unsatisfactory performance and/or behavior†	5.4%	5.5%	5.0%	3.8%	2.9%	4.2%
Medical reasons‡	2.5	3.4	2.7	2.9	2.0	2.6
Death§	1.1	1.3	1.5	0.9	0.4	1.0
Other reasons¶	1.3	1.4	1.3	1.1	0.7	1.0
Total of Above	10.3%	11.6%	10.5%	8.7%	6.0%	8.8%

* Men separating from service after completing their active duty tours are not shown as attrition.
† This category includes unsuitability, unfitness, misconduct, unsatisfactory performance, etc.
‡ The major reason for medical discharge is for physical defects which existed prior to entry into service.
§ The largest single cause of death is battlefield action.
¶ This category includes dependency and hardship discharges, and does not relate to the performance or behavior of the men attrited.

TABLE 8: PERCENTAGE DISTRIBUTION OF ENTRANTS BY PAY GRADE AFTER 19-21 MONTHS OF SERVICE*

Service	Accession Group	PERCENT AT EACH GRADE LEVEL					
		E-1	E-2	E-3	E-4	E-5	Total
Army	New Standards	4.3	7.7	18.8	58.9	10.3	100.0
	Control Group	1.1	3.1	16.9	61.3	17.6	100.0
Navy	New Standards	0.8	32.5	65.8	0.9	—	100.0
	Control Group	—	2.4	50.1	45.9	1.6	100.0
Air Force	New Standards	2.6	4.1	93.2	0.1	—	100.0
	Control Group†	0.2	1.8	97.8	0.2	—	100.0
Marine Corps	New Standards	5.0	19.6	44.7	30.4	0.3	100.0
	Control Group	2.1	5.6	41.8	46.4	4.1	100.0
Total DoD	New Standards	3.8	10.7	33.2	44.7	7.6	100.0
	Control Group	0.8	3.0	37.2	47.9	11.1	100.0

* Pay grade data as of 30 September 1968, for new standards men entering service January–March 1967 and for control groups with the same length of service.
† Estimated for Air Force.

TABLE 9: SUPERVISORY RATINGS OF NEW STANDARDS ENTRANTS AND CONTROL GROUP, BY SERVICE 30 SEPTEMBER 1968

ARMY

RATING CATEGORY

Group	Unsatisfactory	Fair	Good	Excellent	Total
New Standards	1.4%	0.8%	3.2%	94.6%	100.0%
Control Group	0.7%	0.3%	1.4%	97.6%	100.0%

NAVY

RATING CATEGORY

Group	Inadequate	Adequate	Effective	Highly Effective	Extremely Effective	Total
New Standards	2.1%	10.1%	36.2%	42.7%	8.9%	100.0%
Control Group	0.2%	2.2%	16.4%	54.2%	27.0%	100.0%

AIR FORCE*

| Group | | | | | RATING CATEGORY | | | | | | |
	0	1	2	3	4	5	6	7	8	9	Total
New Standards	0.9%	1.2%	2.1%	3.0%	3.9%	5.7%	9.6%	20.1%	32.0%	21.5%	100.0%
Control Group	0.2%	0.7%	0.2%	0.7%	1.4%	2.5%	5.2%	20.9%	33.5%	34.7%	100.0%

MARINE CORPS

| Group | RATING CATEGORY | | | | | | |
	Unsatisfactory	Poor	Fair	Good	Excellent	Outstanding	Total
New Standards	—	0.4%	7.8%	66.2%	25.0%	0.6%	100.0%
Control Group	—	0.3%	3.6%	50.6%	42.7%	2.8%	100.0%

* Rating categories are numerical only. Rating guidelines recommended by Air Force are as follows: 15% of men may be rated 9 (highest rating), 40% as 8 or higher, 65% as 7 or higher, and 90% as 6 or higher.

Discussion

BY *JAMES G. SCOVILLE* °

Under Project 100,000 the armed services annually accept 100,000 men who failed to meet the standards of the Armed Forces Qualification Test, who fall in the range between the 10th and 30th percentile. Not unnaturally, their characteristics are akin to those of disadvantaged individuals throughout American society: they are more heavily Negro, less schooled, and far below average in reading ability. In sharp contrast to the private programs discussed earlier, men taken under these lowered standards are not treated by the armed services with paternalism, special care, or coaching. No one, not even the inductee himself, is told that a particular person has failed the test. Remedial classes were set up at the time the program was begun; however, men taken under Project 100,000 were stated to be no more than half the total referred to them.

Analyses of the benefits to an individual from military training do not yield unambiguous results. On the one hand, surveys find that substantial numbers feel that training received while in service has been useful in their civilian occupations; on the other hand, detailed standardization of data by age, race, schooling, and region suggests that veterans earn no more, and possibly earn less, than nonveterans. These mildly conflicting findings apply to the general population and not primarily to the low-aptitude group inducted under Project 100,000. Hence, any attempt to assess the probable influence of Project 100,000 on the future employment experience and income of its inductees must use finer criteria.

In evaluating the program, one must consider it from two standpoints, that of the individual, and that of the military. In this latter regard, the low-aptitude inductees appear to have a satisfactory performance record in the services. For an estimated marginal cost of $300 per man, the project seems to have dipped into a usable reserve of manpower for military purposes. From the armed services' point of view, it is largely these cost and performance figures which count, and they spell success.

° James G. Scoville is an associate professor of economics and industrial relations at the University of Illinois.

From the standpoint of the individuals involved, evaluation of Project 100,000 is more difficult. For one thing, there is the divergent occupational pattern which arises for this group through the natural operations of the military internal labor market. Assignment of inductees to occupational specialties and training courses on the basis of aptitude and qualifications leads directly to a greater concentration of new standards men in lower-skilled jobs. Fifty-eight percent find their way to combat or service-supply specialties in contrast to 42 percent for inductees as a whole. Civilian jobs that require the skills of combat training or involve service or supply work are either rare or generally ill paid. Coupled with the fact that the goal of remedial reading classes is fifth grade level, this would indicate that training under the project will make little impact on the postservice disadvantagedness of inductees.

There is, of course, the further possibility that new standards men might turn to the market that does exist for these skills, and choose to make a career in the military. The stereotype Southern sergeant, and the more tangible Negro re-enlistment rate of nearly 50 percent, suggest that other disadvantaged groups have responded in this fashion. There are, however, a number of regulations and other barriers to re-enlistment by Project 100,000 inductees, which appear to preclude extensive adoption of military careers. Current standards require that men be judged promotable within the noncommissioned ranks to be eligible for re-enlistment. The services should explore this problem in greater detail to pinpoint areas where greater re-enlistment flexibility can be introduced. At present, any tests of the employment relevance of Project 100,000 must center upon work experience outside the armed forces. Toward the goal of such an evaluation, the Defense Department should follow up the new standards men in some detail. Such data would likely confirm our doubts about the long-run value of the program to the individuals so far inducted, but might indicate directions for improvement.

While Project 100,000 focuses on getting a new segment of the population into the services, Project Transition intends to facilitate getting men out of the military and into civilian jobs. This program is too young to provide much material for assessment, and the Wool and Flyer discussion gives as thorough an interim report as possible. I will confine myself to two observations.

The mild statement that "initial counseling . . . is recognized to be one of the critical links in the success of the program," and reference to the "nationwide shortage of qualified counseling personnel," conceal the hard facts of the matter. As in other quarters, there was a deep dissatisfaction with the work being performed by the state employment services which are responsible for this part of the program. The discussion revealed considerable bitterness about the inefficiency, ignorance, and racial discrimination which characterize some of the employment service offices involved. The armed forces are attempting to escape such situations by developing their own counseling staffs, thus infringing upon the jurisdiction which the employment services jealously defend. Insofar as internal politics dictate that such work must largely continue to be their province, then it seems clear that Project Transition provides yet another argument for federalization of the state services.

Second, let me suggest that the authors need not be so nervous about the danger that their training agencies will select "the most promising prospects . . . rather than those most needing help." Practically speaking, neither can nor should the whole world be run with sole emphasis on the least advantaged. Extensive services should be aimed toward those who, although not hard core, are certainly not among the favored few. Moreover, to the extent that men emerge from military service prepared to fill shortages in middle-level skills, rational use of national manpower resources dictates that they be matched with jobs. The basic lesson to be learned is that a single-purpose program is not likely to meet multiple objectives. To assist those needing the most help (who may or may not be *disadvantaged* in the current sense of the word) may require a separate set of programs. One notes that introduction of a remedial literacy program would probably be part of the solution.

As a final observation, the results of both Projects 100,000 and Transition are of considerable relevance to possible changes in military manpower procurement methods. If, at the extreme, one moved to a volunteer basis (at least for the Army), questions of entry and re-enlistment standards immediately arise. Hence a major question would center upon potentials for redesign of the military services to facilitate careers by low-aptitude men. In addition, counseling and training for transition back to civilian life would become commensurately more important for those who could not make the grade.

9

Programs to Employ the Disadvantaged: A Labor Market Prospective

BY *PETER B. DOERINGER*

INTRODUCTION

Because poverty is foremost a problem of low earnings, manpower programs have been seen as major instruments in the antipoverty efforts of the last four years. Such programs can provide immediate income to improve living standards and weaken other elements of the poverty culture. Moreover, they are highly visible symbols of society's concern with the plight of the disadvantaged community. Program design however has been hampered by inadequate understanding of the dynamics of ghetto labor market behavior.

The proliferation of urban labor market studies in the 1940's and 1950's dealt with the broader patterns of job search and hiring practices in the economy, offering few in-

* Portions taken and adapted from Peter B. Doeringer, "Manpower Programs for Ghetto Labor Markets," Industrial Relations Research Association, *Proceedings of the Twenty-first Annual Winter Meeting,* Chicago, December, 1968, Gerald G. Somers (ed.) (reprinted by permission); and from Peter B. Doeringer, "Ghetto Labor Markets—Problems and Programs," American Academy of Arts and Sciences, Conference on Transportation and Poverty, June 7, 1968 (reprinted by permission).

This paper is based largely upon materials developed as part of a research project on manpower programs and manpower policy in Boston. This project is sponsored by the United States Department of Labor under the authority of Title I of the Manpower Development and Training Act of 1962, as amended. Points of view or opinions stated do not necessarily represent the official position or policy of the Department of Labor.

I wish to thank my graduate assistants, Penny Feldman, David Gordon, and Michael Reich, and my research assistants, Ellen Marram, Carole Richardot, and Virginia Sullivan, for their major contribution to this research.

sights into the unique problems which might confront the ghetto worker.[1] Much of our knowledge of ghetto labor markets therefore must be assembled from a variety of sources: census surveys, aggregate studies of unemployment and income, manpower program evaluations, sociological studies of low-income neighborhoods, and so forth. While the data from these sources are not entirely consistent, they do support a number of generalizations concerning the labor market experience of the disadvantaged.

1. The suburban rings of major metropolitan areas are expanding most rapidly in terms of population and job opportunities, whereas the inner cities are increasingly dominated by nonwhite families with low incomes.[2]

2. Low-income urban neighborhoods are characterized by high unemployment (especially among teen-agers), low wages, involuntary part-time employment, and below average labor force participation rates among adult males.[3]

3. Employment patterns, especially of nonwhites, are skewed towards low-skilled occupations which offer poor earnings potential and which are most vulnerable to adverse economic conditions.[4]

4. Many of the disparities between whites and nonwhites with respect to income and employment can be explained by differences in formal educational levels and in the relationship of residence to work place.[5]

---

[1] The recent Chicago labor market study, under the direction of Albert Rees and George P. Shultz, should provide new information on these problems. See, for example, Joseph C. Ullman and David P. Taylor, "The Information System in Changing Labor Markets," *Proceedings of the 18th Annual Meeting of the Industrial Relations Research Association,* December 1965, pp. 276-89; and David P. Taylor, "Discrimination and Occupational Wage Differences in the Market for Unskilled Labor," *Industrial and Labor Relations Review* (April 1968), 375-90.

[2] See *Report of the National Advisory Commission on Civil Disorders* (New York: Bantam Books, Inc., 1968), pp. 236-50; and John F. Kain, "Housing Segregation, Negro Employment, and Metropolitan Decentralization," *Quarterly Journal of Economics,* May 1968, 175-97. Also, John F. Kain, "The Distribution of Jobs and Industry," in *The Metropolitan Enigma,* ed., James Q. Wilson, Chamber of Commerce of the United States, 1967.

[3] See *Report of the National Advisory Commission on Civil Disorders,* pp. 251-65; and U.S. Department of Labor, *A Sharper Look at Unemployment in U.S. Cities and Slums,* Office of the Secretary of Labor, 1967.

[4] U.S. Department of Labor, Bureau of Labor Statistics, *Social and Economic Conditions of Negroes in the United States,* Report No. 332 (Washington, D.C.: Government Printing Office, 1967), pp. 39, 40, 42.

[5] See Harry J. Gilman, "Economic Discrimination and Unemployment," *American Economic Review* (December 1965), 1077-96; Kain, "Housing Segregation"; and Taylor, "Discrimination and Occupational Wage Differences," 375-90.

THE QUEUE THEORY
OF THE LABOR MARKET

On the basis of these findings, it is frequently suggested that urban labor markets operate according to "queuing" principles. Stated in its simplest form, the *queue theory* asserts that workers are ranked in the labor market according to the relationship between their potential productivity and their wage rates. Employers seek to hire the most productive workers from the queue, leaving the less productive workers unemployed. Thus, the characteristics of the unemployed are determined by total labor demand, the wage structure of the economy, and the relative worker productivities.

Disadvantaged workers are, by definition, those who (1) are farthest back on the more desirable hiring queues, (2) are employed in the lowest paid jobs, and (3) are most likely to experience involuntary unemployment. As the demand for labor increases, the probability of a disadvantaged worker becoming employed rises as employers that are motivated to fill job vacancies in order to meet production goals undertake to hire poorly qualified workers who would be unacceptable under less stringent labor market conditions.

Between 1962 and 1967, 7.7 million new jobs became available—one million, or 13 percent, going to nonwhites. During the same period the overall unemployment rate fell from 5.6 to 3.9 percent, while the nonwhite unemployment rate fell from 10.9 to 7.4 percent. These employment gains from economic growth can be contrasted with the 1.2 million persons who received training under the Manpower Development and Training Act during the same period. Although many of the employment gains for nonwhites were in low-skilled jobs, the period 1960–1966 brought a 50 percent increase in the number of nonwhites in managerial and professional jobs and a 48 percent increase in nonwhite skilled employment.[6]

It is apparent that policies to increase aggregate demand create

---

[6] See *Manpower Report of the President, 1967* (Washington, D.C.: Government Printing Office, 1967); Garth L. Mangum, "Evaluating Federal Manpower Programs," *Proceedings of the 20th Annual Meeting of the Industrial Relations Research Association,* December 1967; Garth L. Mangum and Sar A. Levitan, "Making Sense of Federal Manpower Policy," *Institute of Labor and Industrial Relations, Policy Papers in Human Resources and Industrial Relations,* No. 2; U.S. Department of Labor and U.S. Department of Commerce, *Social and Economic Conditions of Negroes in the United States,* Bureau of Labor Statistics Report No. 332 (Washington, D.C.: Government Printing Office, 1967); and Garth L. Mangum, "Manpower Programs in the Anti-Poverty Effort," in *Examination of the War on Poverty,* Vol. II, Report prepared for the Subcommittee on Employment, Manpower and Poverty, U.S. Senate (Washington, D.C.: Government Printing Office, 1967).

substantial incentives to employers to undertake the adjustments in recruiting techniques, hiring standards, and training necessary to avoid production bottlenecks; still, these activities are not without their costs. Most obvious are the costs of more intensive recruitment and of formal training programs. Less easily measured, but probably more important, are the costs of informal training, such as reduced productivity among new hires, and the inefficiencies of high turnover.[7]

As expanding demand induces employers to hire increasingly less preferred workers, the costs of raising the productivity of the disadvantaged to a level consonant with existing wage levels and established performance standards are likely to rise. These costs may, in turn, contribute to an already inflationary situation. Thus, currently, when over 96 percent of our labor force is employed, we are experiencing an annual rate of price increase of over 4 percent. Further attempts to increase the employment and income levels of the disadvantaged solely through the use of aggregate economic policies are likely to accelerate the rate of inflation—a serious prospect in a period of continuing balance of payments crises.

Society's unwillingness to tolerate much higher levels of inflation and continuation of nonwhite unemployment rates at double the white rates suggest that *some* urban employment problems are more appropriately the concern of manpower programs than of aggregate economic policy. These programs are commonly directed toward three perceived sources of labor market disadvantage: (1) deficiencies in labor market information; (2) inadequate levels of productivity; and (3) poor work habits.

LABOR MARKET INFORMATION IN THE GHETTO

There are persuasive a priori arguments for believing that information systems in the ghetto labor market operate less satisfactorily than those in the urban labor market as a whole. Numerous studies have demonstrated the importance of friends and relatives as a source of employment information, especially for low-skilled jobs. In the ghetto, lower employment rates tend to limit the total quantity of job information available to such a system, while increasing the demands placed upon it. Job information derived from friends

---

[7] See Peter B. Doeringer and Michael J. Piore, "Labor Market Adjustment and Internal Training," *Proceedings of the 18th Annual Meeting of the Industrial Relations Research Association*, December 1965.

and relatives is also likely to constrain the area of job search because of the skewed geographical and occupational distribution of the disadvantaged labor force.[8]

EDUCATION AND TRAINING

Since the simple queue theory maintains that the competitive ranking of workers is determined largely by productivity, customary components of urban manpower programs are education, training, and sheltered work experience. The queue theory also suggests that an expanding economy will encourage employers to amend hiring standards, but government-sponsored training and work experience programs attempt to accelerate this upgrading process.

POOR WORK HABITS AND JOB TENURE

While low levels of education and training can limit productivity and do affect the attractiveness of workers to prospective employers, unreliability on the job, rather than lack of skill, appears to be a more serious cause of ghetto unemployment. In Boston, for example, a vast majority of the unemployed adults seeking assistance from ABCD, Boston's community action agency, had been employed in the recent past.[9] This ability to obtain employment is also confirmed by ABCD's referral experience. With the exception of persons with specific employment handicaps and those in need of part-time work, ABCD was able to locate a substantial number of employment opportunities for which the ghetto labor force was qualified without additional training. Between September 1966 and April 1967, for example, over 15,000 referrals were made. Almost 70 percent of the persons referred for work were offered jobs, but about 45 percent of these offers were rejected. Of those actually placed, however, less

---

[8] It has been found that Negroes rely more heavily on formal sources of labor market information than do whites. See Ullman and Taylor, "The Information System in Changing Labor Markets," p. 283.

[9] Much of the data reported herein have been gathered from the records of ABCD. The ABCD client population is drawn primarily from unemployed workers in Boston's low-income neighborhoods. This group has characteristics similar to the unemployed workers in the Department of Labor's survey of low-income neighborhoods in Boston in 1966. While the Boston experience may not be completely representative of ghetto labor markets in all cities, conversations with employers and with antipoverty program administrators suggest that similar problems exist elsewhere.

than half remained on the job for at least a month. Discussions with employers, follow-up surveys, and conversations with ghetto workers indicate that a high proportion of these terminations have been voluntary.

Several correlates of turnover are readily identifiable. Cross classifying the termination rates of ABCD placements by age and wage rates shows that adults tend to be more stable than younger workers, and that tenure tends to be longer on better-paying jobs, as can be seen from Table 1. These findings are consistent with other surveys

TABLE 1: TERMINATION RATES AMONG ABCD PLACEMENTS BY AGE AND WAGE RATE, SEPTEMBER 1967*
(N = 115)

| | WAGE RATE | |
Age	$1.75 per hour or less	$1.76 per hour or more
25 years and under	66.7%	34.6%
26 years and older	40.0	33.3

* Computed from "Why They Stay or Quit," ABCD unpublished memorandum. Employment status was determined 5 to 14 weeks after placement.

of labor mobility and are customarily explained by factors such as the financial responsibilities and greater job security associated with age, and by the relationship between wage rates and job satisfaction.[10]

To test the dimensions of the turnover problem somewhat further, a multivariate model was developed for analyzing the work histories of ABCD applicants.[11] In the absence of an ideal measure of turnover, the dependent variable employed in the model is length of tenure on the previous job.

---

[10] See, for example, Organization for European Cooperation and Development, *Wages and Labour Mobility* (Paris, 1966), pp. 55-57; and Herbert S. Parnes, *Research on Labor Mobility* (New York: Social Science Research Council) 1959, pp. 102-9.

[11] Ordinary least squares techniques were used in estimating the coefficient in the model. Information on sampling procedures and possible biases in the data are available in the final report of the project. Peter B. Doeringer, ed., "Low Income Labor Markets and Urban Manpower Problems: A Critical Analysis," Report submitted to the U.S. Department of Labor, January 1969.

The independent variables are: (1) wage rate of previous job, (2) age, (3) years of education, (4) sex, (5) race, (6) marital status, and (7) birthplace. The general model is specified as follows:

$$T = a + b_1W + b_2A + b_3E + b_4S + b_5N + b_6M + b_7B + u$$

where T = Weeks employed on previous job [12]

  W = Hourly wage rate of previous job
  A = Last two digits of year of birth (beginning with 1900)
  E = Years of education
  S = Dummy variable for males
  N = Dummy variable for nonwhites
  M = Dummy variable for married
  B = Place of birth [13]

The model was applied to a random sample of ABCD's clients, for whom work history data were available, during the period from September 1967 to April 1968. The results of this analysis are shown in Table 2. Equation 1 pertains to the entire sample, Equations 2 and 3 to the data grouped by age. While the model has low explanatory power, and is least satisfactory in explaining job tenure among young workers, several variables are significant.

In all three equations, age has a distinct influence upon job tenure. Since the marital status variable is insignificant in all equations, it would appear that other factors associated with age—such as increasing labor market experience, greater job security, and pension rights—outweigh the financial responsibilities of marriage as factors in determining employment stability.

Sex is significant only in Equations 1 and 3. Surprisingly, adult females can be expected to have longer job tenure than males. This contradicts the view that females generally have a weaker labor force attachment than males, and probably reflects the importance

---

[12] The relationship between age and *potential* job tenure introduces a bias in favor of the correlation between age and *actual* job tenure. The maximum value of the job tenure variable has been constrained to 99 weeks to reduce the degree to which a small number of older workers with substantial job tenure could influence the significance of the age variable. About 20 percent of the pooled sample was affected by this constraint.

[13] The index assumes discrete values from 1 to 8, according to the following definitions: 1 = Boston, 2 = other areas in New England, 3 = Mid-Atlantic states, 4 = Southern states, 5 = elsewhere in the United States, 6 = Puerto Rico, 7 = Cuba, 8 = other. There were few instances of persons in category 8.

TABLE 2: WEEKS OF TENURE ON PREVIOUS JOB—ABCD WORK HISTORY SAMPLE FOR PERIOD FROM SEPTEMBER 1967 TO APRIL 1968

(t value in parentheses)

	a	W	A	E	S	N	M	B	d.f.	R^2
Equation 1 Pooled sample										
Estimated coefficient	72.64 (6.08)	4.83 (1.57)	−1.23*** (7.49)	.34 (.47)	−7.34* (1.82)	.64 (.15)	3.34 (.82)	1.22 (1.32)	309†	.1955***
Equation 2 Young workers (16-25)										
Estimated coefficient	54.01 (2.34)	−2.98 (.78)	−.86** (2.23)	1.56** (2.14)	−3.15 (.93)	−7.59* (1.73)	2.68 (.54)	2.14*** (2.35)	178	.1030
Equation 3 Adult workers (26-68)										
Estimated coefficient	74.98 (4.21)	10.43** (2.33)	−1.06*** (3.61)	−1.19 (1.00)	−12.71** (1.98)	14.14** (2.09)	1.89 (.31)	1.45 (.09)	157	.1310**

† Computer program capacity required reduction in sample size.

*significant at 10% level
**significant at 5% level
***significant at 1% level

of the earnings of the female work force in low-income areas.[14] For young workers, however, differences in sex do not influence job tenure, indicating common job shopping behavior, job security, and labor force attachment among young males and females.

The effect of race differs sharply for younger and older workers. Young, nonwhite workers average seven weeks less job tenure than their white peers, whereas nonwhite adults can be expected to have 15 weeks more job tenure than whites. The shorter job tenure of nonwhite youths is customarily attributed to involuntary turnover, but the Boston data indicate that in a prosperous economy much of the turnover is voluntary, and is concentrated among the young.[15]

Birthplace also influences the job tenure of younger workers. Youths born in Puerto Rico, Cuba, and, to some extent, the South—many of whom are nonwhite—tend to have greater job tenure than their counterparts born in Boston. This substantiates the impression of several employers that recent in-migrants to Boston prove more reliable on the job.

A full explanation of the influence of race and birthplace upon job tenure is beyond the scope and competence of this study. Nevertheless, there is room for several interesting hypotheses concerning the aspirations of nonwhite youths, the value of job security to recent in-migrants to a city, and the possibility of cultural differences in attitudes toward work and job changing.[16]

Educational level is another variable positively related to job tenure among young workers. Education may contribute directly to habits of stability, or it may improve opportunities for employment in satisfying jobs which discourage turnover. It may also be that the educational system acts as a screening device for distinguishing between stable workers and those prone to dropping out, be it from school or work.

---

[14] Female labor force participation rates, for example, are less stable over the business cycle than male rates. See Jacob Mincer, "Labor Force Participation and Unemployment—A Review of Recent Evidence," in *Prosperity and Unemployment*, eds. Robert Gordon and Margaret S. Gordon (New York: John Wiley & Sons, Inc., 1966), pp. 73-107.

[15] See, for example, Samuel Saben, *Occupational Mobility of Employed Workers*, U.S. Department of Labor, Bureau of Labor Statistics, 1967, Special Labor Force Report No. 84, p. 35; and Lowell E. Gallaway, *Interindustry Labor Mobility in the United States, 1957 to 1960;* U.S. Department of Health, Education and Welfare, Social Security Administration, Research Report No. 18, 1967, pp. 88-89.

[16] Claude Brown's description of the difference between his parents' and his own attitudes toward ghetto employment opportunities is enlightening in this regard. See Claude Brown, *Manchild in the Promised Land* (New York: The Macmillan Company, 1965), pp. 278-82.

The wage rate variable is positive and significant only for the sample of adult workers, a finding which is inconsistent with the data on turnover rates presented in Table 1. While it is likely that the influence of wage rates upon younger and older workers is not equivalent when other variables are held constant, statistical problems may also be involved. For example, job tenure is only an imperfect proxy for turnover rates, so that the two sources of data are not strictly comparable. There are also problems of collinearity. To some extent, the other independent variables in the equation can be used to explain wage rates as well as job tenure. Moreover, the causality between wage rates and job tenure presumably works in both directions.

While labor mobility among the disadvantaged labor force in Boston exhibits many of the same features as labor mobility more generally, one major inconsistency does emerge. High rates of voluntary termination seem to coincide with high levels of unemployment.

One hypothesis which resolves this apparent inconsistency is that the ghetto labor market exhibits, or appears to exhibit, excess labor demand. While this may seem paradoxical in view of the high unemployment in the ghetto, two pieces of heuristic evidence are offered to sustain this view: (1) the presence of large numbers of unfilled low-skilled job vacancies frequently reported in or near central city areas,[17] and (2) statements by ghetto workers that menial, less preferred employment is readily available, even to the casual job seeker.

This excess labor demand can be partly explained by the high concentration of less preferred employers on the demand side of the ghetto labor market.[18] These employers possess one or more of the following characteristics: low wages and low fringe benefits, debilitating production speeds, low-status work, unpleasant working conditions, unsympathetic supervision, inequitable industrial relations arrangements, low promotion opportunities, and unstable employment. Hospitals, hotels, warehouses, maintenance service companies, industrial sweatshops, and so forth are representative of such employers.

---

[17] While job vacancy statistics are not available to support this statement, at least since 1967 both ABCD and the Massachusetts State Employment Service have had a continuing pool of unfilled jobs at wage rates near the federal minimum. A similar situation in New York City was reported in *The New York Times* for October 19, 1968, p. 53.

[18] Piore describes this group of employers as belonging to the "secondary labor market." See Michael J. Piore, "On-the-Job Training in the Dual Labor Market," in Arnold R. Weber (ed.), *1969 Research Volume of the Industrial Relations, Research Association.* Forthcoming.

Product market competition and low profit levels often limit the less preferred employers' ability to compete for labor; therefore, they recruit from the disadvantaged stratum of the labor market. Such recruitment practices may be further encouraged by the inelasticity of product demand with respect to quality, and by the low-skilled content of the enterprise's job structure. Finally, fluctuations of product demand may make the development of a stable work force impractical.[19] Since low wages and less preferred working conditions do not encourage worker loyalty, turnover and frictional job vacancies are likely to be higher than average among such employers.

Less preferred employers are also likely to adopt other strategies toward the labor market, which are compatible with turnover and which may be inimical to worker stability. During periods of high labor demand, for example, desired manning levels within these enterprises tend to exceed actual manning levels for sustained periods of time. Adjustments in compensation and improved working conditions are adopted only gradually in response to these labor scarcities. Instead, overtime, speedups, and deteriorations of product quality are substituted for additional employees. The presence of accessible, unfilled jobs tends to make workers independent of particular employers and, when combined with undesirable working conditions, encourages turnover.

Health problems may also be an impediment to stable employment. As can be seen from Table 3, health ranked third among causes of voluntary terminations in the ABCD sample. Many of the ailments seem to be of a low-grade, chronic variety, such as nosebleeds, headaches, and respiratory problems, many of which are aggravated by the work environment.[20]

Finally, the social systems of the ghetto are compatible with turnover. Alternatives to earned income, for example, are available from welfare programs, hustling, and income sharing among friends and relatives, so that ghetto workers can easily withhold their labor services for short periods of time or treat work as a supplementary

---

[19] Lester makes a similar point with respect to a more advantaged labor market. In his Trenton labor market study, the aircraft industry had developed arrangements for operating efficiently in a situation in which turnover was high because of shifting production contracts. See R. A. Lester, *Hiring Practices and Labor Competition*, Industrial Relations Section Research Report No. 91 (Princeton, N.J.: Princeton University Press, 1955), p. 55.

[20] No attempt was made in the context of this study to pursue the health question, and it is recognized that the interview responses may have concealed other reasons for terminations. It appears that, apart from general health surveys, there is too little research in the area of work-related illnesses among low-income populations.

TABLE 3: REASONS FOR WORK TERMINATION—ABCD FOLLOW-UP SURVEY*

Reasons	Number	Percentage
Further training (including school, skill training, and military service)	34	35%
Dissatisfaction with job	20	21%
Personal health	19	20%
Family reasons (child care, health, etc.)	6	6%
Laid off by employer	4	4%
Withdrew from labor force (retired, underage, no longer seeking employment)	13	14%
TOTAL	96	100%

* The follow-up sample was randomly drawn and is based upon 96 responses made 4–8 weeks following placement by ABCD. The sample suffers from considerable under-reporting, but the magnitudes of the voluntary terminations and job dissatisfaction are consistent with the general impressions of the follow-up interviewers.

source of income. In addition, the active social life of the ghetto—much of it centered on the street—can compete with work as a regular activity.[21]

While it has been argued that a high level of voluntary turnover is the major symptom of labor market disadvantage in the ghetto, its role in re-allocating the labor force should not be ignored. Quitting low-income jobs to obtain higher wages is one important means to economic improvement. Moreover, among teen-agers and other new entrants to the labor force, turnover provides an efficient means of becoming oriented to the labor market.

In Boston, however, there seems to be a large amount of job changing which does not lead to wage improvement. Although wage rates are, of course, only a crude measure of total compensation and

---

[21] These points are made by Piore, "On-the-Job Training in the Dual Labor Market," pp. 2-7, 8-9, 11-12, and can be seen in the descriptions of street corner life in low-income neighborhoods. See, for example, Elliot Liebow, *Tally's Corner* (Boston: Little, Brown and Company, 1967); and Herbert J. Gans, *The Urban Villagers* (New York: The Free Press, 1962).

job satisfaction, the ABCD placement history sample indicates that only 36 percent of job changes resulted in higher starting wage rates. A similar figure was also obtained in the ABCD work history data.[22]

THE DUAL QUEUE THEORY
OF THE LABOR MARKET

The preceding analysis of the ghetto labor market indicates that the simple queue theory is not a satisfactory tool for understanding the dynamics of such labor markets. By focusing upon the dividing line between employment and unemployment, and upon the quantifiable criteria which influence ranking along the queue, the problem of turnover and voluntary unemployment has been obscured. If, as the Boston data suggest, many disadvantaged workers are able to move easily in and out of less preferred employment, then the distinction between the employed and the unemployed becomes blurred.

The precision with which ghetto workers can be ranked on a hiring queue must also be questioned. Analysis of both population and establishment data collected in Boston have failed to explain much of the variance in the hiring decision through quantifiable socioeconomic variables. This finding suggests (1) that interviews are important screening devices, (2) that fine distinctions cannot be drawn within the disadvantaged labor force, and (3) that less preferred employers do not attempt to screen the job applicant as carefully as do preferred employers.

The ghetto labor market and, to some degree, labor markets in general can therefore be understood more clearly in terms of two queues. First, there is the *hiring* queue, not neatly ordered by worker productivity and relative wage rates, but consisting of broad groups defined by quantifiable variables such as education, age, and test scores, and by subjective interviews. Second, there is the *job*

---

[22] Except for differences in the average wage level, however, this experience resembles that reported for manual workers in the New Haven labor market study. Reynolds's analysis of work histories in New Haven (1945-48) found that 40 percent of the manual workers voluntarily changing jobs and 17 percent of the manual workers laid off found better paying jobs. See Lloyd Reynolds, *The Structure of Labor Markets: Wages and Labor Mobility in Theory and Practice* (New York: Harper & Row, Publishers, 1959), p. 215. Although this was a period of high labor demand, Reynolds notes that falling overtime may explain some of the low proportion of upgrading through mobility.

The danger with unproductive turnover lies not so much in its opportunity costs but in the likelihood that it will become a habitual pattern of labor market behavior.

vacancy queue, in which employers are ranked by reputation, as informally defined by workers' evaluations of wages and working conditions.

The labor market integrates these queues in two stages. In the first iteration, workers and jobs are matched according to their relative positions on these poorly defined queues. Once an employment relationship has been established, however, a second, and much more precise iteration occurs on the job as employers and workers appraise one another. If either party is considered to be unsatisfactory during the probationary period, the employment relationship is terminated, and the supply-and-demand queues are reassembled. Through this recycling process, the least acceptable workers and the least attractive jobs must be continually rematched.

MANPOWER PROGRAMS FOR THE URBAN DISADVANTAGED

The ghetto labor force can be divided into at least five categories of disadvantage. In cities where jobs are accessible to the ghetto community, the appropriate mix of manpower programs will depend upon the relative size of each of these categories:

1. Teen-agers with little or no previous work experience.
2. Persons with stable, but low-wage, work experience.
3. Adults with a work history of chronic turnover and poor work habits.
4. Persons with clearly defined obstacles to employment, including the aged, mothers with young children, students seeking part-time work, alcoholics and addicts, functional illiterates, and the physically and mentally handicapped.
5. Persons not in the labor force who have sources of income, such as welfare and illicit activities, which are competitive with productive employment.

For all groups, job development and referral services located in the ghetto are useful for expanding the quantity and quality of labor market information. Such a program, by itself, may be sufficient for employing the handicapped and for remedying teen-age unemployment by expediting exposure to work and leaving turnover to diminish with age and work experience. Referral to higher wage jobs may also be sufficient to promote the upgrading of fully employed, low-wage workers. For many, however, job development must be combined with long-term programs in general education in order to accomplish this upgrading.

Current programs for improving vocational skills among the urban disadvantaged should be viewed with some skepticism. It appears, for example, that short-term, institutional training programs do not contribute to improving worker productivity as significantly as many program evaluations would seem to indicate.[23] Such programs are usually too short and lack the sophisticated curricula necessary to provide a broadly marketable skill. Instead, they provide little more than a superficial familiarity with a limited range of equipment, materials, and operating procedures.[24]

Institutional programs can contribute to employability, however, by helping employers to identify reliable workers. The apparent benefits of many training programs can be explained by this screening effect and by the intensive placement efforts which normally accompany these programs.[25]

The problem of excessive turnover among adult workers has generally evaded solution. Some training programs have been able to demonstrate low turnover, especially where the training environment was very attractive or when the training stipend loomed large relative to alternative sources of income. There has not been any demonstration, however, that this stability has carried over to post-training employment. Moreover, to the extent that turnover can be traced to the low quality of the work available in the ghetto, programs for modifying workers' attitudes are misdirected.

Referral to high wage or otherwise preferred jobs does seem to

---

[23] See, for example, R. J. Solie, "Employment Effects of Retraining the Unemployed," *Industrial and Labor Relations Review* (January 1968), 210-15; and Ernst W. Stromsdorfer, "Determinants of Economic Success in Retraining the Unemployed: The West Virginia Experience," *The Journal of Human Resources* (Spring 1968), 139-58. Solie indicates that benefits associated with the training program, taken as a whole, may be attributable to particular components, such as placement.

[24] Such programs also ignore the practical difficulties in substituting formal training for on-the-job training. Most employers value reliability and ability to learn above limited occupational skills when seeking to fill low-skilled or semiskilled entry-level jobs. Not only are most institutional programs ill suited for providing enterprise with specific skills, but they can be counterproductive by teaching work habits which are incompatible with enterprise procedures. See also Michael J. Piore, "On-the-Job Training and Adjustment to Technological Change," *The Journal of Human Resources* (Fall 1968), 435-549 for an extended discussion of on-the-job-training.

[25] In one company in Boston it has been possible to contrast the experience of a "coupled" institutional training program with that of persons placed directly into jobs. Hires from the institutional program were considerably less prone to quitting than were new hires, but, if turnover within the training program is also included, the quit rates were comparable.

encourage stability. Analysis of placements in which turnover has been low, discussions with ghetto workers, and the modest success of some employers with the use of "trainer coaches," [26] suggest that sympathetic manpower management, as well as high wage rates, may be helpful in controlling voluntary turnover.

Relying upon placements with preferred employers to remedy labor market disadvantage, however, poses the basic conflict inherent in the queuing behavior of the labor market. Preferred employers normally seek to acquire advantaged workers and have adopted wage scales and other industrial relations arrangements to permit them the privilege of selectivity. Hiring the disadvantaged and learning to adapt them to the performance requirements of the work place contradicts these selection principles, and will presumably raise unit labor costs.

Because of the nature of the hiring and on-the-job training processes, the Urban Coalition, the National Alliance of Businessmen, and the recent attempts of the JOBS program to encourage employers and unions to undertake to employ and train the disadvantaged on the job are, in principle, encouraging. Delegating the responsibility for program design and implementation to employers and unions should help to avoid some of the problems encountered in earlier programs by: (1) relating training and other adjustment programs directly to the requirements of particular enterprises; (2) opening preferred employment opportunities, with their inherent motivational properties, to the disadvantaged; (3) compensating employers directly for the costs incurred in modifying employment practices in favor of the disadvantaged; (4) improving the management resources available to manpower programs; and (5) decentralizing the program development process so that it can be more responsive to the problem of the individual work place and specific type of disadvantaged worker being employed.

The major flaw emerging in some of these recent on-the-job training programs is that they do not sufficiently blunt employers' preferences for hiring the relatively less disadvantaged. Broad definitions of eligibility for these programs still permit considerable dis-

---

[26] The trainer coach is responsible for combating tardiness, absenteeism, and other work-related difficulties that contribute to labor market disadvantage. In some cases these coaches are stationed at the work place to mediate difficulties arising during working hours, but more commonly they operate in the community. See, for example, the data from the Jobs Now Program in Chicago in Arnold Nemore, "Transferability of Manpower Programs," in *Examination of the War on Poverty*, Vol. II, Report prepared for the Subcommittee on Employment, Manpower and Poverty, U.S. Senate (Washington, D.C.: Government Printing Office, 1967).

cretion in trainee selection.[27] Moreover, if turnover constitutes the most serious short-run employment problem of the disadvantaged, the current programs are likely to miss their mark because of insufficient incentives to retain new hires.

There is also a tendency among employers to shift the initial phase of training and the burden of immediate turnover to out-plant training institutions prior to employing the disadvantaged. While this may be justified as an efficiency measure in the case of small employers, it is less so for large employers. Inasmuch as it may interpose another screening stage into the employment process, it in fact should be discouraged.

The programs are to be applauded, however, as an initial step in encouraging the considerable resources of the private sector to become involved in antipoverty efforts. If the current trend is to be accelerated, the federal government must be prepared to provide the requisite financial incentives and the climate of steady economic growth needed to make these programs a success on a larger scale. Urban manpower agencies, the backbone of today's manpower programs, are likely to play a relatively smaller role in the future. Nevertheless, they should remain an important source of contact between the ghetto and business communities, standing ready to provide disadvantaged workers, unions, and employers with those referral, training, supportive, and consultant services that are most compatible with antipoverty strategies in the private sector.

---

[27] The eligibility criterion for the MA-3 program, for example, is: "Poor persons who do not have suitable employment and who are either: (1) school dropouts; (2) under 22 years of age; (3) 45 years of age or over; (4) handicapped; or (5) subject to special obstacles to employment." (U.S. Department of Labor, Manpower Administration, *Request for Proposal MA-3*, 1968.)